SYMPOSIA
CELEBRATING THE SEVENTY-FIFTH ANNIVERSARY OF THE FOUNDING OF THE AMERICAN SCHOOLS OF ORIENTAL RESEARCH (1900-1975)

ZION RESEARCH FOUNDATION
OCCASIONAL PUBLICATIONS

Edited by
David Noel Freedman

Volumes 1-2

SYMPOSIA
CELEBRATING THE SEVENTY-FIFTH ANNIVERSARY
OF THE FOUNDING OF THE
AMERICAN SCHOOLS OF ORIENTAL RESEARCH
(1900-1975)

Volume 1: Archaeology and Early Israelite History; Held in Jerusalem, 9-10 June 1975
Volume 2: Archaeology and the Sanctuaries of Israel; Held in Chicago, 1 November 1975

Edited by
Frank Moore Cross

SYMPOSIA
CELEBRATING THE SEVENTY-FIFTH ANNIVERSARY OF THE FOUNDING OF THE AMERICAN SCHOOLS OF ORIENTAL RESEARCH (1900-1975)

Edited by
Frank Moore Cross

Published by
AMERICAN SCHOOLS OF ORIENTAL RESEARCH

Distributed by
American Schools of Oriental Research
126 Inman Street
Cambridge, MA 02139

SYMPOSIA
CELEBRATING THE SEVENTY-FIFTH ANNIVERSARY
OF THE FOUNDING OF THE
AMERICAN SCHOOLS OF ORIENTAL RESEARCH
(1900-1975)

Edited by
Frank Moore Cross

Cover design by Madeleine Churchill

Library of Congress Cataloging in Publication Data

Symposia celebrating the seventy-fifth anniversary of the founding of the American Schools of Oriental Research (1900-1975)

(Occasional Publications - Zion Research Foundation; v. 1-2)
Includes index.
1. Jews—History—1200-953 B.C.—Congresses.
2. Shrines—Palestine—Congresses. 3. Palestine—Antiquities—Congresses. 4. Excavations (Archaeology)—Palestine—Congresses. 5. American Schools of Oriental Research. I. Cross, Frank Moore. II. Series: Zion Research Foundation; v. 1-2.

DS121.55.S97 933 79-10226
ISBN 0-89757-503-2

Printed in the United States of America

Contents

Preface

The formal celebration of the seventy-fifth anniversary of the founding of the American Schools of Oriental Research began in Jerusalem on June 9-10, 1975, with an international symposium on the topic "The Archeology and Chronology of the First Period of the Iron Age: Problems of Early Israelite History," a title which I have modified in the interests both of accuracy and brevity in the present publication. The symposium was convened by the Albright Institute of Archaeological Research, in cooperation with the Israel Exploration Society, and coincided with a meeting of the Trustees of the American Schools (on June 11), the first to be held in Jerusalem.

The symposium was made possible by a generous grant from the Zion Research Foundation of Boston, a nonsectarian foundation for the study of the Bible and the history of the Christian church, and by a grant from the American Council of Learned Societies. It appears in the first of a new series, the *Zion Research Foundation Occasional Publications.*

The symposium was introduced by Professor Hayim Tadmor whom we asked to sketch in the background before and after 1200 B.C.E., the cataclysmic era in which the old powers waned and new nations waxed, among them Israel. His paper therefore is designed to give general orientation. Several papers grapple with the thorny problems of "Conquest" or "Settlement" (catchwords of opposing schools represented). Another group of papers focused on the history of individual cities or peoples at the beginning of the Early Iron Age. Unhappily not all of these papers were ready in time to be published in the present volume. Finally, two papers, one on early Hebrew poetry, one on the early alphabetic scripts, were assigned — to permit the first vice president and president of the Schools to participate.

I am grateful to many who have served to organize the Symposium and to bring it into print. Let me single out only two for special mention: William Dever, at the time of the Symposium Director of the Albright Institute, whose energy and organizational powers brought the Symposium into being, and Thomas D. Newman, Administrative Director of the Schools, who found the necessary funds for its support. My warm thanks also go to Philip King, whose lecture on the history of the American Schools brought the celebrations in Jerusalem to their proper climax and conclusion.

FRANK MOORE CROSS
February 1, 1977

Abbreviations

AASOR	*Annual of the American Schools of Oriental Research*
ADAJ	*Annual of the Department of Antiquities of Jordan*
AfO	*Archiv für Orientforschung*
ANET	*Ancient Near Eastern Texts Relating to the Old Testament*, ed. J. B. Pritchard, 3 eds. (Princeton: Princeton University, 1950, 1955, 1969)
AnOr	*Analecta orientalia*
ARA	D. D. Luckenbill, *Ancient Records of Assyria and Babylonia*
ARE	J. H. Breasted, *Ancient Records of Egypt*
ARI I	A. K. Grayson, *Assyrian Royal Inscriptions I* (Wiesbaden: Harrassowitz, 1972)
BA	*Biblical Archeologist*
Bib	*Biblica*
BMB	*Bulletin du Musée de Beyrouth*
BibOr	*Bibliotheca orientalis*
CAH[3]	*Cambridge Ancient History*, 3rd ed. (1970—)
CBQ	*Catholic Biblical Quarterly*
CIS	*Corpus inscriptionum semiticarum*
CTCA	Andrée Herdner, *Corpus des tablettes en cunéiformes alphabetiques* (Paris: Imprimerie Nationale, 1963)
EA	J. A. Knudtzon, *Die El-Amarna-Tafeln* (Leipzig: Hinrichs, 1915)
EI	*Eretz Israel*
IEJ	*Israel Exploration Journal*
JANES	*Journal of the Ancient Near Eastern Society*
JAOS	*Journal of the American Oriental Society*
JARC	*Journal of the American Research Center in Egypt*
JBL	*Journal of Biblical Literature*
JNES	*Journal of Near Eastern Studies*
KAI	H. Donner and W. Röllig, *Kanaanäische und aramäische Inschriften* (Wiesbaden: Harrassowitz, 1962-64)
KUB	*Keilschrifturkunden aus Boghazköi*
PAAJR	*Proceedings of the American Academy of Jewish Research*
PEFQS	*Palestine Exploration Fund Quarterly Statement*
PEQ	*Palestine Exploration Quarterly*
PKB	J. A. Brinkman, *A Political History of Post-Kassite Babylonia, 1158-722 B.C. AnOr* 43 (Rome: Biblical Institute Press, 1968)
RB	*Revue Biblique*
TCS	*Texts from Cuneiform Sources*
UT	C. H. Gordon, *Ugaritic Textbook, AnOr* 38 (Rome: Biblical Institute Press, 1965)
ZAW	*Zeitschrift für die alttestamentliche Wissenschaft*
ZDPV	*Zeitschrift des deutschen Palästina-Vereins*

Volume 1
Archaeology and Early Israelite History

The Decline of Empires in Western Asia ca. 1200 B.C.E.

HAYIM TADMOR
The Hebrew University, Jerusalem

GENERAL REMARKS*

The year 1200 B.C.E. is the accepted chronological milestone marking the dissolution of the political and social order of the ancient world, which had existed for over three hundred years without major breakdowns. By its very nature, the decline of an empire encompasses all aspects of its existence, its economic structure, and its highly developed political framework. It is a complex process in which one cannot make a clear-cut distinction between the different stages, from stability through decline to collapse. It is therefore appropriate to begin the introduction to this symposium with a survey of the period of stability and prosperity — the 15th-13th centuries B.C.E. — which preceded the decline. We shall start with a few brief remarks on chronology and documentation.

The closely interrelated network of synchronisms in the 15th-13th centuries does not leave a significant margin of error for Mesopotamian and Egyptian dates. For Mesopotamia the margin of error is ± 10 years; for Egypt it is ± 14 years, depending whether one follows the higher or the lower astronomically fixed dates for Tuthmosis III and Ramses II — 1504 and 1304 or 1490 and 1290, respectively. The synchronistic chart, below, follows the higher dates.

Fixed dates, however, do not always indicate documentation. Though the names of the Assyrian and the Egyptian kings of the 12th and the 11th centuries, and in many cases the exact numbers of their regnal years, are known from king-lists or contemporary administrative documents, very few historical inscriptions from that bleak period have come to light. The year 1200, therefore, also marks a break in the flow of documentation, for from that time on the written evidence greatly diminishes and in some places ceases almost entirely. With the collapse of the major empires, the use of Akkadian as the *lingua franca* of international communication in the West also ceased. The schools for scribes of cuneiform in the West were either destroyed or abandoned. Those in Alalakh, Ugarit, Qatna, and other major centers in Syria probably perished in the destruction of the cities in about 1200; those of Megiddo and Hazor may, in fact, have existed for a while, but clearly there was no further demand for the few graduates of these schools, since correspondence in Babylonian was no longer necessary in the area; a new generation of scribes was already training in the native alphabetic scripts. Similarly, the heirs of the Hittites in South

Anatolia and North Syria, the Luwians in Malatya, Carchemish, and other Neo-Hittite centers, stopped writing in Hittite cuneiform, previously used in correspondence with the court at Hattusha; instead, they developed their own national script, the so-called Hieroglyphic Hittite.

"THE CLUB OF THE GREAT POWERS"

The synchronistic chart above schematically represents political interconnections in the second half of the second millennium, the period aptly designated by Professor W. F. Albright as the Second International Age of the ancient Near East (implying that the First International Age was that of Hammurabi and his contemporaries in the 18th century B.C.E.). Whereas the scope of the First International Age was confined to Mesopotamia, Elam, and Northern Syria, the Second International Age encompassed all the major civilizations of the ancient Near East. The international character of this period is exemplified at its best by the evidence from the El Amarna, Boghazkoy, and Ras Shamra archives. It shows that the world of the 15th-13th centuries B.C.E. was divided between several major states that formed what might be termed the "Club of the Great Powers," while the minor states were mostly their satellites or vassals. The Great Powers were Egypt, Babylonia (ruled by the Kassite dynasty), the Hittites, Mitanni, and Assyria. Membership in that league, however, was not as stable as it may seem. When we first learn of its existence from the archives of El Amarna in the 15th century, Assyria is not yet a major power. It attained its international role only after Mitanni was subdued by the Hittites in the early 13th century and almost entirely annexed by Assyria. Toward the close of the 13th century, in a treaty between Hatti and Amurru, her vassal state, the major powers of the time are specifically mentioned. A new claimant, the Ahhiyawa, appears here, though the name was crossed out by the scribe. Powerful as they were, the Ahhiyawa were not considered worthy to join the established, civilized powers of the ancient Near East.

The relationships among the powers of that league were not dissimilar to those of the empires of the 19th century or of today. They were reflected in political pacts, voluminous political correspondence, and especially in the strict rules within the international community: etiquette, use of appropriate titles in verbal give-and-take, subtle protocol for honoring a king according to his status with delivery of appropriate gifts (often a euphemism for mercantile relations). The powers within that league were bound by a network of agreements and were constantly in touch in spite of occasional wars or conflicts. A rival or a friendly monarch is a "great king" and is addressed as "brother ." In times of war he will be addressed as "my enemy." The vassal, on the other hand, is always addressed as "son" or simply by his name.

The international community of the great powers of the Late Bronze Age in western Asia collapsed toward the end of the 13th century, with the advent of the "Sea Peoples," the Israelites, and the Arameans. This was an age of migrations, which continued in the west for over a century, and in Mesopotamia for an additional two centuries. It was mainly these migrations and ethnic movements which brought about the collapse of Egypt's hold on Asia, the destruction of the Hittite Empire, and the eclipse of Babylonia.

In the case of Egypt, no new evidence has been added in recent years to what was already known concerning its decline in about 1200. Naturally, our interest in Egypt is limited to her role as a Western Asiatic Empire. That empire originated in the days of Tuthmosis III, diminished in the days of Amenophis III, and gained new impetus in the days of Ramses II, when the borders between the Hittite and the Egyptian realms were delineated in the treaty of Ramses' twenty-first year. This dominion, which extended as far as Amurru in Syria, receded, as is well known, in the reign of Marneptah and practically ended during that of Ramses III. Faced with grave internal problems, and threatened by the fierce onslaughts of the Libyans and the Sea Peoples, Egypt withdrew from Asia; for the first time in many centuries even Canaan was beyond her reach. The Egyptian claim on Asia, now limited to the coastal strip — that is, the area where the Philistines had settled, not without the assistance of Egypt — was to reappear, in spite of Egypt's rapid decline, occasionally in the first millennium, during the reigns of the militant Libyan and Nubian pharaohs, and especially under the Saite 26th dynasty.

Whereas for Egypt one speaks of "decline" and "recession," it is fully justifiable to use the terms "fall" and "destruction" for the Hittite empire, Egypt's main rival for dominion over Western Asia. Indeed, the fall of the Hittite empire is one of the most intriguing and mysterious chapters in the history of the ancient Near East; the more documents that are discovered and published, the more problematic the main issues become.

About two decades ago, a leading Hittitologist wrote: "Great mass-movements of population were afoot which the brittle Hittite confederacy was utterly unable to withstand."[1] At that time, even less was known of the last years of the Hittite empire. The main sources were from a King Tudhaliya — believed to be the IVth — the contemporary of Ramses II and Marneptah, and his son Arnuwanda, then believed to be the fourth of that name but now considered the third. From the reign of Arnuwanda's brother and successor Suppiluliuma II only a single document was extant.

As for Tudhaliya, a large fragment of his annals describes his war in the west of Anatolia, in the lands of Arzawa and mainly in the lands of Wilusa, Taruisa, and Assuwa.[2] These three toponyms excited great interest from the moment they were deciphered. Emil Forrer and Albrecht Goetze, the pioneers of Hittite studies, and scholars who followed them, identified — with some plausibility — "Wilusa" with Wilion/Ilion and "Taruisa" with Troy, whereas "Assuwa" was explained as the origin of the later name of "Asia." These campaigns of Tudhaliya seem to represent the farthest penetration westward of any Hittite king. Indeed, they demonstrate a remarkable synchronism with the Homeric tradition and toponomy.

---

*Since this lecture appears in the form in which it was delivered, the notes have been kept to the minimum. Several studies that have appeared since are added in square brackets. Abbreviations of the cuneiform literature follow the *Chicago Assyrian Dictionary*.

[1]O. R. Gurney, *The Hittites*, 2nd ed. (Harmondsworth, 1954), p. 39.

[2]J. Garstang and O. R. Gurney, *The Geography of the Hittite Empire* (London, 1959), p. 121.

Again, another document, the so-called "Indictment of Madduwatta," had been assigned by A. Goetze, its first editor, to the reigns of this Tudhaliya and his son Arnuwanda. A petty prince in northwest Anatolia, he was driven out of his country by the Ahhiyawa ruler and later was accused of conspiracy with the king of Ahhiyawa — a complicated affair, the details of which we shall not describe here. However, this effort clearly points to the involvement of the Hittites in western Anatolia and especially with the Ahhiyawa, who, in spite of almost fifty years of eager debate concerning their identity and location, continue to be associated with the Homeric *Achaioi* or Acheans.[3]

The picture that has emerged and become almost canonical is that the Hittites in about 1230 had to fight against the ever-growing pressure of western tribes, probably newcomers from Mycenean Greece. This pressure, in turn, is duly connected with the great migrations which destroy the Mycenean world, as well as with the Trojan War, of the Homeric tradition. A chronological difficulty, which still cannot be resolved, is the mention of a certain Alaksandus of Wilusa, a western king identified by some scholars with Alexander/Paris of the Iliad, the prince of Homeric Troy. However, this Alaksandus appears in a text from the days of Muwatalli, the adversary of Ramses at the battle of Qadesh, i.e., ca. 1300. Yet the traditional date of the Greek chronographers, counting in terms of genealogical chronology, places the fall of Troy almost a century later!

A number of significant discoveries and researches during the last decade have introduced some meaningful changes in the interpretation of these events: first, the discovery of documents pertaining to Tudhaliya, Arnuwanda, and especially Suppiluliuma II, Arnuwanda's successor, to which we shall turn presently; then, the redating of the annals of Tudhaliya by O. R. Gurney (based on an observation of Edmund Gordon). It now seems likely that it was not the last Tudhaliya who fought in western Anatolia, but rather an earlier Tudhaliya, a predecessor of Suppiluliuma I, ca. 1400. More recently, a Hittite computer study by Ph. H. J. Houwink ten Cate,[4] begun in Chicago by H. G. Güterbock, and one by H. Otten[5] into the grammatical and epigraphical peculiarities of the "Indictment of Madduwatta," have shown that the document should be dated to ca. 1400 B.C.E., rather than to the late 13th century. If so, the Hittites were involved with the western Ahhiyawa about two hundred years before the date of the fall of the Hittite empire and the accepted date of the fall of Troy, and this involvement can have no bearing upon the events of 1200.

[3]D. Page, *History and the Homeric Iliad* (Berkeley, 1959), pp. 1-40, 97-117; J. G. Macqueen, *AnSt* 18 (1968), 178ff.; H. J. Houwink ten Cate, "Anatolian Evidence for relations with the West in the Late Bronze Age," in R. A. Crossland and Ann Birchall, eds., *Bronze Age Migrations in the Aegean* (London, 1973), pp. 142ff.; J. D. Muhly, *Historia* 23 (1974) 129ff. [T. R. Bryce, *Historia* 26 (1977) 24-32].

[4]*The Records of the Early Hittite Empire* (Istanbul, 1970)

[5]*Sprachliche Stellung und Datierung des Madduwatta-Texte* (Wiesbaden, 1969).

What then remains for the reconstruction of the terminal stage of the existence of the Hittite empire? Updated historical evidence, revealed in the archives of Boghazkoy and Ras Shamra and published or quoted in recent years, has shown that the Hittites in the days of the last Tudhaliya were in full control of northern Syria, with the kings of Ugarit, Carchemish, and Amurru as their clients, bound by vassal treaties. The only enemy in sight appears to be the king of Assyria — probably Tukulti-Ninurta I, whose merchants were now barred from trading with Amurru. In addition to Hatti, the Great Powers of the "Club" include Egypt, Assyria, Babylonia, and also the Ahhiyawa whose name, as noted above, was subsequently deleted by the scribe.

Were the Ahhiyawa a source of danger? The evidence is too meager to allow a definite answer. Toward the close of the century — as H. G. Güterbock has recently documented[6] — the Hittites were certainly involved in several battles with Alashiya (i.e., Cyprus, or part of it) which they invaded repeatedly in the reigns of Arnuwanda and Suppiluliuma II between 1230 and 1200. Moreover, Suppiluliuma, the last King of Hatti, speaks of defeating Alashiya in a naval battle: "The ships of Alashiya met me in the sea three times for battle, and I smote them and I seized the ships and set fire to them in the sea. But when I arrived on dry land (?) the enemies from Alashiya came in a multitude against me for battle . . . I fought them . . ."

Clearly, Alashiya is at some point the enemy of Hatti, but the situation is very confusing, and the sequence of events as well as their historical significance cannot be determined yet. The king of Alashiya corresponds with Ammurapi, king of Ugarit, and refers to him as "my son." Is this a familial relationship, or should we see here political dependency? If the latter, how can it be accommodated with the fact that Ammurapi is also a vassal of Hatti? Perhaps this is a case of double allegiance, but the question remains open. In any event, the Ugaritic navy of those years appears to have been very powerful: one hundred and fifty ships are mentioned in one of the "letters from the oven"[7] written just before the fall of Ugarit. At about the same time, or somewhat earlier, a letter sent from Boghazkoy to the king of Ugarit demands that a ship and crew should be furnished by him to transport two thousand measures of grain to the city of Ura in Cilicia, repeating that this is a matter of life and death.[8] In another letter[9] the Hittite king expresses deep concern for one hundred ships from Ugarit with desperately needed grain in a time of famine. This severe famine in Anatolia is known from the records of Marneptah,[10] which tell us that the Pharaoh supplied the land of Hatti with grain in a time of need. Additional "tablets from the oven" indicate a grave situation, if not an imminent catastrophe: the advent of powerful enemies, physical danger, and perhaps even

[6]"The Hittite Conquest of Cyprus Reconsidered," *JNES* 26 (1967) 73-81; cf. J. D. Muhly, *Proceedings of the First International Congress of Cypriot Studies, I* (Nicosia, 1972), 218.

[7]*PRU* V, No. 62.

[8]*Ugaritica* V, No. 33; cf. M. C. Astour, *AJA* 69 (1965) 253ff.

[9]Bo. 2810 = H. Klengel, *Altorientalische Forschungen* 1 (1974) 171-73.

[10]Breasted, *ARE* III, 518.

the destruction of cities. However, these alphabetic texts, fragmentary and elusive, do not mention any specific names of the enemy and thus give no clue as to who destroyed Ugarit.

What happened in Hatti proper? Was the army of Suppiluliuma defeated in battle by the enemy from Alashiya or by a coalition of the "Sea People" coming overland from the West? Or was the Hittite king faced with an internal uprising? Another possibility is that when the king was campaigning with his army in Cilicia, the ferocious Kaska tribes, a powerful enemy from the northeast, sacked and burned the defenseless capital of Hattusha. (The evidence for the sack of Hattusha comes from the excavations, though the identity of its perpetrators and the exact chronological setting of the events are still obscure.)

With the sudden fall of the capital, the empire collapsed. In this connection we should recall that 600 years later the Assyrian empire was not defeated in battle, but fell when the Medes took Nineveh by surprise at a time when the king and his army were fighting in Babylonia. This analogy, however, is no more than a pointer towards the solution of the riddle of the sudden fall of Hatti. The well-known account of the contemporaneous Egyptian historian makes it clear that the Egyptians believed that it was the conglomerate of nations known as the "Sea Peoples" that destroyed Hatti and North Syria and was defeated only upon reaching Egypt.[11] At this stage our sources fall silent as to what happened west of the Euphrates, and our focus must now turn to Assyria.

BABYLONIA AND ASSYRIA

When in about 1360 Ashur-uballit I sent his messengers to Akhenaten of Egypt, Assyria was beginning to emerge as a political power independent of Mitanni (or Hanigalbat), her former suzerain, and was attempting to take a position alongside the other members of the "Club" of the recognized Great Powers. This move, known from El-Amarna letters 15 and 16,[12] is contested by the Babylonian king Burnaburiash, who claims in another letter from Amarna that the king of Assyria is "my vassal."[13] The claim, though exaggerated, should not be dismissed, as it is very likely that in his struggle with Mitanni, the Assyrian king sought Babylonian support, and that the diplomatic marriage between Burnaburiash and the daughter of Ashur-uballit (known from an Assyrian chronistic source) is symptomatic of Assyrian political dependence on the southern power.

The next step in Assyria's attempt to assume a major role in Western Asia is illustrated by a well-known Hittite document about seventy years later; at this time, Adad-nirari I, having defeated Mitanni, wrote to the Hittite king expressing his wish to visit Mount Amanus in North Syria, which, in the light of

---

[11] J. A. Wilson in Pritchard, ed., *ANET*, p. 262.
[12] P. Artzi in *EI* 9 (1969) 22ff.
[13] *EA* 9.

well-known historical antecedents (a symbolic visit to the shores of the Mediterranean Sea, with the "washing of weapons" ceremony and the "cutting of cedar logs," another ceremonial act) might have implied Assyrian intention to get a foothold in North Syrian trade. We do not possess Adad-nirari's letter, but we do have the harsh reply of the Hittite king, perhaps Hattusili III, who declined the offer and resented the appellatives "brother" and "great king," the self-designation of the Assyrian *homo novus.*[14] Yet it is clearly the dangerous proximity of Assyria that moved Hattusili to conclude a treaty with Ramses II and thus end a century-old enmity so that the Hittites would be free from the threat of Egypt. Indeed, the tension between Hatti and Assyria is quite apparent in the reign of Shalmaneser I, the successor of Adad-nirari, and especially in the reign of Tukulti-Ninurta I, who claimed to have defeated the Hittites at the very beginning of his reign and carried off eight times 3600 of their people.[15] To counterbalance the latent animosity with Assyria, the Hittites also concluded treaties with Babylonia, Assyria's foe from the middle of the 14th century onward. In spite of that, the Hittite king not infrequently wrote to the king of Assyria, referring to him as "my brother." Evidently, from the beginning of the 13th century, Assyria did become a full-fledged partner in the community of powers, but was still handled delicately and with suspicion.

At this stage it is helpful to review briefly Assyrian interests in the west before 1200. The borders are clearly defined: west of the Euphrates lies Hatti. Assyria's only aim was free passage for its merchants going to Canaan and Egypt; the Assyrian armies, having conquered most of Eastern Mitanni, reached Carchemish on the Euphrates, but lacked either the desire or the ability to cross over even for a plundering expedition. Mercantile ventures, not unique to Assyria, were the very essence of Mesopotamian relations with the west in the 14th century; in fact, they formed the economic basis of the political-cultural framework of the Amarna period.

The kings of Babylon, for their part, occasionally initiated direct contact with Egypt, clearly bypassing Assyria. The first of these contacts is very early, from the last part of the 15th century. A somewhat garbled passage in a Babylonian chronicle informs us that the Kassite king Kadashman-Harbe I smote the Suteans (an appellative for nomads), constructed fortresses in the west (Mount HI.HI), dug wells for water, and settled people "to strengthen the guard."[16] This often misinterpreted passage indicates, I submit, a Babylonian attempt to trade with Egypt directly through the desert route of Palmyra, circumventing Mitanni. This contact by Babylon with Egyptian-held Canaan may explain the appeal of Canaanite princes to Kadashman-Harbe's son, Kurigalzu II, to assist them in their planned rebellion against Egypt. Kurigalzu, we are told, dismissed their appeal and even notified the king of Egypt of the

---

[14] *KUB* XXIII, 102; Cf. A. Goetze, *CAH*^{3} II/2, p. 258.

[15] Grayson, *ARI* I, p. 118.

[16] "Chronicle P" I:5-9 in A. K. Grayson, *Assyrian and Babylonian Chronicles, TCS* 5 (Locust Valley, New York, 1975), 171-72.

treacherous designs of his vassals. This affair, related in a letter of Kurigalzu's son, Burnaburiash, writing to Amenophis III[17] may perhaps be fictitious, as B. Landsberger claimed. Yet the very fact that distant Kassite Babylonia was considered to have the potential to intervene in the affairs of Canaan in the late 15th-early 14th century is indeed highly illuminating. Though we have no information on further Babylonian ventures to Egypt, there are some indications that the kings of Babylon kept an eye on the Euphrates route controlled by the *Aḫlamû*-tribes, using it for their caravans bound for Hatti; indeed, the *Aḫlamû* nomads occasionally appear as the allies of the Hittites. Apparently, all three, including Babylonia, had a vested interest in keeping the caravan routes of the Euphrates free from Assyrian military intervention.

Thus far we have dealt with Mesopotamian involvement west of the Euphrates prior to 1200. The next involvement, now of a pronounced military nature, occurred ca. 1100, in the reign of Tiglath-Pileser I. In order to grasp its full significance, I must again digress and describe briefly the events of the crucial 12th-century in Mesopotamia.

During the last three decades of the 13th century — at the time when Marneptah was struggling with the influx of Libyans and the Sea Peoples, and when the Hittites were fighting in Alashiya — Assyria and Babylonia were deeply involved in bitter domestic strife, occasionally interrupted by looting incursions by the Elamites, which precluded any involvement west of the Euphrates. At this time Tukulti-Ninurta I of Assyria had already established his hegemony over most of Mesopotamia, defeated the Hittites on the Upper Tigris, and claimed kingship of the world from the Lower Sea to the Upper Sea. The ascendancy of Assyria under Tukulti-Ninurta has been well studied and vividly described in recent years, so the drama and the *dramatis personae* are well known. Having defeated his enemies from the North and Northwest, Tukulti-Ninurta faced in battle his Babylonian adversary, Kashtiliash, defeated him, and dragged him naked and bound to Assyria. And yet the humiliation of Babylonia was not over. The Assyrians captured the city of Babylon, looted the temples, and carried off the statue of Marduk to Assyria. The king of Assyria could now claim the title of "King of Sumer and Akkad, King of Karduniash (= Babylonia), King of the Upper and Lower Sea, King of the mountains and wide plains"[18] — titles which echo the pattern of Mesopotamian unity from the days of Sargon and Naramsin. The Assyrian victory came at a time when Babylonia was fully recognized as the ancient seat of lore and letters for all the cuneiform-writing peoples. In the Babylonian "theo-political" world view, crystallized in this period, Babylon and its temples were the center of the universe and Marduk the king of the gods. The blow inflicted by Tukulti-Ninurta I on Babylon was therefore the severest it had known. Yet this was not a senseless desecration like that of the Elamites in years to come; the statue of Marduk was given full honor

---

[17] *EA* 8.

[18] Grayson, *ARI* I, p. 108; [P. Machinist, *CBQ* 38 (1976), 455-71].

in Assyria, and a temple was built for him in the outskirts of Ashur — "The House of the New Year Festival in the Fields."

However, the supremacy of Assyria was ephemeral. Several years later, the Assyrians evacuated Babylonia, rebellion broke out in Assyria, and Tukulti-Ninurta I was killed, we are told, at the hands of his son. The following decades saw an escalation of the strife between Assyria and Babylonia, in which a third power — the Elamites — played a crucial role. This was their second intervention in Babylonian affairs; the first was when Kidin-Hutrutash looted the cities of Babylonia in the disorders that followed Tukulti-Ninurta I's occupation. We get the impression, though there is no direct proof for the hypothesis, that the Assyrians and Elamites acted at that time in conjunction. This second and decisive intervention by Elam under Shutruk-Naḫhunte and his son Kudur-Nahhunte brought about the fall of the Kassite dynasty, ca. 1160. Again, temples were sacked and looted, the Stele of Hammurabi and that of Naramsin were carried off to Susa, and Marduk's statue (a second one?) was taken as booty to Elam. Babylonian tradition distinguishes clearly between the sack of Babylon by Tukulti-Ninurta and that by Kudur-Nahhunte. The former is described as a voluntary decision by Marduk to leave Babylonia and to reside for a while in Assyria, a residence which blessed Assyria and made it prosperous and wealthy.[19] The sack of the Elamites, on the other hand, is described as a barbarous act of sacrilege, so that revenge was called for.[20]

The revenge, indeed, was forthcoming. Nebuchadnezzar I, the fourth king of a new Babylonian dynasty, defeated Elam, invaded Susa, and triumphantly brought home the image of Marduk. This feat, praised eloquently in the literary compositions of the time, heralded an era of restoration for Babylon. Court poets excelled in magnifying Nebuchadnezzar's valor and Marduk's glory, prophesying that from now on and forever Babylon would remain the center of all, with Marduk the unchallenged master. A remarkable document, edited recently by R. Borger[21] is the so-called "Marduk's Prophecy." Speaking in the first person, Marduk describes his exile in Hatti, Assyria, and Elam, and prophesies that a king will be born and will bring him back from exile in Elam, and that Babylon will be blessed forever. The prophecy is fulfilled, not unlike that about Josiah in 1 Kings 13. A recurrent paean of praise in that composition is "Bring tribute, bring yield to Babylon!" (This "Babylo-centric" worldview was to be reiterated in the days of Nebuchadnezzar II, six hundred years later, and reflected in the "Jerusalemo-centric" prophecies of Deutero-Isaiah.)

The renaissance of Babylon, however, was belated and ephemeral. In the north, Nebuchadnezzar's younger contemporary, Tiglath-Pileser of Assyria, already was repelling the newcomers from Asia Minor and waves of nomads

---

[19] R. Borger, *BibOr* 28 (1971) 16.

[20] H. Tadmor, *JNES* 17 (1958) 137-39; [J. J. M. Roberts in *Ancient Near Eastern Studies in Memory of J. J. Finkelstein*, Memoirs of the Connecticut Academy of Arts and Sciences 19 (1977), 183-87].

[21] *BibOr* 28 (1971) 16-17.

along the Euphrates — the Arameans. Soon afterward, Babylonia too would be overrun by these newcomers from the west, and the decline of the empires would then spread to southern Mesopotamia about a century after the collapse of the "old order" west of the Euphrates.

We come now to the reign of Tiglath-Pileser I (1115-1077). The account on the prism from Assur, relating in detail the events of the first five years of his reign[22] and brief accounts on tablets composed, I believe, in his 20th or 21st year,[23] furnish for the first time in the Middle Assyrian period ample and chronologically reliable evidence on Assyrian military efforts. Assyria was involved in Tiglath-Pileser's reign on three fronts: one traditional, against Babylonia in the South, and two new, against the migrating Anatolian peoples in the northwest and against the Arameans in the west and southwest. Thus, we read that at the very beginning of his reign Tiglath-Pileser defeated a host of 20,000 Mushki (classical Moschoi, northeastern Anatolian tribes associated later with the Phrygians). He says: "They and their five kings for fifty years had held the lands of Alzi and Purulumzi."[24] In other words, this confederation of five kings already had been on the Upper Tigris from about 1160. Clearly, they moved into that region during the decades following the fall of the Hittite empire, driven by other intruders into Anatolia. Now, it appears, they were still on the move eastward, into the land of Kadmuhi on the Upper Tigris, the northwest entrance into Assyria.

In the same region Assyria faced more newcomers from the north and northwest, among them the unsubmissive Kaska, who a century before had harassed the land of Hatti. North of Assyria, in what would later become Urartu, Tiglath-Pileser faced a coalition of twenty-three kings of Nairi with their army and chariotry. Here too he claims a total victory, reaching the Upper Sea.[25]

It appears that Tiglath-Pileser succeeded in his efforts to halt the hordes from the northwest and north set in motion by the great migrations of the 13th century. Tiglath-Pileser now turned to the west, in a short-lived effort to establish Assyrian dominion west of the Euphrates, as far as the Mediterranean coast. This campaign, which might be dated to his 15th year (1101), is described as follows: "At the command of Anu and Adad, the great gods, my lords, I marched to Mount Lebanon (and) cut logs of cedar for the temple of Anu and Adad, the great gods, my lords. . . . Against Amurru I advanced. Amurru in its totality I conquered. I received the tribute of Byblos, Sidon (and) Arvad. . . . On my return I brought the land of Hatti in its entirety under my sway. I imposed tribute and (a levy of) logs of cedar upon Ini-Teshub, king of Hatti."[26]

---

[22]Luckenbill, *ARA* I, pp. 72ff.

[23]E. Weidner, *AfO* 18 (1957/8) 347ff.; [H. Tadmor in *Studies in Memory of J. J. Finkelstein*, Memoirs of the Connecticut Academy of Arts and Sciences 19 (1977), 209].

[24]Luckenbill, *ARA* I, p. 74.

[25]Luckenbill, *ARA* I, pp. 77, 80-82.

[26]Weidner, *AfO* 18 (1957/8) 350:24-30; J. D. Hawkins, *Iraq* 36 (1974) 70; [Grayson, *ARI* II, pp. 26-27].

Obviously, this is an attempt to fill the political vacuum in northern and central Syria, created by the fall of Hatti. Not merely a term for the west, Amurru was the former vassal of Hatti, as was Ini-Teshub of Carchemish. Confident after his victories, Tiglath-Pileser turned south against Babylonia, conquered and pillaged north-Babylonian sacred cities, and set fire to the royal palaces within Babylon itself.

We might have expected at this stage a second Assyrian hegemony over Babylonia, like that of Tukulti-Ninurta. However, times had changed and "Hannibal was at the gates." The new factor that frustrated Tiglath-Pileser's imperial hopes was the Arameans. As is well known, they appear for the first time under this name in Tiglath-Pileser's fourth year, though it is very likely that "the widespread hosts of the *Aḫlamû*" already defeated by his father Ashur-resh-ishi were in fact the Arameans. (The other gentilics in that inscription[27] are also couched in traditional high style.) To quote from Tiglath-Pileser's annals: "With the help of Ashur, my lord, I led forth my chariots and warriors and went into the desert. Into the midst of the *Aḫlamû*-Arameans, enemies of Ashur, my lord, I marched. (The country) from Suhi to the city of Carchemish, of the land of Hatti, I raided in a single day. I defeated them; their spoil, their goods, and their possessions in countless numbers, I carried away. The rest of their forces, which had fled from before the terrible weapons of Ashur, my lord, and had crossed over the Euphrates — in pursuit of them I crossed the Euphrates in vessels made of goatskins. Six of their cities, which lay at the foot of Mount Beshri, I captured, I burned with fire, I laid (them) waste, I destroyed (them). Their spoil, their goods, and their possessions I carried away to my city Ashur."[28]

From that year onward, Tiglath-Pileser crossed the Euphrates every year to fight the Arameans, stretched out along the 500 km between Carchemish and Rapiku on the Babylonian border. In what was apparently his 17th year he reported: "For the twenty-eighth time I crossed the Euphrates, in pursuit of the *Aḫlamû*-Arameans — twice in one year. From Tadmar (Palmyra) of Amurru, Anat of Suhi, as far as Rapiku of Karduniash, I defeated them. Their booty and their goods I carried away to my city Ashur."[29]

Were Tiglath-Pileser's annals our only source, we would have believed that Assyria was at the height of her power and that the Arameans were contained on the west bank of the Euphrates. However, a fragment of a Middle Assyrian chronicle has significantly transformed the picture of Tiglath-Pileser's reign. Though the text is very fragmentary, it appears that famine drove the Arameans into Assyria: they pillaged and looted, reaching Nineveh, and Tiglath-Pileser fled to the northwest. The rest of the story is broken away.

2′) [In the year x a famine broke out in the land of . . .], the people ate the flesh of each other, [. . .]

3′) [ ] . . . the 'houses' (= tribes) of the Arameans

---

[27] Grayson, *ARI* I, p. 147.

[28] King, *AKA*, p. 72:44-76:63. [Grayson, *ARI* II, pp. 13-14].

[29] E. Weidner, *AfO* 18 (1957/8) 350:34-36.

4′) [in order to prevent] the relief, they seized the roads,
5′) [they . . . and] they conquered, they took [the . . .] of Assyria.
6′) [The Assyrians went up] to the mountains of Kirruria [to save their naked] life.
7′) [The . . .] took their [gold], silver, and all their property.
8′) Marduk-nadin-ahhe passed away; Marduk-shapik-zeri,
9′) [his son,] "entered [the house of his fathe]r" (= sat on his throne), Marduk-nadin-ahhe had reigned 18 years.
10′) [In the year x rainstorms broke,] the entire crops of the land of Assyria [were destroyed]
11′) [. . .] became numerous, they seized (or: afflicted) the 'houses' (= tribes) of the Arameans,
12′) [they . . . , occupied] the side of the fortress of Nineveh, the country downstream [. . .]
13′) [. . . Tiglath-]Pileser, the King of Assyria [went] to Kadmuhi.[30]

These lines, though very fragmentary and in parts obscure, are an eloquent testimony to the calamities that befell Assyria at the close of Tiglath-Pileser's reign.

Another fragmentary passage, now in a Babylonian chronicle, informs us that a few years later one hundred and five kings of the *Aḫlamû*-tribes came down to Babylonia and "enjoyed abundance and prosperity."[31] J. A. Brinkman,[32] who suggested this interpretation of that fragmentary passage, connected this migration with the famine described above. The search for food drove the Arameans south to the plentiful land of Babylonia. This was the turning point in Mesopotamian history: in a mutual effort for survival, TiglathPileser's son Ashur-bel-kala of Assyria and Marduk-shapik-zeri of Babylonia signed a treaty, thus ending two centuries of hostilities. The treaty was reinforced by diplomatic marriage in the days of the next Babylonian king, Adad-apla-idina. But the joint effort was in vain; during and especially after the reign of that king, the Arameans and other semi-nomads swept through northern Babylonia, destroying and plundering. Soon afterward, Babylonia entered the "Dark Age" and ceased to exist as a decisive political factor in the ancient Near East.

We have now reached the middle of the 11th century, after witnessing the gradual disintegration of the dominating forces in the ancient Near East: first Egypt and Hatti, then Babylonia and Assyria; Elam, too, at the eastern end of our spectrum was swept by the Iranian tribes from the north. By the end of this period, toward the close of the second millennium, the political scene in the west was transformed and a new reality emerged: the Aramean states appeared in

---

[30] H. Tadmor, *JNES* 17 (1958) 133-34; Grayson, *Assyrian and Babylonian Chronicles*, p. 189.

[31] A. K. Grayson, *Assyrian and Babylonian Chronicles*, p. 180.

[32] J. A. Brinkman, *A Political History of Post-Kassite Babylonia, 1158-722 B.C. AnOr* 43 (Rome, 1968), 132; 388.

North Mesopotamia and in Syria, the most powerful of them being the confederacy known as Aram-Zobah; the national states of Moab, Ammon, and Edom came into existence in Transjordan as early as the close of the 13th century; the confederacy of the Philistines was entrenched in the coastal strip of Canaan; all the while, Israel — the main topic of the present symposium — was evolving from a tribal league to a national state, a process which culminated in the 10th century under David and Solomon.

The Israelite "Conquest" and the Evidence from Transjordan*

MANFRED WEIPPERT
Rijksuniversiteit Utrecht, Utrecht

After having brought Israelite rule in the southern Belqā to a bloody end around the middle of the 9th century, King Mesha of Moab had the account of his conquests inscribed on the famous stele which was discovered in 1868 in the ruins of his city Dibon (the present village of Dhībān).[1] He took advantage of this opportunity to augment the account of his conquests with notes concerning the recent history of those territories and cities which he had either acquired or reacquired for Moab. These notes attempt to justify legally his actions or, where this was not possible, to describe those conditions which were changed by Mesha's military campaigns. Since these accounts are based on facts and first-hand knowledge, the stele is a valuable source of information for the eventful territorial history of the Israelite-Moabite border area.

Only in one instance did Mesha, or his "ghost writer," deviate from his principle of limiting his historical notes to the immediately preceding period. This one instance involves the annexation of the territory of Ataroth. The history preceeding this event had apparently taken a quieter course than that in the other territories. Mesha was, therefore, forced to fall back on a much earlier time in history when he claimed: "The people of Gad lived *m*^{c}*lm*, for time immemorial, in the land of Ataroth" (line 10). For an Israelite with even a little knowledge of history, this piece of information must have been quite surprising. If the Bible may be considered indicative, the Israelites never claimed that they had resided in their land *m*^{c}*wlm*, from time immemorial. Instead, they were convinced that they had taken possession of it at a certain point in history via difficult struggles with its previous inhabitants and through the assistance of their God.[2]

---

*Translation from the German by Margret Clarkson (Tübingen). Professor J. Maxwell Miller (Atlanta, Georgia) and Thomas L. Thompson (Tübingen) read the paper in a final stage of preparation and greatly improved upon style and thought. The writer owes a great debt of gratitude to these friends and colleagues for their assistance.

[1]The stele has not been published in a satisfactory manner. Good hand-copies may be found in R. Smend and A. Socin, *Die Inschrift des Königs Mesa von Moab für akademische Vorlesungen herausgegeben* (Freiburg/Br.: J. C. B. Mohr, 1886), and M. Lidzbarski, *Handbuch der nordsemitischen Epigraphik* (Weimar: Felber, 1898), pl. 1. For the text, see now *KAI* No. 181 (with bibliography). English translation: *ANET* 320f.

[2]For a comprehensive view of the perception of the Israelites regarding their history, see M. Weippert, "Fragen des israelitischen Geschichtsbewusstseins," *VT* 23 (1973) 415-42.

I

The most detailed biblical reports concerning the settlement of the Israelite tribes of Gad, Reuben, and Half-Manasseh in Transjordan are found in the book of Numbers. According to the present context, the events by which these tribes occupied their territory east of the Jordan belong to the time of Moses; they form, as it were, the final phase of the Exodus just before Joshua set out to conquer Canaan by crossing over this river.

The biblical account basically states that Moses sent a message from Kadesh to the King of Edom requesting right of passage through his land for the Israelites. The peaceful character of the migration is particularly stressed. The Edomites, however, refused to grant his request and, instead, manned their borders with troops (Num 20:14-21). The Israelites were then forced to make a detour around the lands of the Edomites and the Moabites (Num 21:4, 10-13). Arriving at the Arnon, the northern border of Moab, the Israelites sent a message to King Sihon of Heshbon with the same request — the right of passage through his land. As the Edomites had, Sihon also refused to grant this request and moved his troops into position against them. Sihon was beaten in the battle of Jahaz, and the Israelites took possession of his land (Num 21:21-26). They also conquered the apparently independent city of Jazer on the Ammonite border (Num 21:32). At this point, one would have expected the Israelites to move straight on to the Jordan in order to reach the land of Canaan west of the river. However, they continued to march toward the north in the direction of the land of Bashan. There they defeated King Og of Bashan and took possession of his land (Num 21:33-35). Only then did they turn toward the Jordan and camp in the *ᶜrbwṭ mwᵓb* across from Jericho (Num 22:1).

The same chain of events is also described in the lesson in history given by Jephthah to the king of the Ammonites in Judg 11:12-27. This text, however, is obviously dependent on Numbers 21-22. Deuteronomy 2 presents an interesting variation. Here the Israelites had no difficulties crossing the territories of the Edomites and the Moabites.

These accounts all presuppose that bonds of "brotherhood" existed between Israel and Edom and probably also between Israel and Moab. This "brotherly" relationship motivated them to avoid both military conflicts and challenging the territorial possessions of these peoples. The relationship with the kingdoms of Heshbon and Bashan, however, was different. The "Amorite" kings, as the texts state, were among those people whom Israel was allowed to wipe out.[3]

[3]The theoretical suppositions of these accounts are clearly set forth in Deuteronomy 2: The Israelites are forbidden by YHWH to harm the Edomites, Moabites, and Ammonites in any way or to expropriate them since YHWH himself had given these peoples their territories. The brotherhood of Edom and Israel is established by the fact that Edom is Esau (2:4f.), the brother of Jacob/Israel (cf. Gen 25:25f.) while the relationship between Israel and both Moab and the Ammonites is traced back to Lot, the nephew of Abraham (2:9, 19). Contrast this attitude with the attitude against the "Amorite" king of Heshbon in 2:24. — With regard to the brotherhood of Israel and Edom, see in general J. R. Bartlett, "The Land of Seir and the Brotherhood of Edom," *JTS* N.S. 20 (1969) 1-20

In spite of the "brotherhood" between Israel and Moab, the book of Numbers also contains a few texts reporting conflicts with the Moabites. One of these texts is that of the Balaam pericope (Num 22:2-24:25), a relatively late composition. (One may well ask whether the poems contained in it are really archaic or only archaistic.[4]) The account of the events at the shrine of Baal-Peor (Numbers 25) also belongs to this group of texts. Here, too, I would not wish to vouch for the early dating of this particular text. The song fragments in Num 21:14f. and 21:27-31, however, are unquestionably old, probably going back before the period of the monarchy. They are attributed to the "Book of the Wars of YHWH" (*spr mlḥmt yhwh*) and to the *mšlym*, the poets and ballad singers. The "Song of the Well" in Num 21:17f. probably also belongs to this group. However, it celebrated a peaceful event. Since those are old and, therefore, particularly important sources, I will use the two songs mentioned first as a starting point for my discussion.

D. L. Christensen has recently dealt with the fragment from the "Book of the Wars of YHWH" contained in the fairly incomprehensible Num 21:14f.[5] Since, by and large, I accept his reconstruction of the text, I will here present only his results and my own interpretation.[6]

ʾt Yhw b-spt	3 : 3
ʾt nḥl-m ʾrnn	
ʾšr nḥl-m ʾšr	3
nṭ l-šbt ʿr	3 : 3
nšʿn l-gbl Mʾb	

YHWH came in the tempest,
He came to the Arnon river,
Crossed the river, crossed it,
Deviated (from the way) to dwell in Ar,
Established himself in the land of Moab.

---

and with respect to Deut 23:8, K. Galling, "Das Gemeindegesetz in Deuteronomium 23," *Festschrift Alfred Bertholet* (Tübingen: J. C. B. Mohr, 1950) 176-91; J. Freund, . . . "לא תתעב אדמי כי אחיך הוא" (דברים כ"ג, ח) *Beth-Miqra* 11:3 (1966) 117-21.

[4]The best treatment of this subject so far is that by W. F. Albright, "The Oracles of Balaam," *JBL* 63 (1944) 207-33, even though I cannot agree with Albright's basic thesis. The possible impact of the "plaster inscription" in Aramaic cursive script found at Tell Deir ʿAllā on the study of the Balaam tradition(s) can at present only be surmised. I have not yet seen J. Hoftijzer's preliminary remarks (*De ontcijfering van Deir-ʿAlla-teksten* [Oosters Genootschap in Nederland, 5; Leiden: E. J. Brill, 1973]).

[5]D. L. Christensen, "Num 21:14-15 and the Book of the Wars of Yahweh," *CBQ* 36 (1974) 359f.

[6]The alterations in Christensen's reconstruction and interpretations proposed by the writer are as follows: *Line 1*: I prefer *b-spt* to Christensen's *bswph*. — *Line 2*: *nḥl-m ʾrnn* "the river Arnon" (*nḥl-m* singular construct with enclitic *mem*) as against "the branch wadis of the Arnon" (*nḥl-m* plural construct with enclitic *mem*; Christensen). — *Line 3*: *nḥl-m* singular absolute (accusative) with enclitic *mem* (for emphasis). The second *ʾšr* should be retained and perhaps be interpreted as [ʾaṯarô] or [ʾašarô] "crossed it (*scil.* the river Arnon)" although one would expect for this rather

While the text provides no information about the concrete historical situation on which it is based, the last couplet — YHWH, the God of Israel, established himself in Ar or in the land of Moab — nevertheless seems to indicate that the Israelites conquered the district of Ar.[7] The fact that YHWH is represented in the song fragment as coming from the south certainly has no relationship whatsoever to the Exodus itinerary[8] but rather stems from the fact that the holy mountain, which traditionally has been Sinai or Horeb, is located in the south. The motif is also familiar in other archaic or archaistic descriptions of theophany.[9]

The common reference to Ar and to the Arnon connects this fragment with the Heshbon song in Num 21:27b-30. This song is regularly constructed and, in general, well preserved.[10] I do not understand verse 30.[11] In light of verses 28f. it appears, however, to refer to a defeat of Moab in which the cities of Dibon and Madeba fell into the hands of the other party. Metrically, verse 29b is too long; the parallelism suggests that the section *lmlk ᵓmry syḥwn* may be deleted as an interpolation.[12] The remaining couplet *ntn bnyw plyṭm / wbntyw bšbyt*, "he

---

<ᵓšrh>. — *Line 4*: *l-šbt* infinitive construct of /WṮB/ resp. /YŠB/, not a noun *šbt* "seat." — *Line 5*: For /Šᶜ N/ N in the sense required by the context, cf. Gen 18:4. — *Line 6*: *gbl* here rather "territory" than "border."

[7]The parallelism between *gbwl mwᵓb* and *ᶜr* in Num 21:15 sugests that Ar is a designation for (the?) territory possessed by the Moabites. This is confirmed by Deut 2:9, 18, 29, and probably also by Num 21:28. Only Isa 15:1 provides some difficulty. Here we have two almost identical sentences showing *ᶜr mwᵓb* and *qyr mwᵓb* (probably = el-Kerak) in synthetical parallelism. This might lend support to the suggestion that here *ᶜr mwᵓb* has to be understood as a place-name. Perhaps, however, the sentences must be interpreted as doublets and *ᶜr mwᵓb* understood as a corruption of an original *ᶜyr mwᵓb*, a variant of *qyr mwᵓb*. Note that 1QIsa[a] reads *ᶜyr mwᵓb* in both instances while the Peshitta shows *ᶜyr mwᵓb* (*qĕrīṯā dĕ Mūᵓāb*) in the first sentence, *qyr mwᵓb* (*šūrēh dĕ-Mūᵓāb*) in the second one (= MT). The translation ἡ Μωαβῖτις in the Septuagint is ambiguous; it may represent *mwᵓb* alone or also *ᶜr mwᵓb* interpreted as a designation for the land of Moab in its entirety. — I do not wish to enter into a discussion of the complex text-critical problems connected with *ᶜr* (*mwᵓb*); it seems that *ᶜr* is text-critically certain only in Num 21:15 (where *ᶜyr* in the Samaritan Pentateuch can be understood as indicating the pronunciation [*ᶜÊr*] like Ηρ in the Septuagint).

[8]Contrast F. M. Cross, *Canaanite Myth and Hebrew Epic: Essays in the History of the Religion of Israel* (Cambridge, Mass.: Harvard University, 1973) 99-105.

[9]Cf. J. Jeremias, *Theophanie: Die Geschichte einer alttestamentlichen Gattung* (WMANT 10; Neukirchen-Vluyn: Neukirchener Verlag, 1965) 7ff.; Cross, *Canaanite Myth*, 99-105.

[10]The Heshbon song has been treated recently by M. Noth, P. D. Hanson, J. R. Bartlett, and J. Van Seters. I refer only to these four writers who have cited much of the relevant earlier literature. See M. Noth, *Das vierte Buch Mose: Exodus* (ATD 7; Göttingen: Vandenhoeck & Ruprecht, 1966) 141, 144f.; P. D. Hanson, "The Song of Heshbon and David's *Nīr*," *HTR* 61 (1968) 297-320; J. R. Bartlett, "The Historical Reference of Numbers XXI, 27-30," *PEQ* 101 (1969) 94-100; J. Van Seters, "The Conquest of Sihon's Kingdom: A Literary Examination," *JBL* 91 (1972) 182-97, esp. 192-95.

[11]See n. 19 below.

[12]See Bartlett and Van Seters. Noth retains *ᵓmry* which he connects with *bšbyt* and translates it as "Kriegsgefangene des Amoriters" ("captives of the Amorite"). Hanson, however, retains *syḥwn* which he likewise connects with *bšbyt* and translates it as "the captives of Sihon." I see no reason why the complete passage *lmlk ᵓmry syḥwn* should not be considered as a gloss which was inserted

(*scil.* Chemosh) made his sons fugitives, his daughters captives," with its 3 : 2 words, corresponds to both couplets in verse 30. In these couplets the meter may be identified as 3 : 2[13] but the meaning remains virtually incomprehensible. The first couplet, verse 27b, probably did not originally belong to the song.[14] The relationship between this sentence and the following one in verse 28a is relatively difficult and certainly not made any easier by the use of *ky* at the beginning of verse 28 regardless of whether the *ky* is to be understood as a confirmatory "for" or an exclamatory "yea." It disrupts the meter and, in my opinion, is secondary. It appears to be inserted in the text only to smooth out the connection between verses 27b and 28a. Mention also ought to be made of the fact that verse 27b uses *ᶜyr syḥwn* parallel to Heshbon for "the City of Sihon" while verse 28a uses the less common and more archaic *qryt syḥwn.*[15] Taking these various aspects into consideration, the following text results:

28 *ᵓš yṣᵓt m-Ḥšbn* 3 : 3
lhbt m-qryt S(y)ḥn[16]
ᵓklt ᶜr[17] *Mᵓb* 3 : 3
blᶜt[18] *bmt ᵓrnn*

---

into the text to make it conform to the tenor of the Sihon story. The 3 : 3 meter of the couplet, as reconstructed by Noth and Hanson, cannot be used as a strong argument against the opinions of Bartlett, Van Seters, and the writer (cf. also Jer 48:15 as another witness for the 3 : 2 meter). Another possible interpretation of the textual evidence is that while the first three couplets display the 3 : 3 meter, the last three show 3 : 2.

[13]See n. 12.

[14]It is, however, retained by the four authors referred to above.

[15]Attention perhaps should be directed to the variations in writing the name of Sihon in the Masoretic version of the song. It is written *syḥn* in verse 28 where it originally belongs to the text, while in the gloss in verse 29, the form *syḥwn* appears, which is also used in verse 27. Probably the form with two *matres lectionis* is younger than that with only one. The shorter form is taken over from verse 28 into the prose narrative in verses 21-26 and appears elsewhere in Numbers (21:34; 32:33), Deuteronomy (1:4; 2:24, 30, 31, 32; 3:2, 6; 4:46; 29:6), and Joshua (2:10). The longer form is common in Deuteronomistic and other late texts (Deut 2:26; 31:4; Josh 9:10; 12:2, 5; 13:10, 21, 27; Judg 11:19, 20, 21; 1 Kgs 4:19; Jer 48:45; Pss 135:11; 136:19; Neh 9:22). For the name of Sihon, see further n. 16 below.

[16]In early Israelite orthography, the original form of the name of Sihon may have been either <*Sḥn*> or <*Syḥn*>. Hanson prefers the form <*Sḥn*> ([*Sīḥōn*] or [*Sīḫōn*]) while the writer is inclined to favor <*Syḥn*>. In my opinion, the form <*Syḥn*> indicates an original pronunciation [*Sayḥōn*] or [*Sayḫōn*] which, in Hebrew, later became [*Sīḥōn*] as the Moabite place name [*Daybōn*] (in the Mesha inscription <*Dybn*>, Septuagint Δαιβον became [*Dībōn*] (whence Arab. *Ḏībān*). Perhaps the original pronunciation of the name of Sihon is reflected in the Septuagint name-form Σηων which may represent [*Sêḥōn*] < [*Sayḥōn*]. Single-word personal and tribal names with a diphthong, a monophthongized diphthong, or a long vowel in the first syllable are frequently found in Transjordan during the first millennium. See, e.g., Ammonite *Šwḥr*, F. Vattioni, "I sigilli ebraici," *Bib* 50 (1969) 379, No. 195, line 2; P. Bordreuil, "Inscriptions sigillaires ouest-sémitiques, I. Épigraphie ammonite," *Syria* 50 (1973) 185, No. 23, line 1, and the Edomite tribal names *ᵓwmr, ᵓwnm, dyšwn/dyšn, hymm, ywbb, lwṭn, ᶜybl, ᶜyrm,* and *šwbl* known from the Bible. I have no suggestion regarding the etymology (from a root /SĪḤ/ or /SĪḪ/?) and meaning of *syḥn.*

[17]For Ar (emended here to **ᶜārê* "cities" by Noth, Hanson, and Van Seters), see n. 7 above.

[18]Bartlett and Van Seters retain the Masoretic version *wbᶜly*, but Noth and Hanson correct it to

29 *ʾy lk Mʾb* 3?: 3
ʾbdt ʿm Kmš
ntn bnw plṭm 3 : 2
bntw b-šbt
30[19] *nrm ʾbd Ḥšbn* 3 : 2
ʿd Dybn
nšm ʿd Npḥ 3 : 2/3?
(ʾšr) ʿd Mydbʾ

28 Fire went forth from Heshbon,
Flame from the City of Sihon,
Consumed Ar-Moab,
Burned the heights of the Arnon.
29 Woe to thee, O Moab!
Thou art ruined, O people of Chemosh!
He made his sons fugitives,
His daughters captives.
30 . . . . . .
. . . . . .

---

blʿh. This emendation is supported by the Septuagint κατέπιεν. For /ʾKL/ and /BLʿ/ as parallels, cf. Jer 51:34. Jer 48:45, a combination of Num 21:28 and 24:17, does not help restore our text.

[19]Verse 30 seems to have been a crux already in ancient times. In the first couplet, the Hebrew *Vorlage* of the Septuagint was virtually identical with the MT. It is, however, likely that it showed *wnynm* for *wnyrm* which was translated as καὶ τὸ σπέρμα αὐτῶν (σπέρμα for *nyn* as in Gen 21:23, cf. Isa 14:22 [for *nyn wnkd*?]. Σπέρμα might perhaps also represent *nyr* in the sense traditionally attributed to the word in 1 Kgs 11:36; 15:4; 2 Kgs 8:19 = 2 Chr 21:7, but see Hanson 310-20. In the second couplet, the Greek καὶ αἱ γυναῖκες ἔτι προσεξέκαυσαν seems to represent **w(h)nšym ʿwd npḥw*; but it may be a forced interpretation of a *Vorlage* identical with the MT. The Masoretic *ʾšr ʿd mydbʾ* is represented by πῦρ ἐπὶ Μωαβ which appears to be a rendering of **ʾš ʿl mwʾb*. Here πῦρ may indicate a real variant attested also in the Samaritan Pentateuch (*ʾš*) and even in the MT where the *reš* of *ʾšr* is dotted, that is, deleted. As a consequence, *ʿd* may have been corrected to *ʿl* while *mwʾb* for *mydbʾ* may be a corruption produced by the accidental loss of the *dālet* and a confusion of *yod* and *waw*. In the Peshiṭta, *wnyrm* is understood as **wĕ-nīrīm* and translated as *ḥaqlātā* "fields" by identifying the word with *nyr* in Jer 4:3, Hos 10:12, and Prov 13:23, while the place name *mydbʾ* is mistaken for *m(y)dbr* "desert." In Jerome's rendering — he tried to follow faithfully his *Vorlage*, identical to the MT — the only interesting feature is his translation of *nyr* by *jugum* "yoke" which seems also to be reflected by *mlkw* "kingdom," "kingship" in the paraphrase of the Targum Onkelos. For some more details regarding the textual problems of this verse, see Hanson 303-7.

Various emendations have been proposed by the modern authors referred to above. Noth's version (cf. in addition to his commentary on Numbers, M. Noth, "Nu 21 als Glied der 'Hexateuch'-Erzählung," *ZAW* 58 [1940/41] 167f., reprinted in *Aufsätze zur biblischen Landes- und Altertumskunde*, I [Neukirchen-Vluyn: Neukirchener Verlag, 1971] 82f.) reads:

wnrm ʾbd ḥšbwn	Aber wir haben die Oberhand gewonnen, Hesbon ist zugrundegegangen;
wnšym ʿwd ʾš ʿl mydbʾ	und wir haben weiter ein Feuer angefacht gegen Medeba.

In this form, it may not be assumed that the campaign against Moab described in the song was conducted by the "King of the Amorites," Sihon of Heshbon, as stated in Num 21:26. Sihon is mentioned only incidentally in the epithet *qryt syḥwn* ascribed to the city of Heshbon. It could, therefore, be understood as an Israelite song of victory. This would then provide an easily understandable reason for its being handed down to us in the Bible. The biblical writers would normally have had no interest whatsoever in such a victory, let alone the songs of victory of enemies long since conquered. If this, in actuality, is the case, the song celebrates an Israelite military campaign which, beginning at the Israelite city of Heshbon, brought the Moabite area north of the Arnon into the hands of the Israelites. In verse 30, Dibon and Madeba could have been district capitals which governed the area between the Arnon (Wādī el-Mōjib) and Wādī el-Wālā on one side and the part of the Mishor north of Wādī el-Wālā on the other. In addition, the possibility may not be excluded that both of these song fragments may even refer to the same event.

It may, therefore, be concluded that Israel did not take the southern Belqā, the land between the territory of Heshbon and the Arnon, away from the "Amorite" King Sihon of Heshbon, but rather from the Moabites. This originally Moabite territory later belonged to the tribe of Gad as indicated by Num 33:24, the incidental reference to Dibon as Dibon-Gad in Num 33:45, and Mesha's notes regarding the Gadite inhabitants of Ataroth. The conquest started from Heshbon, which, along with Elealeh (el-ᶜĀl), Kiryathaim (Khirbet el-Qureiyeh), Nebo (Khirbet el-Mukhayyaṭ), Baal-Meon (Māᶜīn and Shibma (Khirbet Qurn el-Kibsh?), was later considered to belong to the tribe of Reuben

---

The main objection to this reconstruction is that it results in two lines of prose not suitable for a song. This pitfall is avoided by the reconstructions offered by the remaining three authors.

Bartlett:

wnynm ᵓbd ᶜd dybwn	And their seed is destroyed as far as Dibon,
wnšym ᶜd npḥ	And their womenfolk as far as Nophah.

Bartlett interprets *ḥšbwn* as an explanatory gloss to the suffix of *nynm*, *ᵓšr ᶜd mydbᵓ* as a gloss to the rather uncommon place name *npḥ*.

Hanson's reconstruction is the most ingenious:

nr M<ᵓb> ᵓbd	The dominion of Moab has perished
Ḥšbn ᶜd Dybn	From Heshbon as far as Dibon!
nšm <bmt Kmš>	Deserted are the high places of Chemosh
Npḥ ᶜd Mdbᵓ	From Nophah as far as Medebaᵓ!

But while the loss of the consonants -*ᵓb* of *Mᵓb* in the first line of the first couplet might easily be explained as a case of haplography, I cannot see any positive evidence for the insertion of *bmt Kmš* into the first line of the second couplet. This all too free emendation is not accepted by Van Seters either, who suggests the following reconstruction:

wnyrm ᵓbd	Their dominion is destroyed
mḥšbwn ᶜd dybwn	from Heshbon to Dibon.
wnśyᵓyhm ᶜd npḥ	And their princes as far as Nopah,
śry(h)m ᶜd mydbᵓ	(their) commanders as far as Medeba.

according to Num 32:37f.[20] What sort of a shifting in the history of the tribes is reflected here cannot be ascertained.

This also means that the account concerning the defeat of Sihon of Heshbon and the conquest of his kingdom by the Israelites may no longer be considered to be authentic historical tradition. Rather, it is highly probable that this account is based on a fabrication or, to put it less harshly, that it was deduced from the designation of Heshbon as *qryt syḥn.*[21] The theory behind this implies that Canaanites and "Amorites" could be evicted and uprooted but not Edomites, Moabites, and Ammonites, those people joined to Israel by the "bonds of brotherhood." On the one hand, this explains the designation of Sihon as "Amorite,"[22] which is not supported by the Heshbon-song and, on the other, the development of the report which, at first glance, appears to be reliable, in Num 21:26: "Heshbon was the city of Sihon King of the Amorites. He had waged war against the first King of Moab and had taken away his whole land as far as the Arnon." Since the area between the Arnon and the territory of Heshbon was originally known to be Moabite, the events were aligned in this way to prevent a contradiction.

This interpretation of the text still does not provide an answer to the question of who Sihon was after whom Heshbon was called *qryt syḥn.* I must confess that I have no satisfactory answer to this question either. The expression *qryt syḥn* invites comparison with Canaanite place-names containing the element *qryt.*[23] These, however, are real place-names and not epithets. There are no examples among them in which the second word is a personal name. The next analogy is that found in the designation of a quarter[24] in Jerusalem as *ᶜyr dwd*, "City of David," a name which it supposedly acquired as a result of its conquest by King David. If this is the case, Sihon could have been the Moabite or Israelite conqueror or even the founder of Heshbon.[25] Naturally, this is pure conjecture and there are no convincing arguments in support of this theory.

[20]For the territories of Reuben and Gad, see now M. Wüst, *Untersuchungen zu den siedlungsgeographischen Texten des Alten Testaments,* I. *Ostjordanland* (Tübinger Atlas des Vorderen Orients, Beihefte, B 9; Wiesbaden: Ludwig Reichert, 1975) 144-53.

[21]See Van Seters, "The Conquest of Sihon's Kingdom," 195.

[22]For the use of *ʾmry* in the Old Testament, see M. Noth, "Nu 21 als Glied der 'Hexateuch'-Erzählung," *ZAW* 58 (1940/41) 181-89, reprinted in *Aufsätze,* I (n. 19) 94-101.

[23]Cf. Van Seters, "The Conquest of Sihon's Kingdom," 195.

[24]See M. Weippert, *ZDPV* 89 (1973) 96.

[25]The problem is discussed in a similar manner by Van Seters "The Conquest of Sihon's Kingdom," 195). It is made even more complicated by the results from the excavations on the site of Heshbon, Tell Ḥisbān, which have so far not produced any evidence for the existence of a settlement here during the Late Bronze Age. Only during the 1974 campaign were architectural structures connected with Iron I pottery found (in August, 1974, I had the privilege of visiting Heshbon with James A. Sauer who showed me these structures and discussed the problems of the site with me on the spot). From the fact that these building remains obviously were lying on bedrock, it may be concluded that Heshbon was founded in the Iron Age I. The Late Bronze Age center of the Heshbon area may then have been Elealeh (el-ᶜĀl); for the results of the 1962 soundings, see W. L. Reed, "The Archaeological History of Elealeh in Moab," in: *Studies on the Ancient Palestinian World Presented*

The results of the discussion of the two song fragments in Numbers 21 and the Sihon story allow us to reconsider the accounts of the meeting of the Israelites coming out of Egypt with the Edomites and Moabites. The contradiction between the old poetic texts concerning the conquest of the Moabite area north of the Arnon by the Israelites and these texts is obvious. This contradiction shows that the idea of a brotherly coexistence, in this early period, between Israel and its neighbors to the east is pure fiction. It seems to me to be questionable whether one may refer to the story of Eglon and Ehud (Judg 3:12-30) in this context as long as the historical and geographical problems in this narrative cannot be clarified. On the other hand, the campaigns of David sufficiently prove, for the tenth century at least, that the Israelites did not hesitate to attack the Ammonites, Moabites, and Edomites. It could hardly have been much different in earlier periods. S. Mittmann, taking up some of the older proposals — particularly those of M. Noth — has attempted to establish that Num 20:14-21 represents a redactional compilation which is not based on early tradition.[26] In this context, the story then serves to bridge the geographical gap between the wilderness tradition and the Benjaminite conquest tradition which had its starting-point in the *ᶜrbwt mwᵓb*. The Sihon story serves the same function. Since I consider Mittmann's interpretation to be correct, this means that the die has also been cast against the historicity of the later elaboration on the same theme found in Deuteronomy 2. As soon as the Exodus route through Transjordan was firmly established, one had to describe how the native population reacted to the migrating Israelites. The descriptions of the route itself probably refer to the great North-South roads which run through Transjordan. The route of the Syrian Darb el-Ḥajj — followed today by the Ḥejāz Railway and the modern Jordanian "Desert Highway" — suggests itself for the detour around Edom and Moab. A predecessor of the Roman road from Philadelphia (ᶜAmmān) to Aila (el-ᶜAqaba) might have been used to travel through the Edomite and Moabite territories. Mesha of Moab makes mention of the Arnon crossing of this road,[27] which corresponds, by and large, to the modern so-called "King's Highway."[28]

---

to Professor F. V. Winnett on the occasion of his retirement, 1 July 1971 (eds. J. W. Wevers and D. B. Redford; Toronto Semitic Texts and Studies, 2; Toronto and Buffalo: University of Toronto Press, 1972) 18-28.

[26] S. Mittmann, "Num 20, 14-21 — eine redaktionelle Komposition," in: *Wort und Geschichte: Festschrift für K. Elliger zum 70. Geburtstag* (eds. H. Gese and H. P. Rüger; Alter Orient und Altes Testament, 18; Kevelaer: Butzon & Bercker/Neukirchen-Vluyn: Neukirchener Verlag, 1973) 143-49.

[27] Mesha inscription, *KAI* No. 181, line 26: *wᵓnk ᶜśty hmslt bᵓrnn*, "And I made the highway at the Arnon."

[28] *drk hmlk* in Num 20:17 and 21:22 is not the name of a certain road but an *appellative* denoting "public road," "highroad" as Akkadian *ḫarrān šarri*, Aramaic *ᵓrḥ mlkᵓ* (A. Cowley, *Aramaic Papyri of the Fifth Century B.C.* [Oxford: Clarendon Press, 1923], No. 25, lines 6f.), Arabic *darb/ṭarīq sulṭānī*. See E. Weidner, "Assyrische Itinerare," *AfO* 21 (1966) 42-46; B. Oded, "Observations on Methods of Assyrian Rule in Transjordan after the Palestinian Campaign of Tiglath-pileser III," *JNES* 29 (1970) 182f. with n. 41.

The account of the conquest of King Og of Bashan is available for the north of Transjordan. Its earliest witness, on which all others including Num 21:31-35 are dependent, is found in Deut 3:1-7. Even this text, with the exception of the names, contains no old tradition. Rather it is copied from the account of the defeat of Sihon of Heshbon in Deut 2:31-37 which itself is dependent on Num 21:21-26. Og was possibly a figure of the saga traditions among the native population of Late Bronze Age Transjordan (compare Deut 3:11).[29]

The function served by the Og story for the presentation of history by the writers of the Pentateuch is clear. Together with the Sihon pericope, it is intended to cover the conquest of all of Transjordan with the exception of the territories of the Edomites, Moabites, and the Ammonites. To reach this end, the areas ruled by Sihon and Og were greatly exaggerated and a common border on the Jabbok (Nahr ez-Zerqā), which in reality never existed, was assigned to them.[30]

According to a later stylization, northern Transjordan was supposed to have been turned over to "Half-Manasseh." Other reports, however, indicate that one must differentiate more carefully in this area, for the direction of the Israelite settlement basically did not proceed from south to north, as the Og-account assumes, but rather from west to east.[31] The occurrence of the "forest of Ephraim" (2 Sam 18:6) in central Transjordan may well suggest that Ephraimites had moved into this area from the west.

It is also certain that another part of the "House of Joseph" migrated from the west to the east. This was the tribe of Machir which the Song of Deborah places in the land west of the Jordan (Judg 5:14). All the other texts connect it with Gilead. Machir is even designated as "father of Gilead" in the genealogies (Jos 17:1; 1 Chr 2:21, 23; 7:14).

The smaller groups such as Jair (Num 32:41; Deut 3:14) and Nobah (Num 32:42) probably also belong in this context, but we have almost no concrete information about them.

---

[29]The texts locating Og in Ashtaroth in Bashan and the reference of Deut 3:11 to his "bedstead of iron" in Rabba of the Ammonites (ᶜAmmān) cannot be reconciled. J. R. Bartlett ("Sihon and Og, Kings of the Amorites," *VT* 20 [1970] 265-68) argues quite convincingly that two different traditions are involved in the biblical figure of Og, which he traces back to two different groups of Israelites. These Israelites, however, may have borrowed the figure of Og from their Late Bronze Age predecessors.

[30]For the literary history of this boundary line, see M. Wüst, *Untersuchungen*, 13.

[31]For the following, see M. Noth, "Beiträge zur Geschichte des Ostjordanlandes, I. Das Land Gilead als Siedlungsgebiet israelitischer Sippen," *PJ* 37 (1941) 75-81, reprinted in *Aufsätze*, I, 368-73; S. Mittmann, *Beiträge zur Siedlungs- und Territorialgeschichte des nördlichen Ostjordanlandes* (ADPV [2]; Wiesbaden: Otto Harrassowitz, 1970) 209-31. While Mittmann has important corrections to Noth's theses, his own views regarding the location and role of Beth-Rehob conflict with the now well-established localization of this state (Zobah) in the Antilibanus region. See M. Weippert, *Edom: Studien und Materialien zur Geschichte der Edomiter auf Grund schriftlicher und archäologischer Quellen* (unpublished dissertation and Habilitationsschrift, University of Tübingen, 1971) 268-71.

The accounts of the Benjaminite abduction of women in Jabesh-Gilead (Judg 21:6-14) and of Saul's rescue of this city from attack by the Ammonites (1 Samuel 11) could indicate that the Benjaminites maintained relations with Transjordan. Jabesh may even have been founded by Benjaminites.

Consequently, these biblical texts could be used to show that northern Transjordan was a region colonized by Israelite tribes from west of the Jordan. It is striking, however, that Ephraim, Benjamin, and Machir (or rather Manasseh) do not appear in the Song of Deborah as representatives of this area but rather a tribe called Gilead (Judg 5:17) and that the Jephthah account (Judg 10:17-12:6) mentions only the Gileadites, clearly disassociating them from the western tribes.

II

It is generally accepted that the settlement of both the Israelites and their Transjordanian neighbors marked the end of the Late Bronze Age and the beginning of the Iron Age. In as far as Transjordan is concerned, we do not yet have a clear picture of this period of transition.

The Egyptian texts and the Amarna letters, which constitute our extra-biblical written sources, refer only to parts of the area and then only in particular periods. Still, a few Late Bronze Age cities are mentioned in the Amarna letters and in the city-lists of Pharaohs after Tuthmosis III. All of these cities, however, are located in the extreme north, in the Ḥaurān, in the Nuqrā, and in the Jaulān. The southernmost city in this group is Pella. In the written sources prior to Ramesses II, no settlements are mentioned south of a hypothetical line between Pella in the west and Bozra (Boṣrah Eski Shām) in the east; even under Ramesses II, only one settlement is mentioned.[32] The Egyptians designated and described the inhabitants of Seir, that is, of the area south of Wādī el-Ḥasā, as *Š3św*, as nomads, probably from the time of Amenophis III and most certainly from the time of Ramesses II.[33]

These texts could be interpreted to mean that the area between the line Pella-Bozra and Elath (el-ᶜAqaba) did not have a settled population in the Late Bronze Age. Increasing archeological investigations of Transjordan, however, have indicated that this is an erroneous conclusion.

In the last century, it was already established that the statements of the sources about the cities in the extreme north of Transjordan in the second millennium corresponded to Bronze Age tells and other sites in this region. On the basis of surface investigations, Nelson Glueck proposed a thesis for

---

[32]This is the Moabite *btrt* discussed below.

[33]Reference is to the "*Š3św* country of Seir" (Egyptian *t3 Š3św Ś3-ᶜ{-r}-i-r3*) mentioned in Ramesses II's "topographical" list at ᶜAmāra West; see R. Giveon, *Les bédouins Shosou des documents égyptiens* (Documenta et Monumenta Orientis Antiqui, 18; Leiden: E. J. Brill, 1971) 74-77, document 16a, No. 1; M. Weippert, *Edom*, 9 and 31f., No. N93; *Bib* 55 (1974) 270f., 277-79. This list is copied from that of Amenophis III at Soleb where the reference to Seir is not preserved (see Giveon, *Les Bédouins Shosou*, 26-28, document 6a).

Transjordan proper:[34] A large gap existed between the Middle Bronze I and the Early Iron Age settlement of this area, during which nomads lived in the land. In the meantime, however, it has been established that Middle and Late Bronze Age settlements were also present in the area between the Yarmūk in the north and Wādī el-Ḥasā in the south.[35] In his later years, Glueck corrected his earlier thesis correspondingly.[36] In regard to the Middle Bronze Age,[37] I refer to S. Mittmann's survey in the ᶜAjlūn, to Irbid, the tell of Ṣāfūt with its Middle Bronze IIA rampart, to tombs in ᶜAmmān, and to Khirbet ᶜArāᶜir on the northern edge of the Arnon valley. South of the Wādī el-Ḥasā, Glueck reported MB I and IIA sherds from Khirbet Mashmīl.[38] As my survey in Edom showed, these sherds were actually Iron I carinated bowls.[39] In addition to Pella, Late Bronze sites[40] which must also be included here are Irbid, Tell es-Saᶜīdīyeh, Tell Deir ᶜAllā, ᶜAmmān and its environs, el-ᶜĀl, Mādabā, Khirbet el-Mukhayyiṭ and Khirbet ᶜArāᶜir. It is interesting to note that, given the present state of our knowledge, the density of the sites decreases as one moves toward the south. There have been no known Late Bronze finds in the area south of Wādī el-Ḥasā — with the exception of a fragmentary lion-hunt scarab of Amenophis III which is supposed to come from Qilāᶜ eṭ-Ṭiwāl southeast of Wādī Mūsā.[41]

In light of the above-mentioned archeological situation, the reasons for the silence in the texts regarding the area between Pella and Wādī el-Ḥasā are not to be found in the history of settlement; the reasons are, rather, political. This area was located on the other side of the border of the Egyptian Empire while the cities in the north up to the latitude of Pella belonged to the Egyptian province of Upe.

---

[34]See, e.g., N. Glueck, "The Boundaries of Edom," *HUCA* 11 (1936) 141f., *The Other Side of the Jordan* (New Haven: American Schools of Oriental Research, 1940) 21 and *passim; Explorations in Eastern Palestine*, IV (AASOR 25-28; New Haven: American Schools of Oriental Research, 1951) 423.

[35]See the survey of the evidence by R. H. Dornemann, *The Cultural and Archaeological History of the Transjordan in the Bronze and Iron Ages* (unpublished dissertation, University of Chicago, 1970) 32-63.

[36]N. Glueck, *The Other Side of the Jordan* (revised edition; Cambridge, Mass.: American Schools of Oriental Research, 1970) 28 and *passim.*

[37]See in general, R. H. Dornemann, *History*, 32-52; S. Mittmann, *Beiträge*, 256-64 and *passim*; F. Zayadine, in: *The Archaeological Heritage of Jordan*, I. *The Archaeological Periods and Sites (East Bank)* (Amman: Department of Antiquities, 1973) 17-19, 71, and map 5.

[38]N. Glueck, *Explorations in Eastern Palestine*, II (AASOR 15; New Haven, Conn.: American Schools of Oriental Research, 1935) 107f. On the maps the site is called Khirbet el-Mushimmīn (grid ref. 2131.0333). According to an inhabitant of nearby Khirbet Abū Bannah, the name presently in use is Khirbet Mashmīl but the name on the maps is also known.

[39]The significant pottery sherds from the site will be published in my forthcoming book on the Edomites.

[40]See in general, R. H. Dornemann, *History*, 53-63; S. Mittmann, *Beiträge*, 256-64 and *passim*; F. Zayadine, in: *The Archaeological Heritage*, I, 19-21, 72, and map 6.

[41]W. A. Ward, "A Possible New Link between Egypt and Jordan During the Reign of Amenhotep III," *ADAJ* 18 (1973) 45f., pl. XXVII.

In the 13th century, the political changes which were to become characteristic for the first millennium began to make themselves felt in the Egyptian texts. Moab is mentioned for the first time under Ramesses II, probably early in his reign, perhaps even before, or shortly after, his fifth year (1285). The allusion to Moab appears in the representation of a fortress which Ramesses II had ordered drawn on the East Wall of his court in the Luxor Temple.[42] The accompanying legend reads: "The town which the mighty arm of Pharaoh plundered in the Land of Moab, *btrt*." Since it is a standardized vignette of Badawy's type 2b, the drawing does not show how this Moabite *btrt* really looked. By altering only the legend, it was later even used as an illustration for the famous city of *šbdn* south of Qadesh.[43] Consequently, it cannot be established whether Ramesses II conquered a fortress, a fortified city, a village or only a nomad's camp in Moab.[44]

Edom is mentioned for the first time in a model letter in the Papyrus Anastasi VI which is dated in the eighth year of the reign of Merneptah (1216).[45] Up until this time, the Egyptians referred only to the *Š3św*-land or rather the mountains of Seir (which, on the other hand, are known from the Bible as the dwelling-place of the Edomites). In the Papyrus Anastasi VI, the Edomites themselves turn out to be *Š3św*, nomads, who appear with their herds on the eastern border of Egypt and request permission to use the water holes in the Wādī Ṭumīlāt. Since there is little information regarding the location and the extent of Seir in the Egyptian texts, we know nothing about where they came from or how they got to Egypt.

---

[42]See K. A. Kitchen, "Some New Light on the Asiatic Wars of Ramesses II," *JEA* 50 (1964) 49f. with fig. 2 A I A, pl. III. Kitchen 64f. is inclined to identify *btrt* with Khirbet el-Medeiyineh near el-Lejjūn or with el-Miṣnaᶜ near er-Rabbah.

[43]Kitchen, "New Light," 49f. with fig. 2 A I B, Pl. III.

[44]Moab is again mentioned in a "topographical" list of Ramesses II at Luxor; see J. Simons, *Handbook for the Study of Egyptian Topographical Lists Relating to Western Asia* (Leiden: E. J. Brill, 1937) 155, list XXII d. 10. — There are two other representations of fortresses with legends on the exterior face of the east wall of Ramesses II in the Luxor temple which Kitchen wants to connect with Moab. For *Tᵓ-b-w-ᵓ-n-ᵓ* (*Tbn*, "New Light," 52, fig. 3 B IV A), identified by Kitchen with Dibon ("New Light," 53, 63) see S. Ahituv, "Did Ramesses II Conquer Dibon?" *IEJ* 22 (1972) 141f. (I believe that *Tbn*/*Tpn* has to be sought in *northern* Transjordan or even the Nuqrā or the Ḥaurān.) The place-name read *Yn?d*[. . .] "in the mountain of *M-r3-rw-n-3* (*Mrrn*)" by Kitchen ("New Light," 52f. with fig. 3 B III) may tentatively be restored as *Y-w*[ ]*-d*[*-h-m-rw-k*] (*Yd*[*hmrk*]) = "Yad ha-Melek"; see R. Giveon, "The Shosu of Egyptian Sources and the Exodus," in: *Fourth World Congress of Jewish Studies, Papers,* I (Jerusalem: World Union of Jewish Studies, 1967) 194. This place may be located in northern Palestine. Both place-names, therefore, do not belong to Moab.

[45]Pap. Anastasi VI 51-61 (*ᵓ-d-w-m*, lines 54f.), A. H. Gardiner, *Late-Egyptian Miscellanies* (Brussels: Édition de la Fondation Égyptologique Reine Élisabeth, 1937) 76f. The papyrus is usually dated in the reign of Seti II, but at least the model letter referred to is a copy of a letter from the time of Merneptah. Merneptah is mentioned with his name "Merneptah-*ḥtpw-ḥr-m3ᶜt*" in lines 55, 56, 60 (the name of Seti II = "Merneptah II" is "*Wśr-ḫprw-Rᶜ-stpw-n-Rᶜ* Seti Merneptah"). Furthermore, Seti II reigned for only six years but, in line 58, the *8th* year of a Pharaoh is mentioned. Merneptah, on the other hand, reigned for more than eight years. The text of the model letter is translated by J. A. Wilson in *ANET*, 259.

As opposed to Moab and Edom, the Ammonites are first mentioned in the Bible.

In terms of the history of settlement, it has been difficult up to now to understand the change in the conditions in Transjordan indicated by the appearance of the Moabites and Edomites in the 13th century. We have some Iron Age I material from excavations of settlements and fortifications (for example, from Pella, Tell Deir ᶜAllā, Tell es-Saᶜīdīyeh, Khirbet el-Ḥajjār, the southern Rujm el Malfūf on Jebel ᶜAmmān, el-ᶜĀl, Heshbon, Dibon, Khirbet ᶜArāᶜir, el-Bālūᶜ), as well as material from tombs (for example, from Irbid, ᶜAmmān, Saḥāb, Mādabā, Nebo).[46] The majority of the Iron Age I settlements mentioned in the scholarly literature, however, have been discovered only by archeological surveys, primarily those of N. Glueck.[47]

The basic problem with surface investigations is well known.[48] Their findings may be used only as positive evidence. With their help, one may establish that people were present at a site during particular periods. The determination of gaps in settlement *e silentio*, that is, by the fact that pottery from certain periods is missing, is unreliable. Another problem in regard to Transjordan is that, while the *general* framework for the chronology of pottery has been established by comparison with Palestinian pottery development and on the basis of additional criteria, the *details* are still very hazy. N. Glueck's data concerning his finds provide an additional variable. We do not mean to minimize his pioneer efforts when we note that the selection of the sites he investigated was not always representative and that the classifications of his sherds may be challenged to a certain degree today.[49] Unfortunately, however, this does have serious implications for the Iron Age I and its related problems which are being considered within the context of this symposium. I would like to point out briefly some of these implications in that area which I know best — the region of the Edomites south of Wādī el-Ḥasā. Here Glueck found and

---

[46]See in general, R. H. Dornemann, *History*, 79-123 and *passim*; F. Zayadine, in: *The Archaeological Heritage*, I, 21-29, 73-77, and map 7 (not distinguishing the sub-periods within the Iron Age).

[47]See Glueck's four volumes of *Explorations in Eastern Palestine* (AASOR 14, 15, 18/19, 25-28; New Haven, Conn.: American Schools of Oriental Research, 1934/35/39/51) *passim*; and *The Other Side of the Jordan* (revised edition; Cambridge, Mass.: American Schools of Oriental Research, 1970) *passim*; S. Mittmann, *Beiträge*, 256-64 and *passim*. Some material may also be found in the reports on the *Lehrkurse* of the German Evangelical Institute for Archaeology in Jerusalem published in *ZDPV*. Via private communications, I am aware of several other surveys. They have not as yet been published.

[48]See the remarks by S. Mittmann, *Beiträge*, 4f., and for some other aspects of the problem, H. J. Franken, "Einiges über die Methode von archäologischen Oberflächenuntersuchungen," in: *Archäologie und Altes Testament: Festschrift für K. Galling zum 8. Januar 1970* (eds. A. Kuschke and E. Kutsch; Tübingen: J. C. B. Mohr, 1970) 117-25.

[49]Cf. S. Mittmann, *Beiträge*, 1f.; H. J. Franken, "The Other Side of the Jordan," *ADAJ* 15 (1970) 5-10; H. J. Franken and W. J. A. Power, "GLUECK'S *Explorations in Eastern Palestine* in the light of recent evidence," *VT* 21 (1971) 119-23.

described sixty-two Iron Age sites.[50] He consistently classified the sherds from these sites as "Early Iron Age I-II pottery" or, synonymously, as "Edomite pottery." In a very few instances, Glueck provided either a slightly closer dating or differentiated between "coarse" and "fine ware" or "plain" and "painted pottery."[51] On the basis of this, it could be assumed that Edom was covered by a relatively fine network of settlements already in early Iron I. When B. Rothenberg's excavations in Timna[c] showed that the class of "painted Edomite pottery" today called "Midianite" or "Ḥejāz Pottery" extended into the end of the Late Bronze Age,[52] it was then possible to formulate the thesis that the Edomites had settled and adopted a fixed political organization considerably earlier than the Israelites. Some reasons could be given for this.[53] It was also possible to understand the place names in the Edomite king-list found in Genesis 36 as well as the tradition about the conflict between the Edomites and the Israelites during the Exodus within this background. All of this, however, was called in question by C.-M. Bennett's excavations in Umm el-Biyārah and in Ṭawīlān in the region of Petra and in Buṣeirā (probably the location of the Edomite capital of Bozrah).[54] Iron I pottery is not found in any of these sites even though Glueck noted "Edomite" or "Early Iron Age I-II pottery" here. The oldest pottery from Buṣeirā may be dated, at the earliest, in the 10th century; that from Ṭawīlān, at the beginning of the 9th century; that from Umm el-Biyārah, only from the 7th century. A reexamination of Glueck's pottery from forty Iron Age sites and a small survey which I myself conducted in Edom in 1974 revealed similar results.[55] Glueck's use of the term "Early Iron Age I-II,"

---

[50]See the lists in V. R. Gold, *Studies in the History and Culture of Edom* (unpublished dissertation, Johns Hopkins University, Baltimore, Md., 1951) 26-36; M. Weippert, *Edom*, 396f., with map 1 I-III.

[51]See M. Weippert, *Edom*, 402f.

[52]B. Rothenberg, *Timna, Valley of the Biblical Copper Mines* (New Aspects of Antiquity; London: Thames and Hudson, 1972) *passim*, esp. 153-63. The history of the problem of this kind of pottery is described in M. Weippert, *Edom*, 403-7 (details still to be corrected).

[53]M. Weippert, *The Settlement of the Israelite Tribes in Palestine: A Critical Survey of Recent Scholarly Debate* (SBT II 21; London: SCM Press/Naperville, Ill.: Allenson, 1971) 133, n. 17.

[54]Umm el-Biyārah: C.-M. Bennett, "Chronique archéologique: Umm el-Biyara," *RB* 71 (1964) 250-53; "Fouilles d'Umm el-Biyara: Rapport préliminaire," *RB* 73 (1966) 372-403; "Exploring Umm el Biyara, the Edomite fortress-rock which dominates Petra," *Illustrated London News* April 30, 1966, 29-31; "Des fouilles à Umm el-Biyarah: Les Édomites à Pétra," *BTS* 84 (1966) 6-16; "A Cosmetic Palette from Umm el-Biyara," *Antiquity* 41 (1967) 197-201; *Excavations on Umm el-Biyara, Petra* (Publications of the Colt Archaeological Institute; London: Bernard Quaritch, forthcoming). — Ṭawīlān: C.-M. Bennett, "The Excavations at Tawilan, Nr. Petra," *ADAJ* 12/13 (1967/68) 53-55; "Chronique archéologique: Ṭawilân (Jordanie)," *RB* 77 (1970) 371-74; "A Brief Note on Excavations at Tawilan, Jordan, 1968-70," *Levant* 3 (1971) v-vii. — Buṣeirā: C. -M Bennett, "Chronique archéologique: Buseira," *RB* 79 (1972) 426-30; "Excavations at Buseirah, Southern Jordan, 1971: Preliminary Report," *Levant* 5 (1973) 1-11; "Excavations at Buseirah, Southern Jordan, 1972: Preliminary Report," *Levant* 6 (1974) 1-24; "Chronique archéologique: Buseira," *RB* 81 (1974) 73-76.

[55]The work on Glueck's pottery was sponsored by the Deutsche Forschungsgemeinschaft. The results from both investigations will be reported in my forthcoming book on the Edomites.

therefore, in most cases means only that he had collected Iron Age pottery. According to our present information, the main period of settlement in Edom must have been in the early Iron Age II, specifically from the 9th to the 7th centuries.[56] After this, a decline may be noted. Before the 9th century, the settlement of the land was gradual, first of all in the north. I know of six sites from the area between Wādī el Ḥasā and approximately eṭ-Ṭafīleh which have Iron I pottery; from the south, however, I know of only one site.[57]

If the findings from Edom may be generalized, Glueck's statement that he found "Early Iron Age I-II pottery" in a particular place cannot be interpreted to mean that he actually found *Iron I* pottery in each case. This relativizes all statements about the beginning of Iron Age settlement in Transjordan which are based on this kind of information alone, without more exact specifications.

Nevertheless, the results of excavations, more definite statements by Glueck, and recent surveys, particularly that of S. Mittmann in the ᶜAjlūn, tend to indicate that, in the area between the Yarmūk and the Wādī el-Ḥasā, a heavy increase in settlement may be observed in the Iron Age I. Taking into consideration the above-mentioned reservations, this also applies to the area between the Wādī el-Ḥasā and Rās en-Naqb, that is, Edom, even if the development there was more gradual, extending into Iron II. As a whole, the increase in the number of settlements at the beginning of the Iron Age must be related to the establishment of the Israelites, Ammonites, Moabites, and Edomites in Transjordan; it is the basic archeological evidence for this process.

III

One question has been completely left out in the considerations I have mentioned up to now. What caused the settlement movement at the beginning of the Iron Age which so fundamentally altered Transjordan and Palestine?[58] Was it, as the Bible states, the movement of the Israelites from Egypt into the land promised to their fathers? (What about the Ammonites, Moabites, and Edomites, then?) Were there hordes of land-hungry nomads or, at least, nomads

---

[56] This may hold true, in principle, also for other parts of Transjordan.

[57] The northern sites include Khirbet Abū Bannah (grid ref. 2156.0322), N. Glueck, *Explorations*, II, 107, revisited on September 3, 1974; Khirbet Mashmīl (grid ref. 2131.0333), N. Glueck, *Explorations, II,* 107f., revisited on September 3, 1974 (see also n. 38 above); el-Qūsah el-Ḥamrā (grid ref. 2020.0377), N. Glueck, *Explorations*, III, 42f.; Khirbet es-Sabᶜah (grid ref. 2103.0322), N. Glueck, *Explorations*, II, 101, eth-Thuwāneh (grid ref. 2192.0182), N. Glueck, *Explorations*, I, 77; II, 97; III 53, revisited on September 4, 1974; Khirbet Umm Sheᶜīr (grid ref. 2057.0251), N. Glueck, *Explorations*, II, 100. — The southern site is Khirbet ᶜAṭīyeh (grid ref. 1935.9387), N. Glueck, *Explorations*, II, 68.

[58] The following questions (which will not all be answered directly during the course of the paper) refer to some current opinion regarding the Israelite settlement and to hypotheses which could possibly be advanced. For the "nomads willing to settle," the well-known views of A. Alt may be cited, while the expression "hordes of land-hungry nomads" is borrowed from G. E. Mendenhall's polemics against such ideas (*Bib* 50 [1969] 436). For the "revolutionary movement," see again G. E. Mendenhall; for the "plastered cistern," W. F. Albright; for the "agricultural terrace," C. H. J. de

willing to settle whose desire was satisfied during the so-called "Aramaic migration?" Or, contrary to all biblical tradition, was this increase in settlement in the 12th century caused by an expansion of the Canaanite population? Was it a revolutionary movement directed against the existing social order which set up a rural culture — possibly religiously motivated — with elements of a primitive democracy over against the feudalism of the ruling class in the cities? Or, was it rather technological innovations such as the plastered cistern or the agricultural terrace which made it possible to cultivate previously untilled areas? Questions such as these cannot be answered on the basis of evidence from Transjordan alone. It is, therefore, advisable to take a quick look at Canaan, the land west of the Jordan.

I will not attempt to come to grips with the scholarly literature within the scope of this article.[59] Rather, I will present my current views regarding the settlement of the Israelites in Canaan in the form of theses which either have been already substantiated or still need to be proved elsewhere.[60]

I am still convinced that the representation of the systematic conquest of Canaan by the united tribes of Israel under the leadership of Joshua as recorded

---

Geus. References: A. Alt, "Die Landnahme der Israeliten in Palästina" (1925), *Kleine Schriften zur Geschichte des Volkes Israel*, I (Munich: C. H. Beck, 1953) 89-125, English translation: "The Settlement of the Israelites in Palestine," *Essays on Old Testament History and Religion* (Garden City, N.Y.: Doubleday, 1967) 173-221; "Joshua" (1936), *Kleine Schriften*, I, 176-92; "Erwägungen über die Landnahme der Israeliten in Palästina" (1939), *Kleine Schriften*, I, 126-75. — G. E. Mendenhall, "The Hebrew Conquest of Palestine," *BA* 25 (1962) 66-87; *The Tenth Generation: The Origins of the Biblical Tradition* (Baltimore/London: The Johns Hopkins University Press, 1973) *passim* (conveniently summarized in chap IX, pp. 215-26). — W. F. Albright, "The Rôle of the Canaanites in the History of Civilization" (1942), *The Bible and the Ancient Near East: Essays in Honor of W. F. Albright* (Garden City, N.Y.: Doubleday, 1961) 341 and 358, n. 72. — C. H. J. de Geus, "The Importance of Archaeological Research into the Palestinian Agricultural Terraces, with an Excursus on the Hebrew Word *gbī*," *PEQ* 107 (1975) 65-74, esp. 70.

[59]Much of the literature from 1925-66 was included in my book *Die Landnahme der israelitischen Stämme in der neueren wissenschaftlichen Diskussion: Ein kritischer Bericht* (FRLANT 92; Göttingen: Vandenhoeck & Ruprecht, 1967). In the English translation (n. 53), the literature was expanded to include titles up through 1969. In the meantime several very important papers and monographs have appeared. Of these, I mention here only the following: W. F. Albright, *Yahweh and the Gods of Canaan: A Historical Analysis of Two Contrasting Faiths* (School of Oriental and African Studies, University of London, Jordan Lectures in Comparative Religion, 7; London: The Athlone Press, 1968); R. de Vaux, *Histoire ancienne d'Israël*, [I.] *Des origines à l'installation en Canaan;* II. *La période des Juges* (Études Bibliques; Paris: J. Gabalda, 1971/73); Sh. Yeivin, *The Israelite Conquest of Canaan* (Uitgaven van het Nederlands Historisch-Archaeologisch Instituut te Istanbul, 27; Istanbul: Nederlands Historisch-Archaeologisch Instituut in het Nabije Oosten, 1971; see my review in *BO* 31 [1974] 296-99); S. Herrmann, *Geschichte Israels in alttestamentlicher Zeit* (Munich: Chr. Kaiser, 1973) 61-166.

[60]In addition to the book mentioned in n. 59, see M. Weippert, "Abraham der Hebräer? Bemerkungen zu W. F. Albrights Deutung der Väter Israels," *Bib* 52 (1971) 407-32; "Fragen des israelitischen Geschichtsbewusstseins," *VT* 23 (1973) 415-42; "Semitische Nomaden des zweiten Jahrtausends: Über die *Š3św* der ägyptischen Quellen," *Bib* 55 (1974) 265-80, 427-33; article "Canaan, Conquest and Settlement of" in *Interpreter's Dictionary of the Bible Supplementary Volume* (Nashville, Tenn.: Abingdon Press, 1976) 125-30.

in the book of Joshua is unrealistic and reflects the ideas of a later period. If it came to successful military ventures at all, then these were conducted by individual tribes or tribal alliances, operating from their own territory against isolated cities such as, for example, Bethel and Laish/Dan[61] — or against other tribes. Most of the events, however, were of a peaceful nature.

A. Alt has called attention to the fact that the Israelite tribal territories, by and large, were situated outside of the realm of the Late Bronze Age cities on the wooded mountains of Palestine[62] or in the northern Negev. These areas, however, were not unpopulated in the Late Bronze Age. Apart from a few scattered cities, Egyptian texts such as the report of Seti I about the Asian military campaign in the first year of his reign or the satirical letter in the Papyrus Anastasi I indicate that these areas were inhabited by *Šꜣśw*.[63] The *Šꜣśw*, as we know from other texts, were nomads who lived in tents and raised small cattle.[64] One may then conclude that it is among these *Šꜣśw* that the origins of Israel can be found. The same also holds true for the people of Transjordan. I have already noted that Seir was considered to be a *Šꜣśw*-land and that the Edomites at the time of Merneptah were clearly referred to as *Šꜣśw*. If the stele from el-Bālū^{c},[65] which for stylistic reasons is to be dated in the 12th century, is really a Moabite monument, it indicates that the Moabites also came from the *Šꜣśw*. R. Giveon has recently shown that the prince portrayed between the two divinities on the stele wears his hair in the typical style of the *Šꜣśw*.[66] Finally, even the biblical tradition lends support to the thesis that the Hebrew patriarchs, the ancestors of Israel, were nomads.[67] Significant here is that the *Haftorte*[68] of patriarchal tradition, Shechem and Bethel (for Jacob), Hebron and Gerar (for Abraham), and Beer-sheba (for Isaac) are located in the nomadic areas of the Late Bronze Age. Shechem (Tell el-Balāṭah), Bethel (Beitīn), Hebron (Jebel er-Rumeideh in the city of el-Khalīl), and Gerar (location unknown) were urban enclaves in these areas while Beer-sheba (Bīr es-the name implies, was a well. The essentially peaceful relationships between the

[61]Bethel: Judg 1:22, 23-26. Laish/Dan: Judges 18, cf. Josh 19:47. For the literary aspects of the Laish story, cf. A. Malamat, "The Danite Migration and the Pan-Israelite Exodus-Conquest: A Biblical Narrative Pattern," *Bib* 51 (1970) 1-16.

[62]A. Alt, "The Settlement of the Israelites in Palestine," *Essays*, 204; "Erwägungen über die Landnahme der Israeliten in Palästina," *Kleine Schriften,*, I, 126f., 144f.

[63]The relevant passages are collected in R. Giveon, *Les bédouins Shosou*, 39-60, document 11, and 125-31, document 36. See also my remarks, "Semitische Nomaden des zweiten Jahrtausends," 271f., 276f.

[64]See M. Weippert, "Semitische Nomaden des zweiten Jahrtausends," 274f.

[65]Bibliography in R. Giveon, *Les bédouins Shosou* 202f., n. 1f.; M. Weippert, "Semitische Nomaden des zweiten Jahrtausends," 271f., n. 4.

[66]R. Giveon, *Les bédouins Shosou*, 203.

[67]Details in M. Weippert, "Abraham der Hebräer?," 418-22.

[68]The German term *Haftort* (or *Haftpunkt*) cannot be adequately rendered in English. In the words of J. Bright (*Early Israel in Recent History Writing: A Study in Method* [SBT 19; London: SCM Press, 1956] 45, n. 1), it "refers to the place to which a tradition adheres and where it was supposedly handed down."

nomadic patriarchs and the cities could provide indications for a certain amount of interdependence and interaction between both groups. This corresponds exactly to the more recent findings in nomadic research.[69]

I would, therefore, like to conclude that the patriarchal stories refer to the Late Bronze Age nomadic population in the Palestinian mountains and the northern Negev and originally, perhaps, even to the migration of portions of this population into these areas. Abraham, Isaac, and Jacob could have played a role here which might be the reason why the memory of them was preserved. On the basis of this identification of the patriarchs, a few striking traits in the tradition may be explained such as the fact that the patriarchs belong to none of the Israelite tribes even though the *Haftorte* for their tradition are located in particular tribal territories, and the fact that they were not worshippers of YHWH as still shines through the later elaborations of traditions.[70] These traditions originate in a period before the development of the Israelite tribal system and before that process of religious ethnogenesis which gave Israel her unmistakable identity. If, nevertheless, they are made a part of the proto-history of Israel, then this can only mean that the *Š3św* poqulation of Canaan, to which the patriarchs belonged, formed the basis for later Israel. This also easily explains the reference to "Israel" as a "people" in Canaan, probably in Middle Palestine, in the fifth year of Merneptah (1219).[71] There is, therefore, no need for any acrobatic attempts to harmonize it with the Exodus tradition. Based on the evidence of the formation of her name with the divine name El, the original tribal confederacy of "Israel" is still "pre-Israelitish," if one may express it in this paradoxical manner. The groups mediating the experiences of the liberation from Egypt and the rescue at the Sea of Reeds or the worship of the God of Mount Sinai to the tribes joined in the existing tribal confederation and apparently effected something like a "conversion."

The establishment of *Š3św* in those areas where they had already wandered with their herds in the Late Bronze Age hypothetically may be traced back to overpopulation. I think that, due to a natural increase in population and also due to the arrival of other groups in the 13th century, a point was reached in which the traditional nomadic economies were no longer sufficient to feed the *Š3św* population. It can be shown with a text such as Josh 17:14-18 that a movement into the large fertile plains of Palestine was blocked by the superior power of the Canaanite city-states, and, perhaps, by that of the Egyptian Empire (which, by the way, is never mentioned in the Bible). Only the possibilities of emigration to Transjordan and of "internal colonization" remained. In addition

---

[69]See, e.g., M. B. Rowton, "Urban Autonomy in a Nomadic Environment," *JNES* 32 (1973) 201-15 (with bibliography).

[70]See the now classic monograph of A. Alt, *Der Gott der Väter* (BWANT III 12; Stuttgart: W. Kohlhammer, 1929), reprinted with additions (cf. *PJ* 36 [1940] 100-3) in *Kleine Schriften*, I, 1-78; English translation: "The God of the Fathers," *Essays*, 1-100. For a more recent treatment of this subject which has considerably altered the picture, see F. M. Cross, *Canaanite Myth*, 3-75.

[71]"Israel Stele" of Merneptah, line 27, *ANET*, 378.

to the raising of small cattle and temporary cultivation, they were now forced to convert to *systematic* agriculture. This brought with it a gradual settlement. The archeological evidence for this is the many small or large Early Iron Age I settlements in the former *Šꜣśw* land built either on virgin soil or on the site of some city destroyed recently or in the past.[72] Where the opportunity arose, a city found in the *Šꜣśw* area was also conquered and its cultivated lands seized.[73] Generally, however, a peaceful agreement was reached with the cities and they were eventually integrated into the tribes as "clans." These various possibilities may be studied in Gibeon (Joshua 9), in Shechem, Tirzah, etc. (Num 26:29-34).[74]

In Transjordan, the settlement process of the Israelites, Ammonites, Moabites, and Edomites appears to have occured peacefully; at least at present we have no archeological or other evidence to the contrary. The existing Late Bronze Age settlements gradually grew into the new order. Larger conflicts arose only after the tribes and the peoples had consolidated and began to expand as was the case, for example, with the conflicts of the Ammonites and the Israelites in Gilead at the time of Jephthah and Saul, or of the Israelites and the Moabites in the Belqā as recounted in the song fragments recorded in Numbers 21.

---

[72]See M. Weippert, *Settlement*, 135 with n. 24 (in this note, line 4 from the bottom, the word "discovery" has to be replaced by "invention"). The examples can now be multiplied; much pertinent information may be found in M. Kochavi (ed.), יוהדה שומרון וגולן: סקר ארכיאולוגי בשנת תשכ״ח (Jerusalem: The Archaeological Survey of Israel, Carta, 1972). Good examples for the reoccupation of deserted sites are Ai (et-Tell near Deir Dibwān), Tell Deir ᶜAllā, and Hazor (Tell el-Qadaḥ). For Ai, where a short-lived Iron I village was built on the ruins of a large Early Bronze city, see J. A. Callaway, "New Evidence on the Conquest of Ai," *JBL* 87 (1968) 312-20, and the convincing critique of Callaway's historical interpretation of the archeological evidence by A. Kuschke, "Ḥiwwiter in ha-ᶜAi?" in: *Wort und Geschichte: Festschrift für K. Elliger zum 70. Geburtstag* (eds. H. Gese and H. P. Rüger; Alter Orient und Altes Testament, 18; Kevelaer: Butzon & Bercker/Neukirchen-Vluyn: Neukirchener Verlag, 1973) 115-19. For the occupation by nomadic groups of the ruins of recently destroyed Late Bronze settlements at Tell Deir ᶜAllā and Hazor, see H. J. Franken, "The Excavations at Deir ᶜAllā in Jordan, 2nd season," *VT* 11 (1961) 361-72; "The Excavations at Deir ᶜAllā in Jordan, 3rd season," *VT* 12 (1962) 378-82; "Excavations at Deir ᶜAllā, Season 1964," *VT* 14 (1964) 417-22; Y. Yadin, *Hazor: The Head of All Those Kingdoms* (The Schweich Lectures of the British Academy, 1970; London: The British Academy and Oxford University Press, 1972) 129-34.

[73]This was apparently the case with Bethel (Beitīn) and Laish/Dan (Tell el-Qāḍī; see n. 61 above) and perhaps with Hebron (Jebel er-Rumeideh in the city of el-Khalīl) and Debir (Khirbet Rabūḍ; for the identification, see M. Kochavi, "Khirbet Rabûd = Debir," *Tel-Aviv* 1 [1974] 2-33; Judg 1:8-15 = Josh 15:13-19).

[74]See M. Weippert, *Settlement*, 18-20.

Israelite Conduct of War in the Conquest of Canaan According to the Biblical Tradition

ABRAHAM MALAMAT
The Hebrew University, Jerusalem

A major dilemma confronts the student of the Israelite conquest of Canaan, encountered also in other facets of Israel's proto-history: what degree of historicity can be ascribed to the biblical tradition (more precisely, those traditions as formed in Numbers and Deuteronomy) concerning the conquest of Transjordan and (in Joshua and Judges 1) Cisjordan? For this tradition, which crystallized only after generations of complex literary reworking, could only reflect the conceptions and tendentiousness of later redactors and, therefore, might be devoid of any actual historical value.

Our problem becomes acute when we realize that the scores of extra-biblical sources on Canaan in the 13th century B.C.E. — the generally conceded period of the Israelite Conquest, or at least of its central phases — make no mention of these events. Nevertheless, this should not lead to an exaggerated skepticism (often met with) as if the entire episode were fabricated. This deficiency can probably be ascribed to the fact that the Israelite Conquest created no disturbance in the international political scene — in any event, nothing sufficient to make an impression upon contemporaneous records, especially those of Canaan's overlord, Egypt. Thus, in reconstructing the history of the conquest, the Israelite record alone must suffice. This, of course, imposes upon us all the limitations of self-evidence — its subjectiveness and the adherent suspicions of idealization and aggrandizement, subservient to political and religious ideologies. Further, the historical trustworthiness of biblical traditions receded with the lapse of time between events and their literary recording. But this memory gap was not acting alone for, more significantly, two other processes were affecting biblical historiography, gradually obscuring the initial reality.

The first operant was "reflection," which subjected the Conquest to contemplation — why and how Canaan fell — and conjured new assessments and motivations, grafting them onto the early events. Thereby, there arose in the biblical sources a historical treatment subordinate to an explicit theological doctrine.[1] Whereas in the relatively raw, early depictions of the Israelite wars,

---

For full references to the works cited below, see the bibliography. A differently edited version of this article appeared in *Encyclopaedia Judaica, Yearbook 1975/76*, by kind permission of the American Schools of Oriental Research.

[1]Cf. Seeligmann, *P*ᵓ*raqim II*, 273ff.

the mortal and the divine are intertwined, the later redactors (the so-called Deuteronomist) have accentuated and brought to the fore the role of the Lord of Israel, submerging human feats. Thus crystallized the ideology of the Holy War, or rather the "Yahweh War," whether of offensive or defensive nature.[2] Such "real" factors as numbers of soldiers or the weaponry involved are of no consequence here, nor is the disparity in the strength between Israel and her adversaries (as, for instance, in the Gideon and Deborah episodes).[3] The sacred element increasingly outshines the profane: God fights for this people (Josh 10:14) and even sends forth before the Israelites the mysterious *ṣir*ᶜ*ah* (hornet? terror?)[4] to overwhelm the enemy ("not by your sword and not by your bow"; Josh 24:12; cf. Exod 23:27-28; Deut 7:20).

The second operant, "telescoping, " is the compression of a string of events into a unified narrative of a relatively brief time-span. Long, involved campaigns were foreshortened chronologically by late redactors, thereby creating in retrospect a historical account of artificial simplicity.

Thus, there eventually emerged the culminating level of biblical consciousness, what I would term the "official" or "canonical" tradition of the conquest. This tradition presents a more-or-less organic and continuous chain of events, in straightforward narrative: the territory on both sides of the Jordan was occupied in a swift military operation, a sort of *Blitzkrieg*.. Initially under Moses and then under Joshua — and with full divine collaboration — all twelve Israelite tribes acted in concert. Canaan was conquered almost in its entirety (redeeming a divine pledge to the Patriarchs). As hinted above, remnants of variant traditions are found in the biblical sources, occasionally even contradicting the final version just described. An example is the conquest of Cisjordan (that is, western Palestine) according to Judges 1. This source negates the entire depiction of a unified, pan-Israelite conquest upheld by the "official" tradition. Not only does this deviant chapter describe several particularistic tribal conquests, but the very direction of conquest is reversed — from the north-central hill-country toward the Negev in the south. Furthermore, the chapter contradicts the "total conquest" by specifying the alien enclaves which held on in the midst of the domains of the individual tribes, too strong to be dispossessed. Thus, the actual course of events comprising the conquest was very much more complex than the simplistic, streamlined, pan-Israelite description projected by the "official" tradition.

---

[2]The basic study on the Holy War in the Bible is von Rad, *Heilige Krieg*; he restricts this concept to the defensive mode of Israel's wars, as manifest primarily in the book of Judges. Stolz, *Jahwes und Israels Kriege*, however, justly extends it to the offensive aspect, as in the book of Joshua. For the most recent treatment of this subject, see Jones, *VT* 25 (1975), where a sharp distinction is made between "Holy War" — the biblical redactors' retrospective schematization of early Israelite military experience — and that actual experience, preferably termed "Yahweh War." For a comparative study on divine warfare in Israel and Mesopotamia, cf. Weippert, *ZAW* 89.

[3]Cf. Miller, *Divine Warrior*, 156ff.

[4]Garstang, *Joshua*, 251f., in a novel interpretation, assumes that the *ṣir*ᶜ*āh*, "hornet," refers figuratively to the Pharaohs (cf. the hieroglyph *bỉty*, "King of Lower Egypt"), whose thrusts into

ON THE PHENOMENOLOGY OF THE CONQUEST

Having assessed the biblical source material, we may now turn to the task at hand. We shall avoid a factual reconstruction of the course of the conquest, as so often sought by those who presuppose its military nature,[5] and we shall not delve into literary criticism of the biblical text or treat the extra-biblical and archeological material as such. Our less pretentious scrutiny of the extant conquest tradition (and partly that of Judges) is solely from the military viewpoint, and our analysis of real historical situations is complemented by schematized, hypothetical projections. Such an approach, it is hoped, will provide a point of departure for reaffirming the tenability of much of the biblical tradition, and thereby retrieve it from the clutches of current criticism.

We shall presuppose two guiding principles in our working hypothesis. (1) The biblical evidence is basically no more than an ancient theoretical model depicting the conquest as if the Israelites themselves (especially in the "official" tradition) sought to form an articulate concept of their inheritance and domination of Canaan (much like the modern conjectures of biblical research). Despite poetic embellishment and distortion, this ancient "theory" had the advantage of being the product of a close and authentic intimacy with the land, its topography, demography, and military situation, etc. Thus, it provided an operative basis for (2) our "typological approach," which serves to determine and to define the prevalent and underlying phenomena within the traditions of conquest and settlement, avoiding the fetters of the continuity of the biblical account. Several of the outstanding phenomena exemplifying the conquest may be noted at the outset.

(a) It is a basic element of Israelite consciousness that Canaan was "inherited" by force, whether an act of man or God. This tenet, a leitmotif running throughout the biblical sources, diametrically contradicts the widespread scholarly assumption (fostered primarily by the Alt-Noth school of thought),[6] which predicates an initially peaceful occupation, largely through transhumance. This biblical thesis, however, finds weighty support in the archeological evidence, demonstrating that several Canaanite cities (such as Lachish in the south, Bethel in the central sector, and Hazor in the north), which according to the Bible were conquered by the Israelites, were indeed destroyed in the 13th century B.C.E., or, more precisely, in the second half of that century.[7] With a few exceptions (where the archeological results indeed remain

---

Canaan would have paved the way for the Israelite invasion. But the basis for this assumption — his identification of the hieroglyph as a hornet rather than a bee — is precarious.

[5]For recent comprehensive treatments, see, e.g., Mazar, *World History of the Jewish People*, III, and Yeivin, *Conquest of Canaan.*

[6]See Alt, *Kleine Schriften* I, and Noth, *Josua*, and in some of his other works. This critical school of thought has been opposed strongly by Kaufmann, in: *Scripta Hierosolymitana*, 327ff., as well as in his other works cited in the bibliography.

[7]See Albright, *BASOR* 74; in addition, for Bethel, see J. L. Kelso, *The Excavations of Bethel.* (AASOR 39, 1968), esp. p. 32; and for Hazor, Y. Yadin, *Hazor* (Schweich Lectures 1970), esp. pp. 108, 131.

problematic), there is significant agreement between the archeological and biblical evidence, and any denial of this correspondence would appear hypercritical.[8]

(b) Another major feature in the several biblical traditions is that the Israelites leaving Egypt were deflected from forcing direct entry into Canaan by the shortest route, from the south. The road along the northern coast of Sinai, known in the Bible as the "way of the land of the Philistines," was surely blocked to the Israelites, it being the Egyptian military route *par excellence*. The reliefs of Seti I (ca. 1300 B.C.E.) depict a series of fortifications protecting this highway, showing that the Egyptians could readily have stemmed any Israelite movement along it. Indeed, these circumstances may be reflected in the book of Exodus: "When Pharaoh let the people go, God did not lead them by the way of the land of the Philistines, although that was near; for God said, 'Lest the people repent when they see war, and return to Egypt'" (13:17). On the other hand, the Israelite attempt to penetrate northward through the Negev, farther inland, ended in failure, for Canaanite strongholds such as Hormah (cf. Num 14:40-45; 21:1; Deut 1:44) east of Beer-sheba, effectively protected the southern hill-country. Unable to advance, the Israelites made a broad swing around into Transjordan, crossing the Jordan river to invade Canaan from its eastern flank. Thus, they supplanted an ineffective frontal assault with a strategically indirect approach (for this military means, see below).

(c) The Canaanite populace west of the Jordan had no unified, overall military organization with which to confront the invaders. Furthermore, the absence of political cohesion was matched by the lack of any Canaanite national consciousness. Only twice are Canaanite fronts against the Israelites, albeit limited, in evidence: once in the south, five allied Canaanite city-states led by the King of Jerusalem (initially only intended to oppose the Gibeonites), and again in the north, an alliance of four Canaanite kings under the leadership of the king of Hazor, which fought at the Waters of Merom. These instances were exceptional (as was Gezer's aid to Lachish; Josh 10:53), however, and in general the Canaanite cities stood in political and military disunity. Thus, for example, no one came to the aid of Jericho (or, seemingly, Ai) in the hour of peril. This extreme political fragmentation in Canaan is demonstrated by the situation depicted in the Amarna letters, of the mid-14th century B.C.E., as well as in the list of thirty-one Canaanite kings allegedly defeated by Joshua (Josh 12:9-24).

(d) Owing to the lack of a broad Canaanite territorial defense system, no attempt was made to stop the Israelites from fording the Jordan. The river was a potential impediment for the Israelites, and provided the Canaanites with a fine means of forestalling the invasion.[9] That the Jordan could be utilized for military purposes is no idle assumption, for this was demonstrated more than once by the Israelites themselves during the period of the Judges. The fords of

---

[8]Cf. now *inter alia* Bright, *History of Israel*, 127ff.

[9]On rivers constituting military barriers, see Clausewitz, *War*, 433 ff.

the Jordan were seized to cut off an enemy's line of retreat on three occasions: to prevent the Moabite army from escaping to Transjordan, in the days of Ehud (Judg 3:28-29); to prevent the Midianites' retreat to the desert, in the days of Gideon (Judg 7:24-25); and to halt the escape of the Ephraimites, in the days of Jephthah (the Shibboleth incident — Judg 12:5-6).

(e) During the days of the conquest and the first stages of the settlement, the Israelites were successful against the Canaanites only in the hill-country and its western slopes. Indeed — and quite contrary to popular notion — an inferior force (such as that of the Israelites) assailing large bodies of defenders in mountainous terrain (such as the Canaanites) holds a decided military advantage, especially in open battle.[10] Such a mountain mentality in warfare, and the complementary reluctance to engage in lowland fighting, was attributed to the Israelites still many generations later: "their gods are gods of the hills, and so they were stronger than we (the 'Arameans'); but let us fight against them in the plain, and surely we shall be stronger than they" (1 Kgs 20:23; cf. the Syrian taunt to the Jews, in 1 Macc 10:70ff.: "Why do you defy us up there in the hills . . . come down to meet us on the plain . . ."). It was in the lowlands (the Jezreel and Beth-shean valleys and the coastal plain) that the Israelite invaders were unable to dislodge the dense indigenous population. The biblical historiographer realized the military reason underlying this: "he took possession of the hill-country, but he could not drive out the inhabitants of the plain, because they had chariots of iron" (Judg 1:19, on the tribe of Judah; Josh 17:16, on the Joseph tribes; and cf. Judg 1:34, on the Danites). In other words, the Israelite inability to capture the plains was a consequence of the Canaanite chariot, a weapon most effectively employed in flat terrain.

CANAANITE-ISRAELITE DISPARITY

In espousing the principal biblical maxim of a military subjugation of Canaan as the decisive factor in the Israelite takeover, we are confronted by the cardinal question: How could the seminomadic Israelite tribes, emerging from the desert fringes, surmount an adversary of long military experience and possessing a superior technology? How was an unmounted horde able to overthrow an array of strongly fortified cities and well-trained forces, including formidable chariotry? This obvious military disparity was one of the prime motives in weaning many biblical scholars away from the traditional view and leading them to hypothesize the peaceful infiltration of Canaan. Admitting such infiltration side by side with actual military campaigns, it hardly can be considered as the initial or principal factor of the Israelite occupation (as is a prevalent view in biblical criticism). History is too littered with analogous instances of ancient states and even empires being overwhelmed by "uncivilized" tribes, two outstanding examples being the Arab conquest of Byzantine

[10]See Clausewitz, *War*, 417ff.

Palestine and the destruction of the Roman Empire by the Germanic tribes. In seeking a rationale for the Israelite conquest, we must focus upon two prime factors: a relative decline of the Canaanite city-states at this time and the specific conduct of warfare assumed by the invading Israelites.

The Canaanite city-states which flowered in the 15th and 14th centuries B.C.E. were frequently the target of Egyptian military attacks. Having endured a prolonged period of colonial rule resulting from these campaigns, they reached a state of deterioration in the 13th century. This deterioration on the eve of and during the conquest was a factor serving to counterbalance the military deficiencies of the Israelites and to facilitate the relatively rapid overrunning of the country. The insecurity of the countryside is clearly reflected also in the roughly contemporaneous Papyrus Anastasi I (second half of the 13th century B.C.E.; cf. the description in the Song of Deborah, Judg 5:6: "caravans ceased and travelers kept to the byways"). The Egyptian policy of *divide et impera* intensified the incessant disputes among the Canaanite city-states, as evidenced by the Amarna letters (second quarter of the 14th century B.C.E.), which also inform us that the actual numbers of warriors kept by the Canaanite rulers were quite meager. Requests for military assistance from neighbors or Egypt often mention no more than ten to fifty men, while a force of fifty chariots was considered rather extraordinary. Thus, in a letter discovered in the southern part of the country, a prince of Lachish is asked for a consignment of six bows, three daggers, and three swords — arms for, say, twelve men at most.[11] These insignificant numbers reveal the vulnerability of Canaan to even small bodies of invaders who, once they had penetrated, could threaten the city-states and sever communications between them.

The Israelites were able to exploit another Canaanite weakness, the heterogeneity of the population, a veritable mosaic of ethnic groups, as is attested, *inter alia*, in the oft-repeated biblical formula listing the seven peoples of Canaan. The Israelites skillfully manipulated local animosities among these groups, who were further differentiated by political and social factors. A prime example is the treaty which Joshua concluded separately with the Gibeonites, themselves of Hivite (non-Semitic) stock, originating in the north, apparently in Anatolia (Joshua 9).

How, however, were the Israelites able to arrive at an accurate appraisal of the land they were about to invade and to effect the means to assure its conquest? The answer lies in the specific military qualities and skills of the Israelites, aspects which have been treated in part by various experts in both the biblical and military fields.[12] The treatment below, however, attacks the conquest as a subject in itself, by dealing comprehensively with a number of the major fundamentals of early Israelite warfare.[13]

[11]For this letter, found at Tell el-Ḥesi in 1892, see Albright, *BASOR* 87.

[12]See in particular Yadin's thoroughgoing *Art of Warfare*.

[13]For my preliminary study, see *Conquest of Palestine in the Time of Joshua*, 2nd edition, 1954 (Hebrew).

INTELLIGENCE

To assure maximum success, any warlike operation must be preceded by intelligence activities. The conquest cycle abounds in intelligence and espionage operations, demonstrating a developed awareness of this prerequisite among the Israelites. There is frequent mention of reconnaissance units sent out prior to campaigns against regions or cities; these missions yielded vital information on Canaan, its topography, ethnic and demographic makeup, military and political structure, productivity, ecological factors, etc.

These elements receive full expression in the story of the twelve spies dispatched by Moses on first reaching the borders of Canaan. Their explicit instructions reflect a comprehensive strategic probe,[14] reading like a modern intelligence brief: " . . . and see what the land is, and whether they are few or many, and whether the land that they dwell in is good or bad, and whether the cities that they dwell in are camps or strongholds, and whether the land is rich or poor, and whether there is wood in it or not" (Num 13:18-20). Similarly, the data gathered on the fertility of the land, the strength of its defenses and the distribution of the Canaanite peoples (vv 27ff.) have the true ring of intelligence reports. Further, the opposite stands taken by the spies testify to divergent attitudes in the evaluation of intelligence data. Ten of the spies, taking a defeatist stance, rouse the people against the planned operation, while a minority of two (Joshua and Caleb) optimistically presses for its implementation (cf. Num 13:31-32, as against 13:30 and 14:9).

Admittedly, the story of these spies certainly contains poetic-legendary embellishment and has undergone tendentious religious editing. Nevertheless, it is authentic in its pattern of intelligence activities, which are typical of Israelite warfare. This is observed also in the Danite campaign to conquer and settle the city of Laish in the north during the period of the Judges; this tribal story, of more realistic stamp than the episode under Moses, reveals a similar pattern of sending out spies and their reporting back (Judges 18).[15] In other instances, the Bible merely refers to such matters in passing, in a single word. The conquest of the land of Jazer in Transjordan (which fell to the Israelites after the defeat of Sihon, king of Heshbon) is described in this telescoped manner: "And Moses sent to spy out Jazer; and they took its villages and dispossessed the Amorites that were there" (Num 21:32). And prior to the conquest of Bethel: "The house of Joseph sent to spy out Bethel . . ." (Judg 1:23). The specific verbal form in the Hebrew[16] indicates that here, too, we are dealing with the dispatch of a reconnaissance unit before the operation.

In the hitherto-mentioned examples, the Israelites were generally aiming for settlement subsequent to the conquest of the sites and thus resorted to

---

[14]Cf. Yadin, *Art of Warfare*, 110.

[15]For the typology of the two spy episodes, see Malamat, *Bib* 51, 2-7.

[16]The Hebrew *wayyāṭîrū*, in the causative *Hipᶜil* of *ṭūr*, is properly rendered "they caused a reconnaissance to be made."

reconnaissance of a broad, strategic nature to obtain a comprehensive picture of their objective. In contrast, where destruction *per se* was sought, as at Jericho and Ai, the more limited scope of tactical, field intelligence — yielding purely military information — certainly sufficed.

The spies dispatched to Jericho, the first Israelite objective in Canaan according to the "official" tradition, found cover in the house of Rahab the harlot. This particular "contact" was a logical one militarily, for Rahab's house was "built into the city wall, so that she dwelt in the wall" (Josh 2:15); that is, it was located in a vital spot in the city's defenses. Further, Rahab's profession enabled her to come into contact with much of the city's menfolk, especially suiting her to the spies' needs, providing them not only with details of the city's defenses but also of the fighting forces and the morale prevalent within the town (Josh 2:15ff.; Josephus *Ant.* 5.1.2, elaborates on the intelligence gathered). This last matter was of particular interest to the Israelite command: "And they said to Joshua, 'Truly the Lord has given all the land into our hands; and moreover all the inhabitants of the land are fainthearted because of us'" (Josh 2:24).

FAILURE OF INTELLIGENCE

A reconnaissance unit was also sent to the next city in the path of the advancing Israelites, Ai, at the upper reaches of Wādī Makkūk, which leads down toward Jericho. In this instance, however, a mishap in the Israelite intelligence led to the one and only military defeat appearing in the book of Joshua (though the biblical tradition ascribes this failure to divine wrath). The spies not only reported raw information but also delved into military counsel: "Let not all the people go up, but let about two or three thousand men go up and attack Ai; do not make the whole people toil up there, for they are but few" (Josh 7:3). In the initial attack on Ai, this advice was taken, and the small force of 3,000 was routed, with losses. In the second attempt, however, Joshua threw 30,000 choice troops into battle (Josh 8:3ff.); though this number appears exaggerated, it indicates that the force in the first operation was but a tenth of the strength necessary to assure success. Thus, the initial intelligence blunder lay in the inacccurate estimate of the enemy's strength. We may point to another possible failing of the spies, namely their interference in operational decisions, which most likely in biblical times, as in modern intelligence practice, was prohibited to field agents; such decisions belong exclusively to the level of command.

In accord with its historiographical tendency, the Bible attributes the initial setback at Ai to a sin among the Israelites and regards the subsequent success as feasible only after the expiation of guilt (Josh 7:11ff.). From a realistic-military viewpoint, the "transgression" was a breakdown in discipline at the time of the conquest of Jericho — that is, Achan's taking of loot which was under divine ban.[17] The glory at Jericho resulted in an overconfidence which infected the

[17]For the imposition of the divine ban (*ḥerem*) as a deterrent to pillaging in early warfare, see Malamat, *Biblical Essays*, 43ff.

Israelite command no less than the ranks; in the sphere of intelligence, this was manifest at the gross underestimate of the enemy. However, the setback at Ai had a sobering effect upon the Israelites. But Joshua seems to have been concerned less by the drop in Israelite morale than by an external factor of extreme significance: the fear of loss of image (note the indicative words attributed to Joshua in 7:8-9) led him to react swiftly with a force sufficiently large to assure an overwhelming victory.[18]

LOGISTICS

The biblical sources can also be gleaned for information on matters of supplies, materiel and their distribution in the Israelite army — that is, on logistics. The lengthy wanderings with their numerous encampments in the desert, the campaigns in Transjordan, and the later long-range incursions into Cisjordan involved complex problems in this field.

Perusal of the book of Joshua reveals that special attention was paid to organizing equipment and food supplies. Thus, just prior to the crossing of the Jordan, Joshua commanded the people to prepare provisions, setting aside three days for the task (Josh 1:10-11). In the later episode of the outrage at Gibeah in the period of the Judges, one in ten of the troops was involved in quartermaster duties, attending to the provisions of the frontline soldiers (Judg 20:10). The timing for the invasion across the Jordan was apparently determined by logistical considerations, to assure the Israelites of steady supplies. It fell in the early spring, "on the tenth day of the first month [i.e., Nisan]" (Josh 4:19 and cf. "after the year was expired, at the time when Kings go forth to battle"; 2 Sam 11:1) when crops, especially barley, had already begun to ripen in the Jordan valley, but somewhat before harvest in the cooler regions of the land. Indeed, the biblical tradition itself relates that after the Israelites had celebrated the Passover on the plain of Jericho, "they ate of the produce of the land . . . and the people of Israel had manna no more, but ate of the fruit of the land of Canaan that year" (Josh 5:11-12). Despite the legendary elements in this story, it reflects a real situation in logistics. This raping of the land was double-edged, furnishing the Israelites with provisions and furthering the ruination of Canaan at one and the same time. Another important source for supplies lay in the conquered cities themselves: "And all the spoil of these cities and the cattle, the people of Israel took for their booty" (Josh 11:14, concerning Galilee; cf. Josh 8:27, on Ai).

The "official" tradition ascribes a central role to Gilgal, the initial camp of the Israelites after the crossing of the Jordan. It was from Gilgal, between the Jordan and Jericho (its precise location is unknown), that Israelite task forces would set out into the hill-country. Following each operation into southern Canaan, they would retire thence, as after the conquest of Ai, the battle at Gibeon, and even the taking of Canaanite strongholds farther west (Josh 9:6;

---

[18]On the battle of Ai, see below, pp. 49-50, and Gichon in *Zer Li᾿gevurot.*

10:15, 43; cf. 10:6-9). So outstanding a fact has led to various ingenious explanations, for example, the assumption that Gilgal served as a cultic site to which numerous stories became accreted,[19] or that there were several Gilgals, or that the name Gilgal (the Hebrew word conveys the sense of "cairn") was actually a generic term for a fortified campsite surrounded by a circle of stones, the camp being moved with the advance of the invaders.[20]

The central role of Gilgal can be understood readily in terms of logistics and strategy. First, as an operational base, Gilgal was a bridgehead in Canaan, supported by the Israelite hinterland in Transjordan, through which supplies and reinforcements could be channeled as required. Neglect of this vital link would endanger the elongated lines of the invasion and place the Israelite task forces in jeopardy. Second, it was the springboard into the mountainous interior, with routes forking out, along which the force could penetrate. These pathways appear to have stretched through the boundary zone between the territories controlled by the two principal kingdoms in the central hill-country, Jerusalem and Shechem. Such a chink offered the Israelites a means of facilitating their various operations into Canaan as described in the book of Joshua and, indeed led toward the propitiating Hivite enclave in the hinterland to the west.

THE INDIRECT MILITARY APPROACH

After intelligence and logistics, we turn to the very methods which typified Israelite warfare during the period of the conquest and settlement. Our focus is upon the tactical plane, the individual engagements — rather than the broad strategic level (though the distinction is often vague in war) which would lead us, irrelevant to our pursuit, toward a Fundamentalistic acceptance of the overall scheme of the conquest as related in the book of Joshua. The acute military problem facing the Israelites was twofold.

(a) Enemy defense was based upon strongly fortified cities, which appeared to the biblical historiographer as "cities great and fortified up to heaven." These fortresses were a stumbling block even for regular forces, such as the mighty Egyptian army, which at times had to resort to long, drawn-out sieges to overcome them. But the very size of the Canaanite cities may well have become a hindrance to their defenders (an average town extended over 10-20 acres, though Hazor sprawled over as much as 200 acres, with a circumvallation of over 3 km). For on the eve of the Israelite invasion, a weakened Canaan (see above) must have had difficulties in mustering the resources necessary for the defense of such extensive fortifications.

(b) The Canaanites deployed well-trained professional forces, the most formidable arm of which was their famed chariotry. The latter was based on a two-wheeled chariot, a light vehicle providing a maximum of maneuverability in

---

[19]See e.g., Noth *Josua*, 11f., 31ff.; opposed by Kaufmann, *Conquest of Palestine*, 67ff.
[20]This last explanation was put forth orally by Y. Yadin.

battle. Though the tactical role of the chariot has yet to be elucidated satisfactorily, it may partly resemble that of modern armored forces. Contemporaneous Egyptian reliefs depicting the chariot reveal a dual role: forming the protective screen for advancing infantry and pursuing a broken enemy in flight.[21] The Canaanite chariot, like its Egyptian counterpart, served as a mobile platform for the longest-range weapon employed in ancient times — the bow, whose most sophisticated form, the composite bow, had an effective range of 300-400 meters.[22] The tactical combination of chariotry and archery is inferred, *inter alia*, in the two outwardly conflicting descriptions of the fall of King Saul on Mount Gilboa. In reality, these were two views of one and the same circumstance: according to 1 Sam 31:3, Saul was surrounded and "the archers found him, and he was badly wounded by the archers," while according to 1 Sam 1:6, "the charioteers and the horsemen were close upon him." Another aspect of the superiority of chariotry over foot-soldiers was its immense psychological impact, especially the terrifying image of galloping horses (cf. Judg 5:22, and Nah 3:2).

In the face of a superior enemy, the Israelites achieved success through what is termed in modern military science "the indirect approach" — a concept propounded by Liddell Hart (though he applied it mainly to the strategic plane rather than the tactical, as done here).[23] This is revealed by a careful analysis of the various descriptions of battles found in the books of Joshua and Judges. Indeed, the period of the conquest and settlement represents a pinnacle in the application of this approach, in Israelite no less than in general military history; for later, with the institutionalization of a regular army under the Israelite monarchy, the indirect gave way to more direct, conventional modes of warfare. This indirect approach sought to avoid frontal assault and siege warfare as well as straightforward encounters with enemy forces, especially chariotry, in the open field. To achieve this, the Israelites resorted to tactics based on deception — feints, decoys, ambushes, and diversionary maneuvers — any guile to attain surprise in overcoming the enemy. Doctrinal reliance upon such ruses is indicated by a recurring phrase in the book of Proverbs: "Devices are established by plan; wage wars by stratagems" (20:18); "By stratagems you shall wage war, and victory (comes) through much planning" (24:6); and compare: "For want of stratagems an army falls, but victory (comes) through much planning" (11:14) [translation by the author, partly based on the new Jewish Publication Society translation]. The pairing of the Hebrew words *maḥšābôt* and *ᶜēṣāh/yōᶜēṣ* ("devices"/"tactics" and "plan"/"planner") with the clearly

---

[21] Cf. Schulman, *JARCE* 2.

[22] On the "composite bow," see Yadin, *Art of Warfare*, 6ff.; and on the chariot, 4f. and 86ff. On the range of the ancient bow in general, cf. W. McLeod, *Phoenix* 19 (1965) 1-14; 26 (1972) 78-82.

[23] The doyen of British military theorists coined the term "indirect approach" already in the late 1920s; see his classic treatise *Strategy* (last revised edition, 1967). Cf. also my remarks in "The Conduct of Israelite Warfare in the Biblical Period," *Acta of the International Conference of Military History* (Teheran, 1976), Bucharest (in press).

military terms *taḥbūlôt* and *milḥāmāh* ("stratagems" and "war") instills them with a particular tenor here (compare the analogous usage of this pair in Jer 49:20, 30).

The conscious employment of cunning and deception in warfare is noted sporadically in ancient Near Eastern sources already centuries prior to the Israelite conquest.[24] A piquant instance is King Shamshi-Adad's chiding of his son, Yasmah-Adad, in the 18th century B.C.E.: "devise feints (*šibqu*) to defeat the enemy, and to maneuver against him, but the enemy too will devise feints and maneuver against you, just as wrestlers employ feints (*šibqu*) against each other" (*Archives Royales de Mari*, I, No. 5, lines 4-9).[25] This comparison of warfare to a wrestling match, found also in classical literature, anticipates Clausewitz' well-known simile by 3,500 years.[26] Throughout the literature of the ancient Near East, however, the books of Joshua and Judges remain unique in the number and variety of battle schemes gathered. In this regard, we can only ponder on the lost contents of the "Book of the Wars of the LORD" and the "Book of Jashar," both mentioned in the conquest cycle (Num 21:14; Josh 10:13).

Actual collections of stratagems in war have survived, however only from classical times (excluding the Far East). Two comprehensive works of this sort, both named *Strategemata*, are extant, each containing several hundred examples, drawn from the Greek and Roman wars. The earlier collection was compiled by Frontinus toward the end of the 1st century C.E.[27] Of lower military-historical order is the collection of Polyaenus, of the second half of the 2nd century C.E.[28] Whereas the former work was founded upon a methodical, practical classification, the material in the second was arranged according to the generals involved. The partial overlap of examples in the two works reveals that both relied upon earlier compilations. In any event, the perusal of these two sources yields quite a few tactical devices resembling various ruses described in the Bible. As these parallels[29] are of considerable importance in bolstering the credibility of the biblical examples, we shall refer to them below, elucidating, *inter alia*, several instances.

CONQUEST OF FORTIFIED CITIES

Among the early wars of the Israelites, we find no actual description of an outright, successful assault upon an enemy city. The adoption of an indirect

---

[24]For a treatment of such aspects in modern warfare, see Whaley, *Stratagem: Deception and Surprise in War* (hereafter *Stratagem*).

[25]Cf. Sasson, *Military Establishments at Mari*, 43.

[26]See Clausewitz, *War*, 75.

[27]For an English translation, see the Loeb Classical Library; the most recent and accurate edition of the Latin source is by Bendz, *Kriegslisten.*

[28]The standard edition of the Greek text remains that of Teubler, by J. Melber, 1887; the latest translation in a European language is the antiquated and inaccurate German rendering by Blume and Fuchs, 1833-55. On the textual transmission, see now F. Schindler, Die Überlieferung der Strategemata des Polyainos, *Österreichische Akademie der Wissenschaften, Phil.-Hist. Klasse* (1973) 284.

[29]Several of these instances have already been noted by Abel, *RB* 56.

military approach finds expression in two principal tactics employed by the Israelites: covert infiltration — neutralizing the city defenses; and enticement — drawing the defenders out into the open.

(a) *Neutralization of City Defenses*

The fall of Jericho, as described in Joshua 2-6, was a siege culminating in a "miraculous" destruction of the walls (6:20) and a subsequent penetration into the defenseless city. The "official" tradition, however, preserves an early strand, apparently hinting at an actual military conquest of the city.[30] This latter is represented by the episode of Rahab and the spies, an independent literary source which has been worked into the amalgam of the Jericho cycle (the episode begins in Joshua 2, but continues only in Josh 6:22ff.). The etiological element of this particular episode (the survival of a Canaanite family "in the midst of Israel"), like Rahab's confession (Josh 2:9-13), is surely the work of a later redactor. In fact, the story of the spies, of a realistic-secular stamp, is quite out of line with the present tradition, which ascribes the fall of the city to divine providence rather than to human feat (for this historiographical tendentiousness, cf. the introduction above). Indeed, the factuality of an actual battle at Jericho is indicated in the review of Israel's history in Joshua's valediction (24:11): "And you went over the Jordan and came to Jericho, and the men of Jericho fought against you . . . ." Thus, we may conclude that there had once circulated a more realistic account of the capture of Jericho, including an intelligence mission involving a "fifth column" within the city.

We cannot successfully reconstruct that early version of the conquest of Jericho because the suppressed story has been truncated in the extant text and supplanted by the historiographer's *actus Dei*. Nonetheless, some notions can be set forth. Such a version would have Rahab playing a more active role in the Israelite penetration into the city, which was most likely accomplished by stratagem. Thus, when the spies had Rahab tie the scarlet cord *outside* her window in the city wall (Joshua 2:18), it was not to protect her household from the Israelites rampaging *within* the city after the collapse of the walls, as the later redactor would have us believe. Rather, it would have marked the way for a stealthy entry into the city (analogous to the postern at Bethel; see below), as also intimated in the LXX version here.[31]

Could the encircling maneuver around the city, the horn blasts, and the great battle cry preceding the miraculous collapse of the walls (Josh 6:20) also be survivals from that realistic account of the city's fall? The repeated encircling of

---

[30]For the problematic archeological evidence from Jericho, see de Vaux, *Histoire ancienne d'Israël*, 560ff., and now also H. and M. Weippert, *ZDPV* 92 (1976) 147f.

[31]For similar attempts at reconstruction, see Windisch, *ZAW* 37; and recently Tucker, "The Rahab Saga"; cf. also Langlamet, *RB* 78, 321ff. On the battlecry (see immediately below) appearing also in Gideon's stratagem against the Midianites (Judg 7:21), see P. Humbert, *La "Terouᶜa"* (Neuchâtel, 1946) 16ff., 30f.

Jericho on six successive days, the Israelites retiring each day to their camp (Josh 6:3, 14), has sometimes been regarded as a psychological device to lower the enemy's guard, preparing the way for a breach into the city.[32] If so, this stratagem may have been meant to distract the enemy from the specific Israelite design, or it may have been a noted form of surprise, which we may term "conditioning," that is, deceiving the enemy by repeating the same "field exercise" until he has relaxed his vigilance and a decisive blow can suddenly be dealt. Stratagems of this sort have been employed throughout history (cf. below, on the conquest of Ai), and Frontinus cites quite a few examples, one of which is particularly similar to our case. A Roman general marched his troops regularly around the walls of a well-fortified city in northern Italy, each time returning them to camp until, when the vigilance of the defenders had waned, he stormed the walls and forced the city's capitulation (*Strategemata* 3.2.1).[33]

The conquest of Bethel is related only in Judges 1 (vv 22-26; Josh 12:16 merely mentions its king in the list of defeated Canaanite rulers), that is, in a deviant tradition of the conquest of Canaan, as we have noted above. Here, the action is ascribed to the Joseph tribes alone, rather than to pan-Israelite initiative under Joshua. Even so, the cursory description reveals several of the patterns typical of the Israelite campaigns of conquest: preliminary reconnaissance (see above) and divine patronage ("and the Lord was with them," v 22). The latter is indicative of the presence of priests and possibly the Holy Ark at the assault, as at Jericho or in Moses' wars, or of other cultic appurtenances, as on the Danite campaign northward (Judges 18). Though the text is not explicit, the change of the name of the conquered city from Luz to Bethel (v 23) may well be another feature of the pattern, for the renaming of captured sites is not an infrequent phenomenon in the conquest traditions.[34]

The actual conquest of Bethel was effected by a well-known ruse in the history of siege warfare, that is, penetration into a fortified city by means of secret ingress. In this instance, the Israelites took advantage of a postern

---

[32]It might be implied here that the city was captured on the Sabbath, as is held in rabbinic sources; such a timing has a specific import in the history of military conduct.

[33]Cf. Abel, *RB* 56, 326; Yadin, *Art of Warfare*, 99f.

[34]On the various elements typical of the conquest campaigns, see Malamat, *Bib* 51. In this story however, the Luz/Bethel change of name is not explicitly associated with the city's conquest (indeed, cf. Gen 28:19), though this is indirectly indicated by the informer's subsequent emigration to "the land of the Hittites" and his founding there "a city, and he called its name Luz" (Judg 1:26), certainly in commemoration of his native town. The impression gained is of an early, elusive tradition ultimately linking the biblical toponym Luz (*lwz*) with the well-known Hittite city *Lawazantia* (note the Anatolian suffix *-ant/diya*). Significant in our context is the fact that the very name of the latter city, situated between the Taurus and the Euphrates, reappears in the late 14th or 13th century B.C.E. (i.e., close to the period of the Israelite conquest) in eastern Cilicia as attested by the city *Lwsnd* in Ugaritic and *Lusanda* in neo-Assyrian texts. For the latter city, see M. C. Astour, *American Journal of Archaeology* 69 (1965) 257; and idem, *Hellenosemitica* (1965) 30ff., where the transfer of city-names is noted as a common phenomenon in Asia Minor, influenced *inter alia* by the invasion of the Sea Peoples — which brings us chronologically to much the same period as the Israelite conquest.

(Hebrew *mĕbōʾ hāʿîr*, here certainly *not* the city gate), of the type of secret passage actually discovered at several sites in Palestine and the neighboring lands.[35] The Israelite pickets (Hebrew *šōmĕrîm*), who kept the city under surveillance, learned of its existence through the treachery of a citizen. As in the Rahab episode at Jericho, the Israelites assured their informant and his family of safety in reward: "And he showed them the way into the city . . . but they let the man and all his family go" (Judg 1:25). Penetration into the city through the hidden passage here, also recalling David's later conquest of Jerusalem, achieved two aims at one blow — maximal surprise and neutralization of the fortifications — leading to the rapid collapse of the city's defense.

(b) *Enticement of City Defenders*

In the books of Joshua and Judges, the most satisfactory accounts of city conquests, as far as reconstructing the minutiae of planning and execution of the Israelite operations is concerned, relate to Ai (Joshua 7-8) and Gibeah of Benjamin (the latter destroyed in internecine war; Judg 20:18-44). In both instances, almost identical stratagems are described, in similar military terms. This similarity has led many commentators to believe that one or the other of the two accounts served as the literary model, but particularly effective stratagems undoubtedly were reemployed in Israelite tactics. If indeed there was interdependence, the capture of Ai (et-Tell) is more likely the copy of the two,[36] for the archeological evidence there is quite negative.[37] The latter point, however, has no intrinsic effect upon our military analysis below, which focuses upon the biblical tradition as transmitted.

The stratagem employed in capturing these two cities is clear enough, in spite of the awkward and repetitious presentations in the biblical text, which are generally regarded as having coalesced from more than one source. The ruse was based on a diversionary movement intended to decoy the defending forces away from their fortifications (Josh 8:6, 16; Judg 20:31, 32), onto open ground for attack, concurrently enabling another Israelite force to seize the now undefended city.[38] The tactical aim was achieved by splitting the Israelite force: the main body was deployed as if to storm the city walls but, in fact feigned retreat into the wilderness, with the enemy in hot pursuit. Such simulated, controlled flight, which could be reversed upon order, was a difficult maneuver involving a certain amount of calculated risk. The second body, the "ambush," was concealed behind the city (at Ai, to the west) or around it (at Gibeah; Judg 20:29). At Ai, it

[35]Cf. Yadin, *Art of Warfare*, 254.

[36]See the commentaries, as well as Roth, *ZAW* 75, and most recently Rösel, *ZDPV* 92, 33ff.

[37]For the various (sometimes farfetched) attempts to resolve the inexplicable discrepancy between the excavations results at Ai and the biblical account, see now de Vaux, *Histoire ancienne d'Israël*, 563ff.

[38]For the Battle of Ai see, in addition to the commentaries, Gale, *Battles of Biblical History*, 21ff., and especially Gichon, *Zer Liʾgevurot*; and on Gibeah, Kaufmann, *Judges*, 289ff.

is explicitly stated that the ambush took cover during the night, remaining there "in readiness" (Josh 8:4-5); this was probably so at Gibeah as well.

The fate of the battle pivoted upon precise coordination between the two Israelite wings, a complicated task in any situation. The adversary had to be lured not only to convenient ground but also to an optimal distance away from the city before the "flight" could be reversed — to allow the ambush sufficient time to gain control of the city before the enemy could regroup and counterattack, yet not so far as to prevent the ambushing force from joining the fracas afield, blocking the enemy's rear. Coordinated timing was assured by predetermined signal. At Ai, it was given to the ambush by Joshua himself (by stretching out his spear toward the city), who was with the "fleeing" force (Josh 8:15ff.); at Gibeah, the very burning of the city by the ambushing force formed a "smoke signal" initiating the counterattack by the main Israelite body (as explicitly stated in Judg 20:38). At this point, the tables were turned and disorder and panic reigned in the ranks of the enemy, caught in the enveloping movement as so poignantly depicted in the text: "So when the men of Ai looked back, behold, the smoke of the city went up to heaven; and they had no power to flee this way or that, for the people that fled to the wilderness turned back upon the pursuers . . . . And the others [of the ambush] came forth from the city against them; so they were in the midst of Israel, some on this side, and some on that side; and Israel smote them, until there was left none that survived or escaped" (Josh 8:20-22). And in the Gibeah episode: ". . . the Benjaminites looked behind them; and behold, the whole of the city went up in smoke to heaven. Then the men of Israel turned, and the men of Benjamin were dismayed, for they saw that disaster was close upon them . . . . Cutting off the Benjaminites, they pursued them and trod them down . . . as far as opposite Gibeah on the east" (Judg 20:40-43).

In this Israelite stratagem we encounter a factor of as yet unrecognized significance,[39] the fact that in both these cases final success was preceded by abortive attempts upon the fortified cities, each culminating in the actual repulse of the attackers. As noted above, the initial assault upon Ai failed, and in the campaign against Gibeah, there were even two initial setbacks, on successive days (Judg 20:19-25). The true ingenuity and boldness of the battle-plan put into effect in the final Israelite operations against these cities lies in the apparent repetition of the very tactics which previously led to failure. This, then, is another instance of the "conditioning" we noted at Jericho, in which repetitive moves are designed to lull the enemy into a false sense of security. How well the Israelites foresaw that the people of Ai would fall for the ruse: "[The Israelites] are fleeing from us, as before" (Josh 8:6), as would the defenders of Gibeah: "[The Israelites] are routed before us, as at the first" (Judg 20:32; cf. v 39). In other words, the Israelites had learned the negative lessons of frontal attack and applied them by shifting to indirect means of attaining their goals. Resorting to

[39]See already, in brief, Malamat, *World History of the Jewish People* III, 163 and n. 92 (note that the last reference there to *Strategemata* should read Book II [*not* III], 5, 8).

deception and subterfuge, they achieved utter surprise and diverted the enemy's attention from the principal objective. Mastering the factors of "time and space," the Israelites retained the initiative and deprived the enemy of the option of seriously influencing the course of the battle, let alone its outcome.

Stratagems of ambush and feigned retreat in capturing fortifications were esteemed practices in antiquity. Two operations of this sort from Palestine proper are attested in the Greco-Roman period. Interestingly, both were directed against the same formidable target — fortified settlements on the heights of Mount Tabor. The earlier operation was conducted by Antiochus III, who lured the Ptolemaic garrison down from the summit (218 B.C.E.). Similarly, 285 years later, Placidus, one of Vespasian's generals, enticed the Jewish defenders from the mountaintop (68 C.E.).[40]

Frontinus devoted an entire chapter to stratagems of this sort (*Strategemata* 3.10); one of his several examples (3.10.5), found also in Polyaenus (5.10.4) though nowhere else, is particularly relevant to our instances, despite differences in detail.

> Himilco, the Carthaginian, when campaigning near Agrigentum, placed part of his forces in ambush near the town and directed them to set fire to some damp wood as soon as the soldiers from the town should come forth. Then, advancing at daybreak with the rest of his army for the purpose of luring forth the enemy, he feigned flight and drew the inhabitants after him for a considerable distance by his retirement. The men in ambush near the walls applied the torch to the wood-piles as directed. The Agrigentines, beholding the smoke ascend, thought their city on fire and ran back in alarm to protect it. Being encountered by those lying in wait for them near the walls and beset in the rear by those whom they had just been pursuing, they were caught between two forces and so cut to pieces.[41]

Frontinus (2.5.8) gives a yet closer parallel to the biblical episodes of Ai and Gibeah, as far as the underlying military principle of "conditioning" is concerned, though here even the initial retreats are feigned.

> Fulvius, commander in the Cimbrian war, having pitched his camp near the enemy, ordered his cavalry to approach the fortifications of the barbarians and to withdraw in pretended flight, after making an attack. When he had done this for several days, with the Cimbrians in hot pursuit, he noticed that their camp was regularly left exposed. Accordingly, maintaining his usual practice with part of his force, he himself with light-armed troops secretly took a position behind the camp of the enemy, and as they poured forth according to their custom, he suddenly attacked and demolished the unguarded rampart and captured their camp.[42]

---

[40]Col. (Ret.) E. Galili has kindly brought these references to my attention; see his paper in *Maarachoth* 82, 64-66. The first reference is taken from Polybius 5.70.6, and the second from Josephus *J.W.* 4.6.8.

[41]Following the Loeb edition, 238ff.; on p. 240, n. 1 there, the similarity with Joshua 8 is already noted. The Carthaginian seizure of Agrigentum (in 406 B.C.E.) *per se* is attested by Diodorus Siculus and most likely by a Punic stele as well; see now, C. Krahmalkov, *Rivista di Studi Fenici* 2 (1974) 171-77.

[42]Loeb edition, 136f.

SURPRISE ATTACKS

In the book of Joshua there are numerous instances which mention no more than the mere fact of the taking of a Canaanite town. We may surmise that many of these strongholds fell not by deceptive methods of the sort treated above, nor by straightforward siege warfare, but corollary to field victories in open battle. Indeed, two examples of such battles — fought against Canaanite leagues at Gibeon (Joshua 10) and at the Waters of Merom (Joshua 11) — were of far-reaching consequence, leading to the capture of entire blocs of towns.

This leads up to our final question: how did the Israelites attain victory in these rare instances of open clash in the field, especially at the Waters of Merom, where the Canaanites employed formidable chariotry (Josh 11:4, 6, 9)? A hint of the Israelite tactics can be found in the brief descriptions of these battles themselves: "So Joshua came upon them *suddenly*, having marched up all night from Gilgal. And the Lord threw them into a panic before Israel, who slew them with a great slaughter at Gibeon, and chased them by the way of the ascent of Beth-horon, and smote them as far as Azekah and Makkedah" (Josh 10:9-10); "So Joshua came *suddenly* upon them with all his people of war, by the waters of Merom, and fell upon them. And the Lord gave them into the hand of Israel, who smote them and chased them as far as Great Sidon . . ." (Josh 11:7-8). "Suddenly," the key word in both passages, evokes the concept of surprise, which the Israelites utilized in these attacks.

Surprise has always been one of the most elementary principles of war, an essential in engaging an adversary superior in either technology or numbers.[43] Of its multifarious causes, we have already encountered two which are very typical — the subtle device of "conditioning," and outright deception. In the battles just noted, however, surprise took a more forthright manifestation, that is, it was employed in lieu of stratagem. Its vital components are secrecy and speed. In our two cases, the Israelites struck a blow so sudden that the enemy was deprived of the opportunity of assessing his position in order to react effectively. As in any such surprise, the Israelites must have attacked at a time (and location) quite unexpected by the enemy. Moreover, they exploited the product of surprise — the dislocation of the enemy — pressing him beyond the breaking point and relentlessly hounding him in his headlong flight (Josh 10:10, 19; 11:8), in classical application of the "principle of pursuit."

In contrast to the vague circumstances surrounding the battle of the Waters of Merom, the historical, geographical, and military context of the battle at Gibeon is lucid.[44] The treaty between the Israelites and the Gibeonites exposed the northern flank of the kingdom of Jerusalem and threatened Canaanite cohesion throughout the southern hill-country, leading to an immediate military reaction against the renegade city of Gibeon. The bold Israelite plan of action,

---

[43]Cf. Clausewitz, *War*, 198ff.; Erfurth, *Surprise* (see in particular the English translators' introduction); Whaley, *Stratagem*, 86ff.

[44]See Ephᶜal, in *Military History of the Land of Israel.*

rushing to the aid of their vassals, is unfolded in a single verse: "So Joshua came upon them suddenly, having marched up all night from Gilgal" (Josh 10:9). Taking advantage of the hours of darkness, the Israelites made a lightning march from Gilgal to Gibeon (modern el-Jib) — a distance of 25-30 kilometers, involving a climb of over a thousand meters (Gilgal, ca. 250 meters below sea-level; Gibeon, ca. 840 meters above sea-level). The attack upon the astonished enemy apparently took place at dawn, when the Canaanites faced the walls of Gibeon with their rear and flanks exposed most dangerously before the assailing Israelites.

The credibility of the above reconstruction is supported by the renowned verse from the Book of Jashar: "Sun, stand thou still at Gibeon, and thou Moon in the valley of Aijalon . . ." (Josh 10:12).[45] This wondrous picture well reflects an early morning situation before the setting of the moon in the west, over the Aijalon valley, and after the sun had risen in the east, over Gibeon. The Israelite tactics may have taken into account another factor, the very position of the sun on the horizon, blinding the enemy facing the Israelite troops who were attacking him from the east. That this is not solely a modern military consideration is shown by examples in Frontinus (2.2.8) and Polyaenus (8.10.3). Both relate that the Roman general Marius, fighting barbarian tribes, deployed his troops in such a manner as to cause the sun to blind the enemy facing him. Polyaenus adds: "When the barbarians turned (toward the Romans), the sun was in their faces and they were blinded by its brilliance . . . and when they could no longer bear the rays of the sun, they raised their shields to their faces. Thus they exposed their bodies and were wounded, and were destroyed by the Romans."

NIGHT OPERATIONS

Utilization of the veil of darkness in achieving surprise was ingrained in Israelite tactical planning, from the days of the conquest down to the beginning of the monarchy. Though much more demanding than daytime operations — in training, courage and leadership — night activities benefit from security of movement, beside providing psychological bonuses.[46] Indeed, their very nature can nearly nullify the outward superiority of an antagonist, swinging the balance in favor of a weaker force, if it takes the initiative. Israelite night operations took the form of either outright attacks or unobserved convergence upon an enemy prior to dawn or daylight attack — and they are reviewed accordingly below.

Night movements in anticipation of attack in light occur in the following biblical episodes (the first two have been treated above): (1) in the final attack

---

[45] The present position of the "quotation" from the "Book of Jashar" is peculiar, for its true context would seem to be the battle proper at Gibeon, prior to the pursuit of the enemy by way of the ascent of Beth-horon as far as Makkedah; see Kaufmann, *Judges*, 143f. For a novel explanation of the "miracle" conjured by Joshua by calling upon the heavenly bodies, on the basis of the Mesopotamian "omen" literature, see Holladay, *JBL* 87.

[46] On night operations in general, see Boltze, *Das Nachtgefecht*.

upon Ai (Josh 8:3; cf. v 13); (2) at Gibeon (Josh 10:9); (3) in Abimelech's ambush against Shechem (Judg 9:34); (4) in Saul's deployment against the Ammonites besieging Jabesh-Gilead (1 Sam 11:11); and possibly (5) in David's raid on the Amalekite camp (1 Sam 30:17).

Bolder still and more exacting in planning and execution were actual night attacks. The classical example — throughout military history — is Gideon's assault upon the Midianites, described in great detail in Judges 7. Despite the theological tendentiousness and several enigmas in the text, analysis of the story reveals characteristics and maxims of night warfare still valid today.[47] Another instance is the sequel to Saul's victory with Jonathan over the Philistines (1 Sam 14:36). We may also note Abraham's night raid to recover his nephew Lot from captivity (Gen 14:15). Though the historical basis of this latter episode is, admittedly, doubtful, like the other cases it is most indicative of the tried and trusted nature of night operations among the Israelites.

The early Israelites encountered an adversary much superior to them in military strength. By preserving a clear view of the objective and applying means unanticipated by the enemy, a bold and imaginative Israelite leadership was successful in translating what we today would call a specific military doctrine into spontaneous victory. An overriding factor was the Israelite soldier's basic motivation — his deep sense of national purpose. It was this blend which engendered the momentum of the Israelite conquest.

---

[47]For a detailed military analysis of Gideon's battle, see Malamat, *PEQ* 85; and cf. *World History of the Jewish People* III, 143ff. For partly different approaches, see Field-Marshall Wavell in *Soldiers and Soldiering*, and Yadin, *Art of Warfare*, 256ff.

BIBLIOGRAPHY

Abel, F. M., "Les stratagèmes dans le livre de Josué," *RB* 56 (1949) 321-39.

Albright, W. F., "The Israelite Conquest of Canaan in the Light of Archaeology," *BASOR* 74 (1939) 11-23.

Albright, W. F., "A Case of Lèse-majesté in Pre-Israelite Lachish, with Some Remarks on the Israelite Conquest," *BASOR* 87 (1942) 32-38.

Alt, A. "Erwägungen über die Landnahme der Israeliten in Palästina; Josua," in *Kleine Schriften zur Geschichte des Volkes Israel* I, 126-75; 176-92. Munich, 1953.

Boltze, A., *Das Nachtgefecht.*[3] Berlin, 1943.

Bright, J., *A History of Israel.*[2] London, 1972.

Clausewitz, C. von, *On War.* Edited and translated by M. Howard and P. Paret. Princeton, 1976.

Encyclopaedia Britannica,[15] Macropaedia IX, *s.v.* Intelligence and Counterintelligence; XIX, *s.v.* Warfare, Conduct of. Chicago, 1973.

Ephᶜal, I., "The Battle of Gibeon and the Problem of Joshua's Southern Campaign." Pp. 79-90 in *The Military History of the Land of Israel in Biblical Times.* Jerusalem, 1964. (Hebrew).

Erfurth, W. von, *Surprise*. Harrisburg, 1943. Translated by S. T. Possony and D. Vilfroy from the German *Die Überraschung*. Berlin, 1938.
Frontinus, *Strategemata*. Loeb edition, translated by C. E. Bennett. London, 1925.
Frontinus, *Kriegslisten*. Latin and German by G. Bendz. Berlin, 1963.
Gale, R., *Great Battles of Biblical History*. London, 1968.
Galili, E., "The Conquest of Palestine by the Seleucian Army," *Maarachoth* 82 (1954) 57-72. (Hebrew).
Garstang, J., *Joshua, Judges*. London, 1931.
Gichon, M., "The Conquest of Ai — A Historical Military Examination." Pp. 56-72 in *Zer Li᾿gevurot*. Z. Shazar Jubilee Volume, ed. by B. Z. Lurie. Jerusalem, 1973. (Hebrew).
Holladay, J. S., "The Day(s) the Moon Stood Still," *JBL* 87 (1968) 166-78.
Jones, G. W. H., "Holy War" or "Yahwe War"? *VT* 25 (1975) 642-58.
Kaufmann, Y., *The Biblical Account of the Conquest of Palestine*. Jerusalem, 1953.
Kaufmann, Y., "Traditions Concerning Israelite History In Canaan," *Scripta Hierosolymitana* 8 (1961) 303-34.
Kaufmann, Y., *The Book of Judges*. Jerusalem, 1962. (Hebrew).
Kaufmann, Y., *The Book of Joshua*.[2] Jerusalem, 1963. (Hebrew).
Langlamet, F., "Josué II — Rahab et les espions," *RB* 78 (1971) 321-54.
Liddell Hart, B. H., *Strategy: The Indirect Approach*. London, 1954.
MacVeagh, R. and Costain, T. B., *Joshua, A Biography*. New York, 1948.
Malamat, A., "The War of Gideon and Midian — A Military Approach," *PEQ* 85 (1953) 61-65 [revised and updated, pp. 110-23 in *The Military History of the Land of Israel in Biblical Times*. Jerusalem, 1964. (Hebrew)].
Malamat, A., *The Conquest of Palestine in the Time of Joshua*.[2] Jerusalem, 1954. (Hebrew).
Malamat, A., "The Ban in Mari and in the Bible," *Biblical Essays. Proceedings, 9th Meeting, Die Ou-Testam. Werkgemeenskap in Suid-Afrika* (Stellenbosch, 1966) 40-49.
Malamat, A., "The Danite Migration and the Pan-Israelite Exodus-Conquest: A Biblical Narrative Pattern," *Bib* 51 (1970) 1-16.
Malamat, A., "The Period of the Judges." Pp. 129-63, 310-23 in *World History of the Jewish People* III. Rutgers University Press, 1971.
Mazar, B., "The Exodus and Conquest." Pp. 63-93 in *World History of the Jewish People* III. Rutgers University Press, 1971.
Miller, P. D., *The Divine Warrior in Early Israel*. Cambridge, 1973.
Noth, M., *Das Buch Josua*.[2] Tübingen, 1953.
Polyaenus, *Strategemata*. Teubner edition. Edited by J. Melber. Leipzig, 1887.
Polyaenus, *Kriegslisten*. Translated by W. H. Blume and C. Fuchs. Stuttgart, 1833-55.
Rad, G. von, *Der heilige Krieg im alten Israel*. Zurich, 1951.
Rösel, H., "Studien zur Topographie der Kriege in den Büchern Josua und Richter," *ZDPV* 91 (1975) 156-90; 92 (1976) 10-46.
Roth, W. M. W., "Hinterhalt und Scheinflucht," *ZAW* 75 (1963) 296-304.
Sasson, J. M., *The Military Establishments at Mari*. Rome, 1969.
Seeligmann, A. L., "From Historical Reality to Historiosophical Conception in the Bible," *P᾿raqim II*. Jerusalem, 1969-74. (Hebrew).
Shulman, A. R., "The Egyptian Chariotry: A Reexamination," *JARCE* 2 (1963) 75-98.
Stolz, F., *Jahwes und Israels Kriege*. Zürich, 1972.
Tucker, G. M., "The Rahab Saga (Joshua 2)," Pp. 66-86 in *The Use of the Old Testament in the New and Other Essays*. Edited by J. M. Efird. Durham, 1972.
Vaux, R. de, *Histoire ancienne d'Israël*. Paris, 1971.
Wavell, A. P., "Night Attacks — Ancient and Modern," *Soldiers and Soldiering*. London, 1953.
Weippert, M., "'Heiliger Krieg' in Israel und Assyrien," *ZAW* 84 (1972) 460-95.
Whaley, B., *Stratagem: Deception and Surprise in War*. Cambridge, 1969.
Windisch, H., "Zur Rahabgeschichte," *ZAW* 37 (1917/18) 188-98.
Yadin, Y., *The Art of Warfare in Biblical Lands* I-II. Ramat Gan, 1963.
Yeivin, S., *The Israelite Conquest of Canaan*. Istanbul, 1971.

The Transition from a Semi-Nomadic to a Sedentary Society in the Twelfth Century B.C.E.

YIGAEL YADIN
The Hebrew University, Jerusalem

Let me begin by saying that the purpose of this paper is to defend, in broad lines, the Albright school of thought of interpreting both the biblical narrative and the archeological discoveries related to the conquest and settlement of the Israelites in the Holy Land against other schools of thought, and particularly against the so-called Alt school and its derivatives.

Professor Manfred Weippert in his splendid book, *The Settlement of the Israelite Tribes in Palestine* (London, 1971), writes (p. 55) "The fact that the 'schools' of Alt and Albright could, on the same source material and, in the main, on the basis of the same methodology, develop such fundamentally divergent views of the historical course of events involved in the Israelite settlement forces us, in the opinion of George E. Mendenhall, to make a new and thorough examination of the foundations of research in this field, that is, to submit the 'ideal model' which has been utilized in all scientific work on the problem hitherto, to a critical examination."

This is obviously necessary; but the fact that two basic schools of thought arrive at contradicting results does not mean — as Mendenhall believes — that both are wrong and that a third solution should be looked for. It is possible that only one school of thought is right, and proving this is in fact the specific purpose of this paper. Now, when saying this, one must be careful not to generalize, allowing for the possibility that although one school may be right in its general principle it may still be wrong in some of its details; or, vice versa: that one school of thought may be wrong in its general principle and yet be right in some of its details. Yet, before examining this problem more closely, I should like to make a plea for the archeological evidence. In rejecting the archeological evidence brought up by Albright, Weippert states, *inter alia* (pp. 128-29): "This means, however, that archeological finds are essentially silent evidence." I submit that the "silence" of the archeological evidence is so resounding that the very assertion put forward by Weippert is wrong. It all really depends on how one interprets the archeological evidence. Suppose we were excavating not in Israel, so intimately related with historical sources, but — let us say — in some *terra incognita*.

I believe everyone will agree that results of thorough archeological excavations in the last fifty years prove clearly that a certain culture — which we may call the Late Bronze culture — based on fortified city-states, had come to a sudden, abrupt end;[1] cities were destroyed, with many of them showing indications of conflagrations and destructions which could not be attributed to famine or earthquakes. Sometime later — stratigraphically speaking — either on the same site or elsewhere, a new, completely different culture developed, having a rather poor architectural concept which could hardly be called urban and which seems most like the first efforts of settlement of a semi-nomadic people. Nothwithstanding this remark, some sites — although destroyed in the previous period — were immediately rebuilt and could definitely be regarded as proper cities with fortifications and all the necessary attributes and elements. Now, to call such evidence "silent evidence" only because, to quote Weippert again (p. 127): "So far, however, no documents of this nature have come to light in Palestine from the period in question, and, in view of intensive archeological activity since the twenties, it may well be doubted whether discoveries of this nature will be made in future" — to call this evidence "silent" is to deny the principal importance and contribution of archeological discoveries. Let me put this the other way around and bluntly: had the archeological evidence shown (1) that no cities of the Late Bronze period had been destroyed, (2) that the destruction came about in the Iron Age, and (3) that only then were the older cultures replaced by semi-nomadic or nomadic people — had this been the case, and with no documentary evidence from the excavations indicating the identity of the destroyers of the previous cultures and those who replaced them (which presumably would support a certain historical school of thought), would then those supporting this school of thought also have considered the archeological evidence as "silent?" It would have been quoted as remarkable archeological support for the soundness of that school. I ask, therefore, does not the statement that archeological finds are essentially "silent evidence" emanate from the fact that excavation results actually, and in a most amazing way (except in some cases to be mentioned later), support a different school of thought, in fact — the school of biblical historiography? The biblical narrative in broad lines tells us that at a certain period nomadic Israelites attacked the city-state organization of the Holy Land and destroyed many of its cities, setting them on fire; then, slowly but surely, they replaced them with new, unfortified cities or settlements at the first; at the same time, they were unable to occupy certain cities whose residents continued to live side by side with the new invaders. As already indicated, this description — leaving out the words "Canaanite" or "Israelite" — is exactly the picture which the archeological finds present to us: a complete

[1]For the ever-increasing evidence of the destruction of many sites in the Holy Land during the 13th century B.C.E., that is, at the time the Mycenean IIIB pottery was still in use, see recently V. Hankey, "A Late Bronze Temple at Amman: I. The Aegean Pottery," *Levant* 6 (1974) 131ff.; H. G. Bucholz, "Ägäische Funde und Kultureinflüsse in den Randgebieten des Mittelmeers," *Archäologischer Anzeiger*, Heft 3 (1974) 325ff.

system of fortified cities collapsed and was replaced by a new culture of which the material aspect can be defined as the first efforts of semi-nomads or nomads to settle down. If such is the case, one may well ask why or how it is that, notwithstanding such clear evidence, there are eminent archeologists and historians who deny this amazing conformity and attempt to submit different interpretations of either the literal, historical narrative or the archeological finds or both.

To answer this question, one also must analyze the personal approach and starting points of these scholars (all scholars, in fact, all of us are only human and consciously or subconsciously our approaches are influenced by initial biases). If, therefore, in the following I analyze and criticize views held by this or that scholar and try to explain how I believe he might have arrived at his conclusions and why he is trying to prove his point, it should not be construed as minimizing their integrity but rather as an effort to explain how I view their methodology and conclusions and to show how scholars who basically accept the *a priori* approach of the Alt school deny the importance of the archeological discipline and its contribution to the settlement of this problem or interpret it in an impossible way. I must again quote Weippert (p. 135):

> The discussion of the archeological contribution to the reconstruction of the process of the settlement of the Israelite tribes can be brought to a close at this point. The result is largely negative, or at the very best, uncertain; where definite statements are possible, these support the settlement theories of Alt and Noth rather than those of Albright and his followers. In the question of conflagration levels it must be conceded that 'Israelites,' too, could have taken part in the destructions even if they need not necessarily have been their main protagonists. If historical judgments are in the main probability judgments which are achieved by balancing various related or divergent possibilities . . . it seems obvious to me that the archeological side of the balance, both in general and in individual cases, can have only little weight. The weight of proof falls almost entirely on the literary traditions which, in Albright's view too, cannot do justice to this task without additional support. Thus, the search for 'archeological facts' as 'external evidence' for the Israelites' settlement actually leads back in a circle to the point of departure. *There must always be literary, formal, and traditio-historical criticism* (italics by Weippert).

These statements are not only a strong plea and defense of the Alt school of thought, but also in fact a denial of the importance of archeological evidence in solving these problems. Now, in order to examine further the developments which have occurred in this field since Alt put forward his basic teachings and to negate the validity of the methods of other scholars who have followed this school of thought but tried to adjust their views to the archeological discoveries by actually deforming them, which is as bad as denying them, it is necessary once more to summarize very briefly Alt's basic approach to this problem.

Alt's school of thought can best be presented here with quotations from the excellent summary in Weippert's book (p. 5): the

> tribal confederacy did not exist at the time when those who later became the Israelites entered Palestine. It is extremely doubtful whether in that period one can speak at all of 'Israelite' tribes in the later sense. According to Alt, one must suppose, rather, that it was a question of individual clans or confederacies of clans of nomads with small cattle who, during the winter rainy season and the spring, lived with their herds in the border territory between the desert and the cultivated land and who were forced, when the vegetation in that area ceased in summer, to penetrate further into the cultivated land and to come to an understanding with the owners of the land about summer pasturage in the harvested fields and in the woods;

and later on, in Alt's opinion (p. 6)

> the clans who entered the country in this way in the course of a regular change of pasture then gradually settled in the relatively thinly populated wooded areas of the uplands, areas which were not directly exposed to the reach either of the Canaanite city-states or of Egyptian sovereignty, and began to practice agriculture once they had turned these wooded areas into arable land. This peaceful process of transition on the part of nomads to a sedentary life was, according to Alt, the real process of settlement and it was, in the nature of things, a peaceful development since the interest of any landowner there might be would not be harmed by it. Only gradually, at a second stage, did the 'Israelites' expand also into the fruitful plains and valleys which had long been occupied by closely packed groups of Canaanite cities. In this way there occurred isolated military encounters in which the 'Israelites' were not always the victors . . . but in which they nevertheless succeeded from time to time in taking a fortified city, massacring or driving away its inhabitants and themselves taking over the cultivation of its arable land. Alt called this second stage of 'Israelite' settlement in Palestine 'territorial expansion.'

In other words, this means that certain cities which were destroyed in the so-called "territorial expansion" stage would have existed in what — archeologically speaking — we call the Iron Age, or rather, during the course of the 12th century.

Having said this, I would now like to examine a school of thought subsidiary to that of Alt which has been trying to prove the accuracy and validity of such an approach but submitting it to archeological research. Here I must examine more closely the research and views — often changed radically — of my colleage, Professor Aharoni and analyze the results of the archeological evidence in the city of Hazor, which, all will agree, plays a major role in the literary sources about the conquest of the country by Joshua. Here, indeed, as Aharoni said correctly at the beginning of his research, should be the testing-ground — both historically and archeologically — of the Alt school of thought.

Let us examine more closely how this line of approach developed and faced the archeological evidence.[2]

Basically accepting Alt's line of approach of a peaceful penetration and infiltration preceding the destruction of some of the Canaanite cities, Aharoni made an important discovery in his archeological survey of upper Galilee. He discovered quite a number of tiny Iron Age settlements which he attributed to the peaceful phase of the Israelite infiltration preceding the downfall of Hazor. Avoiding for the moment the denial of Albright's assertion that all collared-rim pottery automatically and necessarily must be attributed to producers who were ethnically Israelite, I believe there can be no doubt that Aharoni was right in attributing these Upper Galilee settlements to the Israelites. If the Alt school of thought and Aharoni's interpretation of these settlements were correct, then the destruction of the great Canaanite city of Hazor should have occurred sometime after this phase of settlement. But here a new element had to be taken into account, and this is the contradiction between the biblical narrative in Joshua 11 concerning the conquest of Hazor and the mention of King Jabin in Judges 4. Alt's approach to this question, to refer again to Weippert's book (p. 33), was that he hesitates as to whether in the lost original of the narrative, all the Israelite tribes were mentioned or only the Galilean ones or even, perhaps, only Naphtali whose territory lay closest to the place in question. However, he places the historical event behind the tradition in the period of "territorial expansion" and interprets it as an attempt to gain access from the area to the south of Merom and Hazor to new territory for settlement farther north by breaking through the Canaanite encirclement. According to Alt, the mention of King Jabin of Hazor in Judges 4 would place the event described in Josh 11:1-5 in a fairly late period.

Professor Mazar, who has studied the battle and the two narratives in Joshua and Judges very analytically and penetratingly and generally has accepted some of Alt's assertions, claims nevertheless that the battle of Deborah *preceded* the fall of Hazor as recorded in Joshua.[3] Moreover, he proposed that both Joshua and Judges reflect historical events but in reversed order, placing the destruction of Hazor as described in Joshua after the one mentioned in Judges 4. Now, Aharoni, accepting this interpretation by Mazar of Alt's basic approach as well as Albright's date for Deborah, came to the natural, obvious, and logical conclusion that the great Canaanite city of Hazor was destroyed by the Israelites at *the end of the 12th* century, i.e., a generation or so *after* the date of the Upper Galilee Iron Age settlements. All this was based on the flimsy results of the excavations at Hazor by Garstang, whose conclusion was that Hazor had been destroyed sometime in the 15th century.[4] This led, of course, to

---

[2]For a detailed examination of Aharoni's views, and the related bibliography, see my *Hazor*, The Schweich Lectures (London, 1972), pp. 9-10; pp. 129ff.

[3]See my *Hazor*, pp. 9-10; pp. 129ff.

[4]*Hazor*, pp. 18-19.

both the etiological interpretation of Alt and the theories presented by Mazar and Aharoni, which meant that the city of Hazor to be sought in relation to the battles of Deborah and Joshua must be a later city in the 12th century B.C.E.

Then came our extensive excavations of Hazor, in which Aharoni took part (and if I may say so, he was at that time the only member of the staff who had a clear-cut view of the historical interpretation of events). The results of our excavations were a shattering blow to these theories. It became clear throughout the many areas excavated and without exception that the large Canaanite city was suddenly destroyed and set on fire in the 13th century B.C.E. or, in archeological terms, at the end of the Late Bronze Age, at a time when Mycenean IIIB pottery was still in use. Taking the dates for this particular pottery as set by Furumark, this meant that the city was destroyed sometime before 1230 or, let us say, before the very end of the 13th century B.C.E.[5] An archeological fact, just as important — not "silent" — was that on the rather thick debris of the destroyed Canaanite city on the tell proper a new settlement had been discovered, poor in nature, obviously of semi-nomadic character, and identical in pottery and other material aspects with the settlements discovered earlier by Aharoni in Upper Galilee which allegedly preceded the destruction of the large Canaanite city which at that time was thought to have existed at the *end of the 12th century.*

These discoveries rocked the basic approach of the Alt school, and presented a serious challenge to the theories developed by Aharoni. Not only was the nature of the archeological evidence "noisy," showing that the sequence of events had been just the opposite, but it proved beyond any doubt that there had been no proper city at Hazor in the 12th century!

Much as I regret it, I must now analyze the reactions and archeological interpretations which followed our discoveries, because only by so doing can we better understand some of the new challenges to the Albright school of thought and prove that those who wish to adhere at all costs to a historical concept based on a certain interpretation of literary sources may reach conclusions that deny the validity of archeological facts which are — irrespective of the settlement problem — well anchored chronologically and culturally. Aharoni's first reaction was that the last Late Bronze city which we discovered was not necessarily the last city at Hazor. But that was only the very beginning; when further excavation proved beyond doubt that there was no other city but City XIII, Aharoni began to challenge the dating of the destruction of the Late Bronze city, which was based on the existence of Mycenean IIIB pottery. For a while, he asserted rather vigorously that the Mycenean IIIB pottery did not

---

[5]See above, n. 1. Based on the discovery at Deir ᶜAlla of a burned faience vase with the cartouche of Queen Tewosret, the tendency now is to extend the date of Mycenean IIIB down to 1200 B.C.E. (see particularly Bucholz, Ägäische Funde, p. 478). But since in the same cache there were found early Mycenean IIIB (III A-B) materials, it is possible that the Mycenean pottery was accumulated in the sanctuary throughout the 13th century, and Tewosret's date should serve only as an *ante quem* date (so, Hankey, p. 133).

actually prove that the city had been destroyed in the 13th century, that there was no proof that Mycenean IIIB pottery had not been used in the first half of the 12th century, and that therefore the archeological evidence did not contradict the theory that the city of Hazor had been destroyed in the 12th century, after the initial phase of the peaceful infiltration in the early days of the Iron Age.

Mazar, on the other hand, was quicker to recognize that the archeological evidence pointed clearly to the fact that the city of Hazor was destroyed in the 13th century, and, still adhering to the belief that Joshua and Judges had historical nuclei, he offered a new suggestion, that Deborah lived in the 13th rather than the 12th century. This is definitely a possibility — although I, personally, do not believe it — and at least it tallies with the archeological discoveries. It does, however, exclude the possibility that a theory of peaceful infiltration is compatible with the archeological discoveries. I am happy to note that, after a long time, Aharoni faced the bitter but unchallengeable archeological fact and in his recent book he now mentions that all now agree that the Mycenean IIIB pottery was 13th century and that Hazor actually was destroyed in the 13th century B.C.E. This was a courageous admission, bowing to the archeological evidence which again is not "silent" at all.

I should like to mention here an interesting and characteristic fact, that Noth — perhaps the greatest exponent of Alt's general school of thought — immediately conceded when faced with the archeological evidence from Hazor. To quote again from Weippert (p. 36-37) Noth agrees "that the destruction of the town at the end of the 13th century B.C., confirmed by the excavations of Yadin at *tell el-qedaḥ*, does admit of a link with a capture of it by 'Israelites' and thus with the event that stands behind Josh 11:1-15. He now dissociates himself explicitly, and correctly, from the classification of the narrative as an aetiology." This view was expressed by Noth in two articles, one characteristically entitled "Hat die Bibel doch recht?" (in the festschrift for Günther Dehn [Neukirchen, 1957] pp. 14ff. and again in Supplements to Vetus Testamentum 7 [1960], pp. 273ff.).

But now came the most interesting development in interpreting the archeological evidence. Having conceded that the archeological results at Hazor show conclusively that the city was destroyed in the latter half of the 13th century, but still adhering to the basic theory of the Alt school of a peaceful infiltration preceding the expansion phase, and still believing that the Iron Age settlements he had discovered in Upper Galilee were indicative of the earlier phase, Aharoni came to an *opposite* conclusion from the archeological point of view. Unable to prove that the 13th-century Bronze Age culture belonged to the 12th century, he wants us now to believe that the Iron Age I settlements were actually 14th-13th centuries in date! This assertion was unacceptable archeologically, as was his previous claim concerning the dating of the Mycenean IIIB and the Late Bronze cultures in the 12th century.

Let us examine his archeological arguments for dating the collared-rim in the 14th and 13th centuries B.C.E., i.e., in the Late Bronze period. To start with, there is the two-and-a-half letter inscription in the Proto-Canaanite script on a jar handle found at Khirbet Raddana.[6] Aharoni, on the basis of this script, dated it before 1300 B.C.E. or in his words: "Thus the suggested minimum date of c. 1300 B.C. gives a *terminus ad quem* for the introduction of the collared-rim ware." This contradicts the conclusion reached by Cross and Freedman (*BASOR* 201 [1971] 19-22) that "the inscription should be dated to about 1200 B.C." It is not for me to refute Aharoni's assertion that "Cross and Freedman evidently were influenced by the generally accepted dating of the 'collared-rim ware' to which the inscribed jar handle belongs, i.e., the twelfth-eleventh century B.C." Let them explain the criteria for dating it. But when the views of expert epigraphists contradict his conclusion by 100 years, it would seem a bit far-fetched to state (p. 135): "In any case the epigraphic analysis of the Raddana inscription furnishes a first clear *terminus ad quem* for the early wave of settlements in the hilly region in the fourteenth century B.C., contributing further and apparently *most conclusive* (italics are mine — Y.Y.) evidence for the date of the Israelite conquest and settlement." That this date is impossible archeologically was shown also by Moshe Dothan,[7] who pointed out that several iron implements were discovered with these finds. Aharoni's "archeological" proof that the collared-rim was contemporary with the Late Bronze period is even less convincing and obviously methodologically wrong. He singles out the occurrence of two fragments of a collared-rim jar, which in the publication of *Megiddo II*[8] are ascribed to Locus 2064 of Stratum VIIB, i.e., to the Late Bronze period. However, examination of the locus in question shows clearly that they were intrusive and do not belong to that stratum at all. The locus is in a building adjacent to the temples of Stratum VIIB, Area BB. On this particular locus we read in *Megiddo II* (p. 105): "Most of the remaining construction of this building lies immediately beneath, or is interwoven with, the stratum IV stables." Indeed, the examination of the plans in figs. 258 and 403 show it clearly to be a most disturbed area, and sherds found there could theoretically belong to VIIA, VIB, VIA, VB or V. Most amazing methodologically is the fact that Aharoni would like to base a whole system of chronology on two isolated sherds, contrary to his basic approach of not dating strata on the evidence of isolated sherds. In the same article on the Khirbet Raddana inscription in which he tries to show that the inscribed jar handle might belong to the earlier phase, he says (p. 135): "This is an enlightening admission that sherds are stratigraphically not reliable, even if found in a clear stratigraphical context, and that more emphasis than usual should be laid on the reconstruction of vessels found *in situ*." We can therefore see that there is no archeological proof that the Iron Age collared-rim pottery goes back to the 14th or 13th centuries, and this negative evidence in fact is one of the strongest arguments against accepting a

---

[6]*IEJ* 21 (1971), 130ff.

[7]Orally, in a lecture at the Israel Exploration Society Thirtieth Archaeological Convention, September, 1972.

[8]Pl. 64, No. 8.

theory of coexistence of these two cultures in the 14th and early 13th centuries B.C.E. The complete absence of both cultures together is strong — not "silent" — archeological evidence indicating a sequence of cultures, not contemporary ones.

Similarly, one should reject the interpretation of the single scarab found recently on the surface at Tell Mashash for dating the earliest Iron Age settlements at this particular site. Kempinsky would like to date this scarab to the days of Ramses II[9] or Seti II;[10] but here, again, it is quite unclear that this particular scarab is 19th and not 20th dynasty and even later. The comparisons suggested by the excavators are unconvincing, since not enough emphasis is put on the fact that the weapon held by the Pharaoh is a straight sword rather than a sickle-shaped one and the fact that the whole repertoire of the pottery is typical Iron Age and to date has not been found in any context of the Late Bronze Age cultures.

Having demonstrated that, archeologically speaking, there is no support for a general picture of peaceful Israelite infiltration before the collapse of the main Canaanite cities of the Late Bronze culture, and that the earliest signs of Israelite settlements *follow* (and not always immediately) the collapse of the Canaanite cities destroyed by the Israelites according to the book of Joshua, we should now turn to another extreme theory which challenges Albright's basic approach. This time the motive for the challenge is just the opposite from that which motivated Alt and his followers — not the critical examination of biblical sources, but rather what one may define as a more Fundamentalistic approach to biblical sources. I am referring to the theory recently proposed by J. A. Callaway, subsequent to his excavations at Ai, which reaffirmed the fact — already noted by Marquet-Krause — that there were no Late Bronze Age remains on the site of et-Tell. Not accepting the etiological aspect of the story of the conquest of Ai as narrated in Joshua — or to use his words in the article "New Evidence on the Conquest of ᶜAi,"[11] "I am persuaded that there is too much historical evidence to call the conquest of ᶜAi a legend or etiology" — Callaway came to the conclusion that "Josh 8:1-29 reflects a conquest of ᶜAi in Iron Age I, or in the 12th century B.C." Having discovered at Ai two phases of occupation with slightly different types of collared-rim pottery, Callaway then presented the theory that the first phase of occupation was Hivite and that this was the very settlement conquered by the Israelites and that its date was conceivable "before some of the last Late Bronze cities fell." As proof for the existence of this type of collared-rim pottery in a Late Bronze context, he adduces the sherd mentioned by Aharoni as well as another type of jar published in *Megiddo II*, pl. 83.1.[12] But examination of all the loci in which this type had been discovered shows these without exception to be ascribed by their excavators to Stratum VI! Based on his interpretation of the Ai evidence, as

[9] *Qadmoniot* 27-28 (1974) 132.
[10] *ZDPV* 89 (1973) 203.
[11] *JBL* 87 (1968) 316ff.
[12] P. 316, n. 25.

explained above, Callaway came to a general conclusion that (p. 320): "Albright's view that the conquest of ᶜAi reflects a Late Bronze capture of Bethel is also, in my opinion, untenable; in fact, I think we can no longer take for granted that the conquest of Canaan by invading Israelites accounts for the Late Bronze destructions of Bethel, Lachish, Tell Beit Mirsim, or Hazor." In other words, Callaway concludes that the conquest occurred in the Iron Age and that the cities captured by the Israelites were not necessarily all fortified, but could have been just villages or hamlets, so characteristic of the early phase of the Iron Age, except for places such as Megiddo and Beth-shean, of which the biblical tradition says explicitly that they were not captured by the Israelites. This, I submit, is again a wrong interpretation of the archeological evidence, ignoring the biblical descriptions of the capture of the big cities which have no etiological character.

Here we may also mention a very recent — and I may add, desperate — theory, presented by V. Fritz.[13] Fritz, admitting the strength of the archeological evidence that the city of Hazor XIII fell during the 13th century, yet being unable to accept — for historical reasons — the possibility of the Israelites conquering the city, offers a suggestion — unwarranted by any source — that the city of Hazor fell as a result of attacking Sea Peoples. In other words, everyone is a potential destroyer of Hazor, even if not mentioned in any document, except those specifically mentioned in the Bible as having done so! Perhaps, if we had, instead of the Bible, an external document describing the Israelites as the Desert Peoples, it might have been easier for scholars to accept the possibility that just as the Sea Peoples managed to destroy some of the Canaanite cities in Syria and Palestine in the west, so the Desert Peoples could destroy the Canaanite cities in the mainland.

Having reviewed briefly, without doing full justice to all the views, the difficulties encountered by the various schools of thought if examined in archeological terms, may I at the end try to present my interpretation of the biblical narrative, the external evidence, and archeological evidence. I believe the basic mistake of the extreme schools of thought on both sides is their totalitarian attitude, namely, that either the whole narrative in Joshua is wrong, or that it had to be accepted *in toto* as true, even if sporadic details (admittedly etiological in nature) were clearly contradicted by the archeological data.

I believe it is in the true nature of Albright's broad line of approach — although not necessarily in its details — that we must examine biblical evidence open-mindedly and compare it with the archeological evidence in each case, without prejudice or bias or any preconceived total idea. Wherever we find agreement between the biblical narrative and the archeological evidence, there is no reason to doubt the historicity of that particular biblical source. On the other hand, wherever the archeological evidence bluntly contradicts the biblical narrative — as in the case of Ai — we should examine the possibility that that particular chapter in the Bible is either etiological, a later interpolation or an

---

[13]V. Fritz, "Das Ende der spätbronzezeitlichen Stadt Hazor stratum XIII und die biblische Überlieferung in Josua 11 and Richter 4," *Ugarit-Forschungen* 5 (1973) 123ff.

editor's misunderstanding, as, for example the case of Judges 4. Let us not be dogmatic and try to find a solution which will satisfy all the sources in the Bible; yet at the same time let us not dismiss *a priori* the basic historiographic approach of the Bible — which I believe is fully confirmed by archeological excavations — that there was a phase in the Late Bronze Age in which the Israelite nomads, like nomads from other parts of the country, managed to attack the decadent Canaanite settlements and then slowly but surely moved into the next phase in Israel's history, the sedentary settlement of the tribes in the country on the ruins of previous Canaanite cities.

One may finally ask: how was it possible for the nomadic Israelites to conquer such a culture? A solution to that need not necessarily be found in the archeological evidence only. I have my own view and shall now present it briefly.

Although I have tried to challenge Weippert's conclusions "that the archeological side of the balance, both in general and individual cases, can have only little weight," I agree with his picture of the state of affairs in Canaan in the last phase of the Bronze Age (p. 133), i.e.,that there was already a dissolution of the city-state system as a result of the "decline in political and economic stability"; but this does not mean that "the self-dissolution of the city-state then made possible, of course, the infiltrations of nomads who later, when they had become sedentary, formed a confederacy of the twelve tribes of Israel." This dissolution was not the *cause* of their collapse but, at most, *expedited* it. I would make a somewhat different emphasis: the decline of the city-state system, not only through internal problems but also as a result of the hammering and destruction wrought during the 14th and 13th centuries in Palestine by the Egyptian pharaohs themselves, had weakened it to a degree that enabled even the semi-nomadic Israelites not only to infiltrate into the country but also to capture and give it the *coup de grace*. We do not have to visualize impregnable, strongly fortified Canaanite bastions but rather degenerated cities with weak fortifications. I should mention a fact which has not been given enough attention, though confirmed by archeological discoveries, that in many cases the Late Bronze Age people did not actually build new fortifications but rather reused Middle Bronze fortifications, strengthening them where necessary. This also explains the situation at Jericho, where archeologists were trying in vain to find a Late Bronze city wall and where obviously the Middle Bronze wall could have been in use even in that settlement of the Late Bronze which the spade has shown to have existed there. I would like, in fact, to revive, in a slightly different way, the theory offered many years ago by Garstang,[14] namely that even the biblical tradition recognized the fact that the repeated destructions of Canaanite cities in Palestine by the Pharaohs prepared the way militarily for the Israelites. I refer to the hornet mentioned in Josh 24:12: "I sent the hornet before you which drove them out." The "hornet" could refer to the Egyptian Pharaohs,

[14]*Joshua, Judges* (London, 1931) 258ff.

whose title, denoting the kingship of Lower Egypt, was probably the hornet, commonly taken for a bee. Even if this explanation of the verse is unacceptable, the numerous Egyptian reliefs and annals are clear evidence that many of the fortifications of the Canaanite cities were systematically destroyed by the Egyptian Pharaohs of the 14th and 13th centuries. In other words, Canaan of the 13th century was ripe politically, economically, and militarily for a conquest of the type described in Joshua.

Shechem: Problems of the Early Israelite Era

Lawrence E. Toombs
Wilfrid Laurier University, Waterloo, Ontario

The excavations of the Drew-McCormick, later the Joint, Expedition to ancient Shechem, between the years 1956 and 1969, explored the transition between the Late Bronze and Iron Ages at five principal locations on the site. This extensive sampling of the data includes two fields associated with the wall system (Fields I and III), two in housing areas between the city wall and the Acropolis (Fields VII and IX), and one adjacent to the temenos area on the northeast side (Field XIII). Additional data of a supporting nature are provided by the fill within and in front of the Fortress Temple (Field V).[1] The evidence for the transition derived from these fields has been published piecemeal and in brief form in the annual preliminary reports of the expedition,[2] and in part was summarized by G. Ernest Wright in *Shechem: the Biography of a Biblical City,*[3] but the data bearing on the transition have never been gathered together and presented as a unity.[4] For the sake of clarity and completeness, each of the major fields will be dealt with separately and an attempt will then be made to bring the results together into a composite picture of the sequence of events for the city as a whole.

The extensive area-excavation in Field VII, the upper residential quarter of the city, provides a convenient starting point for this process.[5] In this field the latest phase of Late Bronze Age occupation is marked by portions of several buildings of somewhat random construction and not, as far as could be

---

[1]For the location of these fields, see fig. 1.

[2]G. Ernest Wright, "The Second Campaign at Tell Balâtah (Shechem)," *BASOR* 148 (December 1957) 11-28; Lawrence E. Toombs and G. Ernest Wright, "The Third Campaign at Balâtah (Shechem)," *BASOR* 161 (February, 1961) 11-54; Lawrence E. Toombs and G. Ernest Wright, "The Fourth Campaign at Balâtah (Shechem)," *BASOR* 169 (February, 1963) 1-60; Robert J. Bull, Joseph A. Callaway, Edward F. Campbell, Jr., James F. Ross, and G. Ernest Wright, "The Fifth Campaign at Balâtah (Shechem)," *BASOR* 180 (December, 1965) 7-41. Robert J. Bull and Edward F. Campbell, Jr., "The Sixth Campaign at Balâtah (Shechem)," *BASOR* 190 (April, 1968) 3-41; Edward F . Campbell, Jr., James F. Ross, and Lawrence E. Toombs, "The Eighth Campaign at Balâtah (Shechem)," *BASOR* 204 (December, 1971) 2-16.

[3]McGraw-Hill (New York, 1965), *passim*, but esp. pp. 57-79, 123-38.

[4]The transition between the Late Bronze and Iron Ages takes place between Strata XII and XI in the overall stratification of the site: see fig. 2. This chart is reproduced from *Annual of the Department of Antiquities*, The Hashemite Kingdom of Jordan 17 (1972) plate 2.

[5]The basis of the analysis of Field VII is the unpublished Field Report for the 1964 season prepared by Edward F. Campbell, Jr. For a brief summary see *BASOR* 169 (February, 1963) 20-26. The stratigraphy of the transition in Field VII, Area IX, is illustrated in fig. 3.

determined in the excavated areas, oriented in any coherent plan. The type of soil layers encountered indicated industrial activity of an undetermined kind, and agricultural activity and food-storage and processing seem to have taken place in the immediate neighborhood. This final Late Bronze Age phase rests on a layer of destruction debris, which seals all earlier levels and indicates that a major disaster, probably military in origin, struck at least this part of the city toward the end of the Late Bronze Age.

In the next phase, succeeding the buildings just described, collar-rimmed store-jars and cooking pots with elongated, triangular rims begin to appear. These forms are usually taken as indicative of the Iron Age. Architecturally, the phase contains the remains of two buildings, one of which is a mere reuse of a building of the final Late Bronze Age phase. Further evidence of continuity between the Late Bronze and Iron Ages is the continuation of industrial activity in the area.

Thus, the evidence from Field VII indicates a destruction late in the Late Bronze Age, followed by a rebuilding on a modest scale, with the intrusion of agricultural activity within the city walls. The beginning of the Iron Age shows repair and reconstruction, but no major destruction of the buildings.

The impression of continuity between the Late Bronze and Iron Age occupation at Shechem gained from Field VII is confirmed and strengthened by evidence from Field IX, the lower residential quarter.[6] The final phase of Late Bronze Age construction represents a decline from the sophisticated building tradition of the earlier Late Bronze Age levels. As in Field VII, a destruction level exists between the flowering of the Late Bronze culture and its final phase.[7] The latest levels of Late Bronze in Field IX show two principal architectural features. The first is a sanctuary which dominates the western portion of the field; the second is a number of house walls to the east of the sanctuary. Both of these architectural zones continue into the Iron Age. The sanctuary is reconstructed and the house walls are rebuilt and, occasionally, realigned, but the Late Bronze Age traditon is maintained. The construction technique is, however, sufficiently novel to lead the supervisor of the field, Joseph A. Callaway, to conclude that the evidence indicated the appearance of a new people. Not only do characteristic Iron I pottery types begin to appear, but the construction is more massive and functional than that of the Late Bronze period and involves the use of roughly-finished plaster, not seen in the earlier sanctuary. The Iron Age sanctuary and adjacent buildings were destroyed by a violent fire, which buried the structures under more than a meter of ashes and collapsed walls.

In summary, Field IX shows a destruction layer in the later part of the Late Bronze Age followed by a cultural decline. The Late Bronze Age building

---

[6]The discussion of Field IX is based on Joseph A. Callaway's unpublished Field Report for 1964, briefly summarized in *BASOR* 180 (December, 1965) 9-15. See also fig. 4.

[7]*BASOR* 180, p. 11.

tradition extends, with significant technical innovations, into the Iron Age. No evidence of destruction marks the transitional period.

The excavation in Field XIII agrees in the main with the results obtained in Fields VII and IX and provides some additional information.[8] During the early phases of Late Bronze, Field XIII was the site of a large house built around a central courtyard. This building was destroyed and its remains covered with a layer of compacted earth containing decayed bricks and a great deal of charcoal and ash. This layer is clearly destruction debris, spread about in order to create a level foundation for a new construction. The building erected on this platform was a simple rectangular structure with two rooms. This structure provides important ceramic evidence for the transition from the Canaanite to the Israelite period. The fill on which it rested and the makeup for its lowest floor contained Late Bronze Age pottery. The forms are those of LB IIB and include late forms and local imitations of Cypriote "bilbils" and of hemispherical bowls of late White Slip II; but the quantity of imported wares is relatively small and only three Mycenean body sherds were found.

No diagnostic Iron I sherds were recovered from these foundation layers, the pottery of which showed a general deterioration both in fabrication and in the application of painted design. The pottery indicates a foundation date in the late 14th or early 13th century. The two-room building underwent one major reconstruction in which a new floor level was laid. It is in association with this reconstruction that the first Iron I sherds appear. The building remained in continuous use throughout Iron I until it was destroyed and its remains covered by the debris of the destruction.

This evidence agrees closely with that provided by Fields VII and IX — a major destruction late in the Late Bronze Age, followed by an impoverished rebuilding, the new structure continuing, with repairs and renewals of its floors, into Iron I.

Thus far we have reviewed the available data from within the city. We now turn to the situation at the city wall. In Field I, the guard-rooms, which flanked the East Gate on its southern side during the Late Bronze Age, reveal a sequence of layers remarkably similar to those of the building in Field XIII.[9] The Late Bronze Age surfacing is represented by a series of five plaster floors, separated in each case by a layer of occupational debris 5 cm. to 10 cm. in thickness. The pottery from these layers was consistently Late Bronze in date. Overlying the uppermost floor was a gray, compact layer, heavily infused with plaster and brick fragments, 30 cm. in thickness. The associated sherds were LB II in date.

---

[8] The description of Field XIII evidence is derived from Lawrence E. Toombs' unpublished Field Report for 1968, a brief summary of which appeared in *BASOR* 204 (December, 1971) 7-17. The ceramic situation became clear during studies made for a forthcoming publication of the Late Bronze Age pottery from Shechem. Fig. 5 shows the nature of the transition in Field XIII, Areas 1 and 2.

[9] The basis of the description of the East Gate guard-rooms is the unpublished Field Report of Lawrence E. Toombs for 1957, summarized in *BASOR* 148 (December, 1957) 22-23.

Above this debris was a further series of floors, fourteen in all, and in the occupational debris covering these floors, the first Iron Age sherds began to appear. Above the latest floor level lay a second destruction layer, in which were found, among other Iron I forms, two fragmentary lamps with flattened rims, radically pinched spouts, and rounded bases — a lamp form at home in Iron I.

This stratigraphic sequence shows that, after a destruction during the Late Bronze Age, a sequence of floors was laid down in the guard-rooms, beginning in LB II and continuing without violent interruption until the end of Iron I on the site.

The evidence from the East Gate guard-rooms, which may be regarded as structures directly related to the defensive system, is supplemented by data obtained from two squares immediately behind the guard-rooms and within the city proper.[10] Here, at the high point of Late Bronze Age occupation, an area of well-laid cobblestones represents a roadway or open square. This open area was in use for a considerable period of time and was frequently repaired and completely rebuilt at least once. The latest phase of the cobbles was covered by a layer of destruction debris 75 cm. to 1 m. in thickness, piled up against the back wall of the guard-rooms. A wall, running parallel to the back wall of the guard-rooms, was dug into this destruction debris. It had the effect of producing a narrow roadway at the back of the guard-rooms where the cobbled surfaces formerly had been. The foundational pottery for this wall displays only LB II forms, but the sherds associated with the surfacing of the narrow roadway show characteristic Iron I types. Once again, as in the fields previously examined, the sequence is a Late Bronze Age destruction, after which the rebuilding, still in the Late Bronze Age, represents the efforts of a financially enfeebled community. The reconstruction continues in use, with repairs and refurbishing, into the Iron Age.

The last body of data comes from Field III, a trench over the city walls in the northeast quadrant of the site.[11] It is disappointingly scanty and does not reach as late as Iron I. The Late Bronze Age material is also badly disturbed. Iron I is represented only by an earth layer containing sherds of the period, but without associated structures. Structures belonging to the Late Bronze Age are present, but their nature and function are difficult to determine, and it is not until Middle Bronze Age levels are reached that the stratigraphic situation becomes clear. The field, therefore, does not yield a sequence of layers covering the transition from Late Bronze to Iron I. It does, however, as will be shown later, produce evidence bearing on the destruction of the city in LB II.

The data reviewed above are monotonous and repetitious, with only minor variations in detail from field to field. The remarkable concurrence of the

---

[10]Based on Lawrence E. Toombs' Field Report for 1966, summarized in *BASOR* 190 (April, 1968) 3-4. For the sequence of layers described below, see fig. 6.

[11]Based on the Field Report of Robert W. Funk for 1957 and summarized in *BASOR* 148 (December, 1957) 17-20.

evidence, however, argues for the soundness of the results, and the following sequence of events in the history of the site may be regarded as fairly firmly established.

1. During the Late Bronze Age, Shechem enjoyed a long period of considerable prosperity, characterized by high population density, sophisticated building techniques, and impressive public works.

2. Before the end of the Late Bronze Age this state of affairs altered suddenly and radically. Archeologically, there is no discernible period of decline preceding the disaster. It overtook a flourishing city in the form of a general destruction, probably the consequence of a military attack. While general throughout the site, the Late Bronze Age destruction does not seem to have had the ferocious violence of the earlier obliteration of the Middle Bronze city or the later destruction of Iron I Shechem. Rebuilding took place without a marked break in occupation. Although all the field reports of the expedition refer to the presence of destruction layers during the Late Bronze Age, they have not been emphasized in the preliminary reports, nor has their significance been discussed.

3. In the aftermath of the disaster, the city was depopulated and impoverished, and its rebuilding took place with poorer materials in less-splendid buildings than its forerunner.

4. The life of the city in this state of diminished resources and vigor continued for a lengthy period, which begins in the Late Bronze Age and ends with the destruction of the Iron I city. Although a full sequence of layers cannot be established in the sacred area, because much of the Late Bronze and virtually all of the Iron I evidence was removed by the German expeditions,[12] the history of the Fortress Temple also indicates the continuity between the Late Bronze and Iron I periods. On the massive foundations of the last MB IIC temple (Temenos 7), a lighter building, oriented at an angle of five degrees from the axis of its predecessor, was constructed (Temenos 8). It demonstrably was established in the Late Bronze Age. Its successor (Temenos 9) has precisely the same plan as Temenos 8, and on presumptive evidence is equated with the Temple of Ba^{c}al-Berith mentioned in Judges 9 in connection with the kingship of Abimelek. The missing link in the argument, of course, is positive evidence for destruction between Temenoi 8 and 9.

5. The Iron I city underwent violent destruction, which obliterated its buildings and left the site a wilderness of ruins. At the time of its destruction, the culture of the city was fully-developed Iron I. The end of the Iron I city is almost certainly to be attributed to its capture by Abimelek (Judges 9).

While the archeological sequence is relatively secure, the dates to be assigned to its various elements and the historical events with which they are to be correlated is more problematical. The era of prosperity for Late Bronze Age

---

[12]The most significant of the preliminary reports of Sellin and Welter are to be found in *ZDPV* 49 (1926) 229-36, 304-20; 50 (1927) 265-74; 51 (1928) 119-23; 64 (1941) 1-20. For a digest of their results, see Wright, *Shechem*, chap. 3.

Shechem probably began in the reign of Thotmes III (1490-1436 B.C.E.), whose conquests to the north provided a shield behind which cities like Shechem could enjoy political security and, in consequence, flourishing trade.

These favorable conditions continued into the Amarna Age, when Labʾayu, king of Shechem, made his influence felt throughout the highlands from Jerusalem to Megiddo. His devious policies earned him the hostility and possibly the envy of neighboring states; and at least one abortive attempt was made to kidnap him. He was finally killed by the troops of Biridiya of Megiddo. His sons continued their father's agressive policies, and the animosity against the rulers of Shechem among its neighbors continued.[13]

There is no documentation, so far as I know, for a destruction of Shechem during the Late Bronze Age, but on the testimony of the Amarna Letters such an event would be far from unexpected. If the dynasty of Labʾayu ever proved to be weak or ineffectual rulers, there were neighboring kings only too willing to bring the city to ruin. Labʾayu's name had become a by-word for perfidy in the region, so that when Shuwardata wished to insult Abdi-Heba and to arouse suspicion against him, he could think of no better way than to call him "another Labʾayu" (280:30-35). The archeological evidence would indicate that the expected did occur — and Shechem was destroyed.

If we follow the chronology for the Amarna Letters suggested by Edward F. Campbell, Jr.,[14] the reigns of Labʾayu and his sons would bring us well into the time of Ikhnaton, i.e., to approximately the middle of the 14th century. The destruction of the city, then, took place in the latter half of the 14th or at the very beginning of the 13th century. Shechem's period of prosperity thus extended from approximately 1480-1300 B.C.E., a period covering LB IB, LB IIA, and possibly part of LB IIB.

The destruction of Shechem at the end of this period of prosperity is not irrelevant to the nature of the transition which took place on the site between Late Bronze and Iron I. Many sites in the hill-country and in the plains and valleys show destruction levels datable to the 13th century and attributable either to the Israelites or the Philistines.[15] Shechem, however, does not display this phenomenon. The transition from Canaanite to Israelite occupation took place during a period of relative poverty and cultural decline in the life of the city. Moreover, it occurred without the evidences of violent military attack and, probably, gradually over an extended period of time — by infiltration perhaps, rather than by conquest. Does the destruction of Shechem, possibly in reprisal

---

[13] A convenient summary of Labʾayu's career is given by Edward F. Campbell Jr., in *The Biblical Archaeologist Reader 3*, (New York: Doubleday, 1970) 71-73. A more detailed discussion is that of Weber in J. A. Knudtzon, *Die el-Amarna-Tafeln* (Leipzig, 1915) 1306f.

[14] *The Chronology of the Amarna Letters* (Baltimore: Johns Hopkins University, 1964).

[15] G. Ernest Wright, "The Archaeology of Palestine," in *The Bible and the Ancient Near East*, G. E. Wright, ed., (New York: Doubleday, 1961) 94.

for the expansionist policies of Labʾayu,[16] create the military precondition for the peaceful transition of Shechem from Late Bronze to Iron I?

The excavation in Field VII indicated a rather underpopulated condition within the city, with some portions of the site being available for farming or gardening. The weakened condition of Shechem both in resources and man-power may have made it physically impossible to oppose the advance of the newcomers, and the inhabitants may have judged it more expedient to admit them without conflict than to oppose them with inadequate means of defense.[17]

Archeological evidence to support or refute this hypothesis is unfortunately scanty. The missing ingredient is firm evidence as to the state of the city's defenses at the end of Late Bronze. The North Gate and its adjacent structures had been cleared to Middle Bronze Age levels by the German excavators. The area exposed at the East Gate was not extensive enough to elucidate the Late Bronze Age wall system, beyond suggesting that the fortifications of the period employed the inner line of the MB IIC wall. There remains, then, only the evidence from Field III which contains many ambiguities. The Field Supervisor, Robert W. Funk, recognized the problems in his Field Report, declaring that the interpretation of the Late Bronze fortifications must "remain conjectural."[18]

A wall of well-coursed stone 1.5 m. in thickness was constructed squarely on top of the rear line of the MB IIC defenses. This wall, clearly of Late Bronze date, presented two puzzling features. It seemed too slight a structure to have served as a defensive wall, and the plaster surface associated with it was a little over one meter higher than the floors of a large Late Bronze building to the west. Funk suggested that the defensive system may have followed the outer wall of the MB IIC fortifications and that the slighter stone wall was part of a subsidiary circumvallation within the main line. Funk's original conjecture may be correct, but the evidence gathered from the other fields suggests an alternative possibility which, in my judgment, is more convincing. The defense system of the main Late Bronze Age phases followed the inner line of the MB IIC defenses as it did at the East Gate. This was breached and broken down during the Late Bronze Age destruction, and in the impoverished rebuilding which followed, was replaced by the slighter wall. In the troubled times of the mid-13th century, this weak defense system proved inadequate to protect the city and became a factor in the peaceful acceptance of the new political order. This

---

[16]The connection between the destruction of LB II Shechem and the dynasty of Labʾayu is, of course, only one possibility among many. There were enemies aplenty toward the end of the 14th century, including a resurgent Egypt, to account for the destruction of the city.

[17]This paper deals in the main with the archeological evidence. The possibility that the decline of 13th-century Shechem made it possible for tribal groups, related to later Israel, to take control of the city before the Hebrews from Egypt arrived on the scene, or even the possibility that these tribal groups conquered Shechem about 1300 B.C.E., would require fuller discussion in another context.

[18]Field Report, p. 13. Fig. 7 shows the stratigraphic features incorporated in the description below.

reconstruction accounts directly for the difference in surface levels between the wall and the adjacent building. The former belongs to the post-destruction phase, and the latter to the pre-destruction phase. A hasty repair to the guard-room walls at the East Gate and crude attempts to buttress the weakened corners may belong also to the post-destruction phase.

The frequently noted absence of Shechem from the "conquest narrative" in Joshua 1-12 offers a "support from silence " for the hypothesis of a non-violent passage of Shechem from Canaanite to Israelite control.[19] The failure of the narrative to mention the capture of so important a city may be taken as presumptive evidence that no such capture did occur. The other side of the coin is seen in Judges 1 where the name of Shechem does not appear among the cities that remained in Canaanite hands.[20]

Shechem disappears from the biblical narratives after the Dinah incident of Genesis 34[21] and does not reappear until the account of the covenant mediated by Joshua to Israel, when it is already an acknowledged center of Israelite life (Joshua 24). This is precisely the situation one would expect if Shechem had passed peacefully into Israelite hands.

This paper, then, argues that there was a hitherto unrecognized conquest of Shechem during the Late Bronze Age, probably in the late 14th or early 13th century. This conquest, which may have come about as a reaction by other city-states to the expansionist policies of the dynasty of Labᵓayu, greatly weakened and impoverished the city and, thus, became an important factor in the subsequent peaceful passage of Shechem into Israelite political control.

---

[19] A useful summary of Shechem in biblical and extra-biblical references is given by Walter Harrelson and Bernhard W. Anderson in *BA* 20 (1957) 2-19.

[20] An alternative to the hypothesis offered above must be mentioned. If the conquest traditions took form between 1150 and 975 B.C.E., when Shechem was a small agricultural and stock-raising village, the site was possibly omitted because of its comparative insignificance at the time the narrative was compiled.

[21] It is tempting, indeed, to see in the destruction of the city by Simeon and Levi, a biblical memory of the late 14th-century destruction of the city.

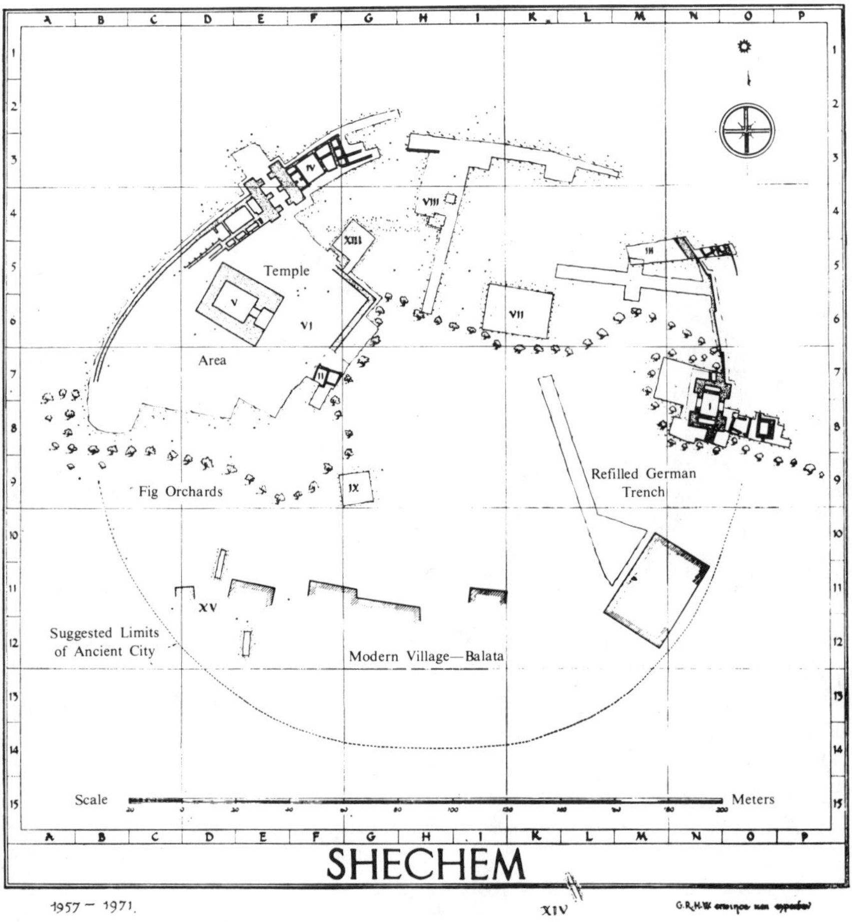

Fig. 1. General plan of the site of ancient Shechem showing the location of the fields discussed in this paper.

Stratification Of Tell Balâṭah–Shechem

Period	Stratum	B.C. Date	Field I	Field II	Field III	Field IV	Field V-VI	Field VI-2	Field VII	Field VIII	Field IX	Field XIII
Hellenistic	I	ca. 150/128–107	Debris	Hellenistic House	Debris	German Excavation	German Excavation	German Excavation	Stratum I	Excavation	Phase 1	Excavation
	II	ca. 190–150/128							II		2	
	IIIA	ca. 225-190	401		Phase 1. Walls				IIIA		3a	
	IIIB	ca. 250-225							IIIB		3b	
	IVA	ca. 300-250	170		Phase 2. Walls				IVA		4a	
	IVB	ca. 331-300							IVB		4b	
	ABANDONMENT Ca. 475–331. B.C.											
Persian	V	ca. 600-475	Sherds		Sherds Present In the Wash-down the slope	German Excavation			V	German —	5	
Iron IID	VIA	ca. 724–600	412A					German Excavation	VIA		6	
	VIB								VIB			
Iron IIC	VII	ca. 748-724	412B	Iron II Building			Granary		VII		7	German
	VIII	ca. 810-748	412c						VIII		8a 8b	
Iron IIB	IXA	ca. 860-810	175						IXA	Phase 1.	9a	
	IXB	918-860							IXB		9b	
Iron IIA	XA	ca. 950-918	176 and floors 490	Early Iron II Building					XA	2.	10	Surface as A.D.–1934 Poor Rebuild
	XB	ca. 975-950							XB			
	ABANDONMENT Ca. 1150/1125 — 975 B.C.											
Iron IA	XI	ca. 1200 1150/25	178 179		Debris behind Wall B		Temenos 9	LB Phase 1	Phase 11–12 (Layers 3-4)	3.	11	Phase 1
LB IIB	XII	ca. 1350/10 1200	127A				Temenos 8	2.	13-15 (Layers 5a-c)		12 a	(LB Phase 1) [2]
LB IIA	XIII	ca. 1400–1350 10	127B		"Palace"			3.	16a (Layers 6a)	4.	12 b.	(LB Phase 2) [3]
LB IB	XIV	ca. 1450-1400	127					4.	16b (Layer 6b)		12 c.	(LB Phase 3a-b) [4]
	ABANDONMENT Ca. 1550–1450 B.C.											
MB IIC	XV	ca. 1600-1550	WALL B		MB Phase 1a-d	WALL B	Temenos 7	MB IIC Phases 1-3	17 (Layer 7)	5 6	13	MB II C House In Area 4
	XVI	ca. 1650-1600	WALL A		MB Phase 2a-b	NW-Gate Erected	Temenos 6 (Fortress-temple)				14	MB II C Drain
MB IIB	XVII	ca. 1675-1650	WALL C Earthen Embankment		WALL C Earthen Embankment	Earthen Embankment	Temenos 5 909-910	Earthen Embankment			15	Earthen Embankment
	XVIII	ca. 1700-1675					Temenos 4 901				16	
	XIX	ca. 1725-1700					Temenos 3 902					
	XX	ca. 1750-1725					Temenos 2 939 Wall D	WALL D			17	
MB IIA	XXI	ca. 1800-1750					Temenos 1b 999	Cobbled Pavement			18	
	XXII	ca. 1900-1800					Temenos 1a 968				19-20	
Chalcolithic	XXIII						Chalcolithic A (Ghassulian)	Same				
	XXIV										Chalcolithic B (Pre-Ghassulian)	
	Virgin soil over marl (huwwar) bedrock Was reached In Fields V, VI, VIII and IX											

Fig. 2. Chart showing the overall stratigraphy of Shechem. The transition from Late Bronze to Iron I takes place between Strata XII and XI, or more precisely, during the early phases of Stratum XI.

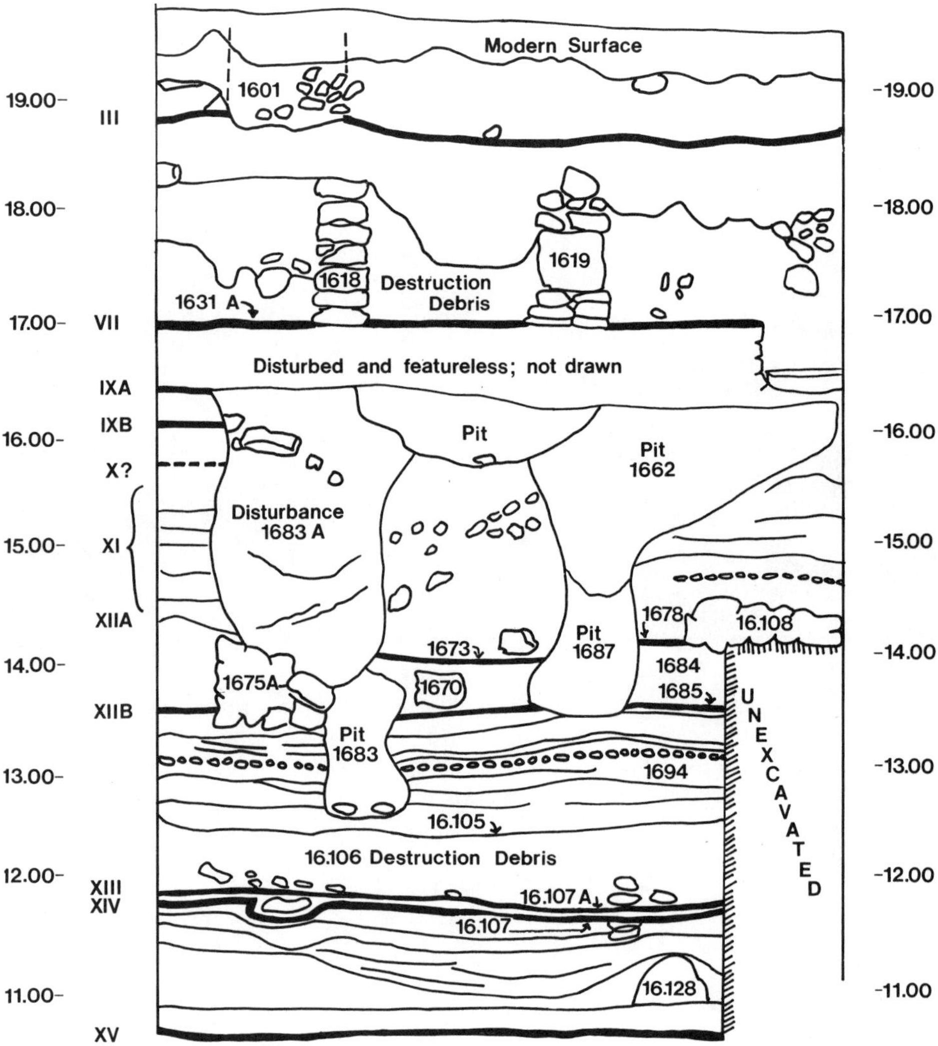

Fig. 3. Section of east balk of Field VII, Area 9. Locus 16,106 is the Late Bronze destruction debris sealing Late Bronze floors 16,107 and 16,107A. Iron I sherds begin to appear in quantity at Locus 1694.

Fig. 4. An unfinished maṣṣebah lying on the floor of the Iron I shrine. The walls in the foreground belong to building of the final Late Bronze Age phase. The decomposed brick and other debris of the Abimelek destruction overlies the Iron I sanctuary. Photo by Lee Ellenberger.

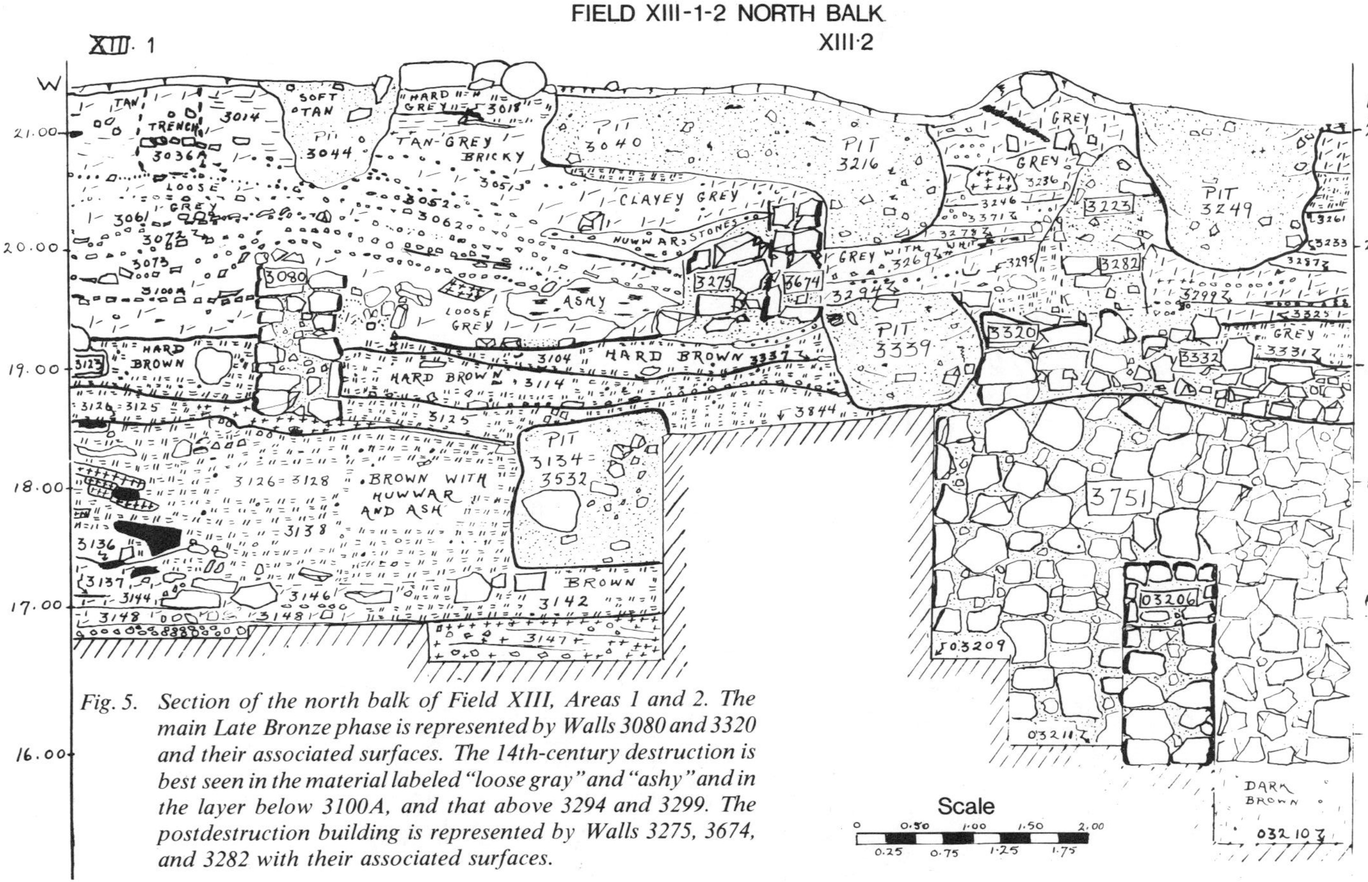

Fig. 5. Section of the north balk of Field XIII, Areas 1 and 2. The main Late Bronze phase is represented by Walls 3080 and 3320 and their associated surfaces. The 14th-century destruction is best seen in the material labeled "loose gray" and "ashy" and in the layer below 3100A, and that above 3294 and 3299. The postdestruction building is represented by Walls 3275, 3674, and 3282 with their associated surfaces.

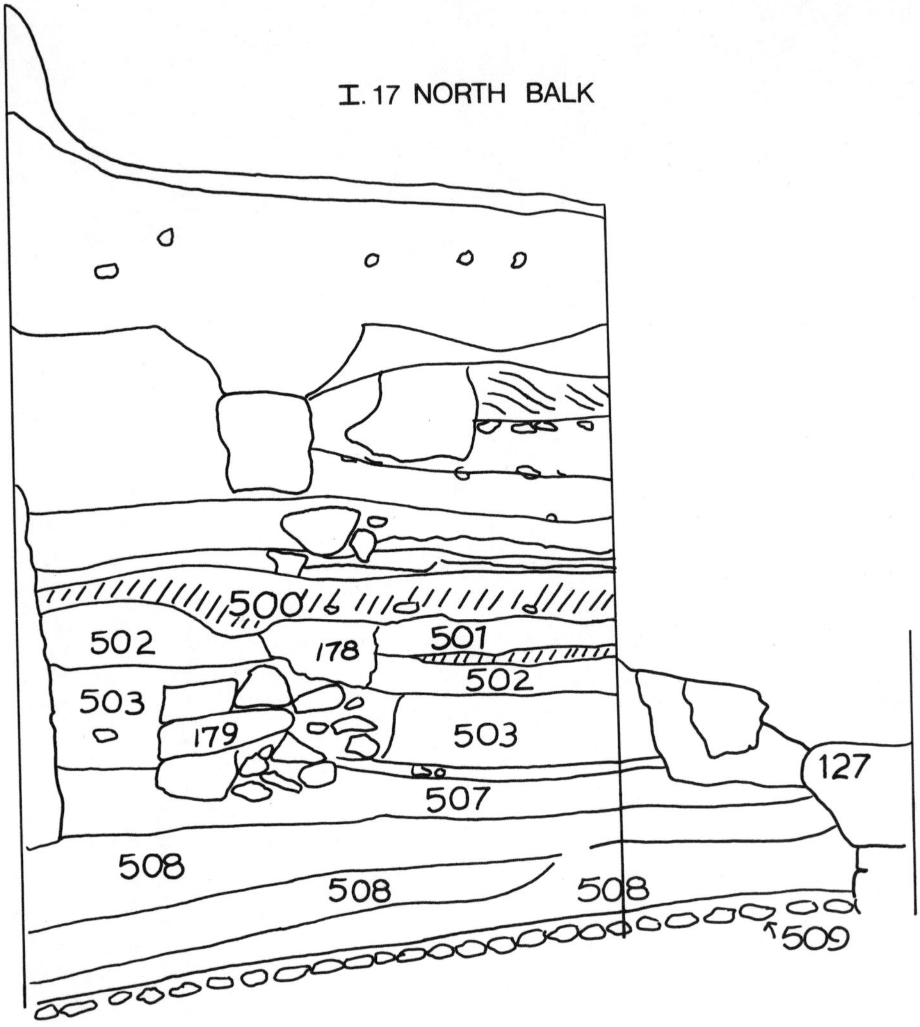

Fig. 6. Field I, Area 17, north balk. Wall 127 is the north wall of the guard-room with its uppermost stones collapsed to the west. 509 is the latest cobbled surface of the Amarna period. 508 is raw destruction debris from the 14th-century destruction. 507 is the leveled top of this debris. Wall 179, rebuilt as 178, is the wall constructed during Late Bronze and used throughout Iron I. Layers 503, 502, and 501 are the buildup of surfaces against this wall. Layer 500 is Iron I destruction.

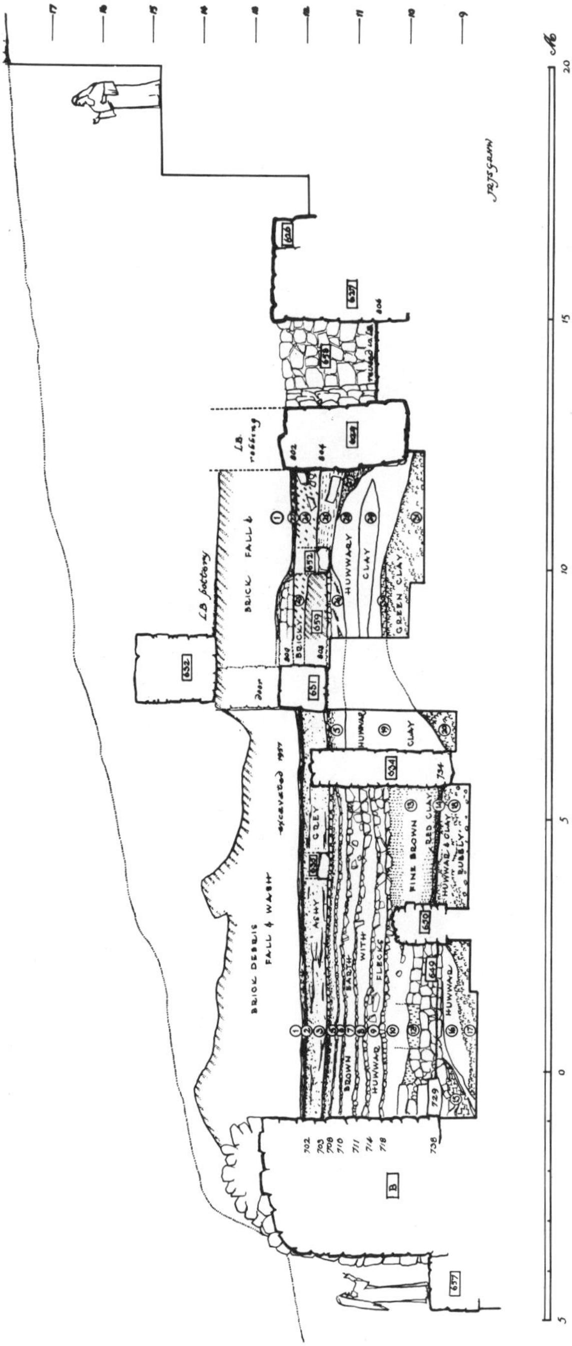

Fig. 7. Section of Field III, south face. The Late Bronze wall is seen founded on the MB IIC structure below. A fragmentary floor extends westward from the wall. This floor is almost a meter higher than Late Bronze surfacing to the west.

Early Israelite Poetry and Historical Reconstructions

DAVID NOEL FREEDMAN
University of Michigan, Ann Arbor, MI

In a series of papers of which this is the third, I have presented the thesis that the early poetry of Israel constitutes a prime source for the reconstruction of Israel's history and that these materials have, to a considerable extent, been neglected or misinterpreted and misapplied to the questions at hand.[1] In my view, this corpus of poetry should be restudied in an attempt to recover authentic historical information, to supplement, correct, and revise existing models of the early Israelite experience. In order to accomplish this objective, several problems need to be resolved, including the following: (1) To determine the scope and date of the corpus; I note in passing that the date of a poem is not necessarily correlative with the accuracy of its contents. An early date does not guarantee historical validity or precision, a late date does not exclude them. In general, however, the earlier the date, the greater the reliability of the contents. (2) To assess the contents of the poems for their historical usefulness. It is important to bear in mind that poetry is not prose, that we cannot expect in the poems to have a journalistic account of events and circumstances, or a chronicle produced by a historian as a result of research and reflection. There are, however, corresponding advantages in poetry roughly contemporary with the events and circumstances: songs often capture the spirit of the occasion and focus on what is centrally important. Inevitably they also contain direct factual information, which can be appropriated by the careful historian. (3) To cope with methodological issues, such as the comparative value of arguments from evidence and arguments from silence. The former as a class are superior to the latter, but occasionally inferences based on the absence of data can be quite compelling.

Then the relationship between the poems and the prose narratives needs to be considered. Traditionally, the approach has been harmonistic, and in practice this has meant the subordination, if not suppression, of the poetic tradition, in favor of the more comprehensive and coherent prose account. As a result there

---

[1]The two earlier papers are now in print: (1) "Divine Names and Titles in Early Hebrew Poetry," in F. M. Cross et al., eds., *Magnalia Dei* (Essays in Honor of G. Ernest Wright; New York: Doubleday and Co. 1976) 55-107; (2) "Early Israelite History in the Light of Early Israelite Poetry," in H. Goedicke and J. J. M. Roberts, eds., *Unity and Diversity: Essays in the History, Literature and Religion of the Ancient Near East* (Baltimore: Johns Hopkins University, 1975) 3-35. Other studies in the series are in preparation.

has been a marked tendency to minimize or ignore the contribution of the poems to historical reconstructions. Without elevating a contrary procedure to the level of principle, namely, that there is a necessary conflict between the poems and the prose accounts, nevertheless, each should be dealt with independently of the other and analyzed, interpreted, and evaluated in terms of its own content and structure. In the general comparison of poetic and prosaic sources, two points may be made: (1) that the early poems are closer to the events than any surviving prose accounts (e.g., the Song of Deborah in Judges 5, and the prose account in Judges 4; the Song of the Sea in Exodus 15 and the prose account in Exodus 14; (2) the transmission of poetry tends to be more faithful than that of prose, even though the former may be predominantly an oral phenomenon and the latter a written tradition. This is so because word selection and placement as well as rhythmic and stylistic factors are central in poetic composition and contribute to the preservation of the material in its original form. Contrariwise, except for mechanical blunders, it is easier to protect the sense of a prose composition, while indulging in editorial revisions.

There have been numerous studies of individual poems in the premonarchic corpus, and important historical inferences have been drawn from them: I need only mention the classic studies of W. F. Albright and those of his pupils.[2] Few scholars, if any, have doubted the importance of the Song of Deborah as a historical source, difficult as the poem is to interpret, or that it mirrors the circumstances and occurrences at a particular time and place in the period of the Judges (probably the latter half of the 12th century B.C.). In a very vivid way it brings us into direct contact with the actions and thoughts, the manners and morals of particular people in that context. The same would be true of the lament of David over Saul and Jonathan of a later time. It is our contention, however, that there is a substantial corpus of such poetry, which can be profitably considered, and that valuable historical information can be gleaned from this material. Furthermore, any general reconstruction of early Israelite history would have to incorporate the data of the poems, and in other ways deal with the picture they present.[3]

The corpus of which we have been speaking consists essentially of the premonarchic poems which have been preserved in the biblical text, having survived the wholesale reordering of priorities and restructuring of Israelite traditions which took place under the impact of the monarchy.[4] As a result of such direct and deliberate influence, especially in the days of David and Solomon, the great

[2]The latest treatment of the corpus by W. F. Albright is to be found in his *Yahweh and the Gods of Canaan* (New York: Doubleday, 1969), especially chap. 1. Other pertinent studies by him, his students, and other scholars are listed in the two papers mentioned above.

[3]The paper on "Early Israelite History" specifically addresses this problem.

[4]All the major literary strands of the Primary History (Genesis through Kings), come from the period after the formation of the monarchy and reflect its influence. For the significance of this basic change in Israel's experience and condition, see G. E. Mendenhall, *The Tenth Generation* (Baltimore: Johns Hopkins University, 1973) chap. 7.

prose narrative was composed and compiled, and subsequently, the other literary strands, which together make up the Primary History of the Hebrew Bible (i.e., the Torah and Former Prophets). Our concern, however, is with the principal poems, which antedate these prose works and, we believe, escaped revision at the hands of monarchistic scribes. While the poems have been incorporated into the larger literary complex, we contend that they are independent of it.[5]

On the basis of the work of many predecessors and contemporaries, chiefly that of my teacher W. F. Albright and my colleague and friend of long standing, F. M. Cross (including his independent studies and our collaborative efforts), certain basic conclusions may be drawn about this corpus of poetry. It consists of five major poems, along with a few small pieces and some fragments.[6] These are to be found in the Primary History as follows:

The Testament of Jacob	(Genesis 49)
The Song of the Sea	(Exodus 15)
The Oracles of Balaam	(Numbers 23-24)
The Testament of Moses	(Deuteronomy 33)
The Song of Deborah	(Judges 5)

This is a minimal list, but I think a reliable one. In agreement with a growing consensus among scholars, I hold that all of these poems are pre-monarchic in composition and may be dated in the 12th and 11th centuries B.C. with considerable confidence.[7] In general my views agree with those of Albright (which are elaborated in his volume, *Yahweh and the Gods of Canaan*), which will hardly come as a surprise, but there are some important differences. Thus Albright dated the Song of the Sea (Exodus 15) to the early part of the 13th century, while in my judgment it must be dated a century later, i.e., in the early 12th.[8] I may add, in passing, that his date depends upon a critical emendation, the only one he insists on in the poem, but all the more revealing (and unjustified) for that reason.[9] He included the Song of Moses (Deuteronomy 32) in this corpus, following Eissfeldt's original proposal concerning the relationship of Deuteronomy 32 to Psalm 78 and the dates of composition of these poems.[10]

---

[5]The arguments and evidence for this conclusion are summarized in the two papers mentioned, which in turn cite books and articles by a sizable group of scholars.

[6]In addition to the major poems cited, mention may be made of Exod 17:16; Num 6:24-26; 10:35-36; 12:6-8; 21:17-18, 27-30; Deut 34:7b; Josh 10:12-13.

[7]See the discussion in "Divine Names and Titles."

[8]For Albright's latest view of the Song of the Sea, cf. *Yahweh and the Gods of Canaan*, 12-13. For mine and other views, see "Divine Names and Titles" and "Early Israelite History."

[9]Albright, *Yahweh and the Gods of Canaan*, 45-47. See his earlier comment in Cross and D. N. Freedman, "The Song of Miriam," *JNES* 14 (1955) 249; cf. our mediating remarks, p. 248, n. 44.

[10]Albright, *Yahweh and the Gods of Canaan*, 17-19; O. Eissfeldt, "Das Lied Moses Deuteronomium 32:1-43 und das Lehrgedicht Asaphs Psalm 78 samt einer Analyse der Umgebung des Mose-Liedes," *Verh. Sächs. Acad. Wiss. Leipzig, Phil.-hist. Kl.*, Vol. 104, No. 5 (Berlin, 1958) 26-41.

It seems to me that the Song of Moses cannot be earlier than the 10th-9th centuries, and therefore it should not be included in any pre-monarchic corpus.[11]

With regard to the corpus of poetry as defined, our next objectives are to organize them according to date of composition, i.e., to establish a sequence-dating, relative in terms of order, absolute in terms of external events and circumstances, and to classify their contents with relation to each other and in chronological order. At the end of this process we will offer a hypothetical outline of the principal events in the early history of Israel.

In the two earlier papers, I attempted to fix the dates of composition of a dozen poems (including the five in our corpus) about which there has been a good deal of discussion and more than a little controversy; and I also tried to reconstruct in a very partial way the history of Israel in the 12th century on the basis of an analysis of two of the poems in the list (Exodus 15 and Judges 5).

Briefly summarized, my conclusion about the dates was that the two earliest poems are the Song of the Sea and the Song of Deborah, both being composed in the 12th century. Of the two, the Song of the Sea is earlier, coming from the first half of the century, and the Song of Deborah is later, coming from the second half of the same century. The other three poems all belong to the 11th century, with the order of composition less easy to determine and not directly pertinent for our purposes. Perhaps Genesis 49 is somewhat earlier in the century and Deuteronomy 33 somewhat later, with Numbers 23-24 somewhere around the middle.

With respect to the contents of the poems and the historical situations presupposed or reflected in them, the chronological order is somewhat different. There is always some time lapse between an occurrence and the report of it — in the case of a poem composed chiefly to celebrate such an event the time-span may be very short indeed, a matter of days or weeks — and the gap may vary widely from poem to poem. On the basis of previous examination of the two 12th-century poems (Exodus 15 and Judges 5), and current investigation of the three remaining poems in our group (Genesis 49, Numbers 23-24, and Deuteronomy 33), I propose the following chronological order according to content (in contrast with composition):

1. Genesis 49. Pre-Mosaic, non-Yahwistic: late 14th-early 13th century.
2. Exodus 15. Mosaic, Yahwistic: around 1200, or early 12th century.
3. Numbers 23-24: 12th century, a little later than the situation in Exodus 15.
4. Deuteronomy 33: 12th century, roughly contemporary with Numbers 23-24.
5. Judges 5: 12th century, latter half.

---

[11]See the discussion in "Divine Names and Titles" and references provided there, especially G. E. Wright, "The Lawsuit of God: A Form-Critical Study of Deuteronomy 32," in B. W. Anderson and W. Harrelson, eds., *Israel's Prophetic Heritage* (New York: Harper & Brothers, 1962) 26-67.

This arrangement happens to agree with the order of the poems in the Bible, i.e., from Genesis to Judges. It shows that the editor or compiler of the biblical narrative had essentially the same insight into and appreciation of the historical background of the poems. The attributions of authorship cannot be defended, to be sure: e.g., in both Deuteronomy 33 and Judges 5 the assignment of authorship is based on the occurrence of the name of the principal figure in the poem (i.e., Moses in Deuteronomy 33 and Deborah in Judges 5) but involves a misinterpretation of his or her role in the poem. In neither case can the poem properly be attributed to the person named, in contrast with the lament over Saul and Jonathan, which can safely be assigned to David himself. There is no reason, however, to question the validity of the reference or the proximate relation of the poem to the events described.

All this means is that the editor or compiler of the great prose work correctly understood the place of the poems in the developing history of Israel and put them in a plausible place in the narrative. The organization of the narrative also illustrates a major, if questionable, conviction on the part of the compiler of the biblical narrative, namely that the twelve-tribe confederation was already in being in the Wilderness Wanderings and that Moses was directly related to it. The assumption was part of a larger synthesis which combined patriarchal traditions with the narratives of the Exodus and Wanderings, Conquest, and Settlement, integrating everything around the themes of promise and fulfillment, and the migration from Mesopotamia to Canaan to Egypt and back by way of the wilderness to permanent settlement in the Holy Land.

A detailed examination of the poems produces a somewhat different picture of the sequence of events and of the relationship of the several narrative strands:

(1) The Song of the Sea links the tradition of the Exodus from Egypt with the crossing of the sea and the march through the wilderness to the holy habitation of Yahweh, the sacred mountain of the deity. There is nothing about a tribal confederation (the name Israel does not occur in the poem) and no connection with patriarchal traditions or promises about the land of Canaan. On the contrary, the horizon of the poem is limited to the southern wilderness, the traditional home of Yahweh.[12]

(2) The Oracles of Balaam share the same outlook and horizon as the Song of the Sea. Terror-stricken Moab of the Song of the Sea is the focus of attention, and its leader summons Balaam to counterpoise his magic to that of Yahweh. The results are predictable, but the exact location of Israel remains uncertain. While the prose narrative places Israel in the plains of Moab, and that is a possibility to be reckoned with, the description of Israel dwelling apart, presumably at an oasis, in its tents, reminds us of the description in Exodus 15 of the wilderness habitation. Egypt and the Exodus are the immediate past references, and Canaan remains beyond the concern of the poet. There is no

[12]See the presentation of evidence in "Early Israelite History."

substantial overlap in the names of peoples and places between the two poems (especially if we include the addenda to Numbers 24, vv 20-24). As the compiler correctly recognized, Israel is not yet settled in its permanent home.

(3) The Song of Deborah is linked with Exodus 15 through Yahweh's march from Sinai to Canaan. Sinai is the point of departure (Egypt and the Exodus and the march through the wilderness are not included), and Canaan and the great struggle with the Canaanite city-states are the immediate target of the poet. Through the intervention of Yahweh the One of Sinai, his people Israel, organized into a confederation of tribes, is victorious in this life-or-death struggle. The tribal list in Deborah ties that poem to the two remaining poems in our group, the Testaments of Jacob (Genesis 49) and Moses (Deuteronomy 33). The order, relationships, and historical implications of these three early tribal lists are the next subjects of our inquiry.

As noted, the tribal group is identified as Israel in the Song of Deborah. An Israel, presumably not very different in composition is mentioned in the Marniptah stele of the latter part of the 13th century, so the presence of this community in the holy land at that time seems reasonably certain.[13] In fact, an earlier constitution of this community may be posited on the basis of information provided in the book of Genesis. The name itself is assigned to the patriarchal era as the alternate designation of Jacob, the last of the Fathers and the eponymous founder of the twelve-tribe league. It is reasonable to apply the statements in Gen 33:18-20 to the federation and observe that the God of the league is called El (i.e., the patriarchal deity) and that at one time its headquarters were at Shechem, whose well-known shrine was dedicated to El, *baᶜal bĕrît*.[14] The presumption is that the league traced its origins to the patriarchs, or at least to Jacob (the wandering Aramean), and that it was non-Yahwistic and pre-Mosaic in its initial stages. This view is supported by the tradition preserved in the Exodus narrative, that the twelve-tribe structure was already in existence before the departure from Egypt and in particular before the introduction of the name Yahweh to the Israelites by Moses. The narrator assumed that this development from individual to tribe took place by natural generation in Egypt, whereas the evidence suggests that the tribal league was organized in pre-Mosaic times in the land of Canaan, quite possibly under the aegis of Jacob himself, and dedicated to the worship and service of the patriarchal El, one of whose titles was *ʾăbîr yaᶜăqōb*. It is worth noting that the name Israel does not occur in the Song of the Sea, that those who departed from Egypt, crossed the sea, and came to the mountain sanctuary are called the people whom Yahweh redeemed and purchased. But there is no tribal league there, and they are not called Israel. The combination: Israel, the people of Yahweh, occurs for the first time in the Song of Deborah; that expression is

---

[13]A convenient translation is given in *ANET*, pp. 376-78.

[14]See the discussion by Cross in *Canaanite Myth and Hebrew Epic* (Cambridge, MA: Harvard University, 1973) 39 and nn. 156-58; 47 and n. 16; 49 and n. 23.

reflected in the statement that Yahweh came from Sinai to Canaan and presumably involved the conversion of the league (or the major part of it) to faith in the God of Moses.

Turning back to the tribal lists, there are six possible arrangements of the tribal groupings preserved in the three poems.[15] According to the previous analysis, the oldest of the three is Judges 5, which we date to the latter part of the 12th century, whereas both of the others, Genesis 49 and Deuteronomy 33 have been placed in the 11th century. If we were to assume that the chronological order of the lists was the same as the order of the composition of the poems, then we would start with Judges 5 and try to explain the development of the other two from the earlier grouping. We would posit a ten-tribe league (since only ten tribes were mentioned in Deborah) at the beginning was expanded to eleven in Deuteronomy 33 (or possibly twelve if we do not accept the consolidation of two tribes, Ephraim and Manasseh [or Machir] into Joseph, mentioned earlier). Such developments are possible, though explanations are difficult to come by, especially since the two testaments are roughly comparable in date, and yet their lists are apparently incompatible. Some other hypothesis would seem to be required, and without running through all the remaining possibilities, I wish to suggest another approach to the relationships among the three lists. An incidental finding in the course of the sequence-dating analysis of the divine names and titles used in early poetry was that Genesis 49 is unique among poems with divine names (n.b., David's Lament over Saul and Jonathan makes no reference to the deity, at least by name or title), in that the name Yahweh does not occur in any of the blessings (it appears once in v 18, commonly regarded as a liturgical aside).[16] The absence of the name Yahweh and the presence of the divine names derived from patriarchal times (e.g., El, Shadday, possibly ᶜAl, vv 25-26) suggests rather strongly that the tradition embodied in this material is pre-Mosaic or at the very least earlier than the time of Deborah and the confirmed association between Yahweh and the tribal league. The inference to be drawn is that the list in Genesis 49 is the earliest, with the others following. On further reflection it seems to me somewhat more likely that Deuteronomy 33 follows Genesis 49 and precedes Judges 5, but the case is hardly decisive. The critical points are those which involve changes from one list to the next, especially omissions or alterations in status. Since neither time nor space will permit a detailed examination of the three lists here, we will concentrate attention on the following entries (1) Joseph, including Ephraim and Manasseh (or Machir as in Judges 5); (2) Judah; (3) Simeon and Levi.

With respect of Joseph and its subdivisions, the order of development would seem to be from the single tribe Joseph (Genesis 49) to the two sub-tribes within the larger unit (Deuteronomy 33) and then the emergence of separate

---

[15]On the order of composition and the dating of the two testaments, see Albright, *Yahweh and the Gods of Canaan*, 17-20, and Addenda, 265-66.

[16]See the discussion in "Divine Names and Titles."

tribes, in this case Ephraim and Machir (from Manasseh). The reverse would be more difficult to rationalize, especially since the Joseph oracles in Genesis 49 and Deuteronomy 33 have very archaic features: e.g., the ABC // ABD pattern in Gen 49:22 (*ben pōrāt yōsēp // ben pōrāt ᶜălē-ᶜayin*), and the specification of Joseph's origin in Mesopotamia, or the identification of Yahweh as the bush-denizen in Deut 33:16, an allusion to the Sinai (*sĕnēh*-bush) tradition. The increase and expansion of the Joseph tribe is described in the book of Joshua, and in view of tribal losses elsewhere, the division into two sections makes sense.[17] In later formulations of the list of tribes, both traditions were preserved: in some lists Joseph occupies a single place, in others, Ephraim and Manasseh hold two spots, and in some instances, the three are grouped as in Deuteronomy 33.[18]

With regard to Judah, the evolution, or devolution, seems to proceed from Genesis 49, where Judah is accorded an exalted status, being promoted over the heads of three older but undeserving brothers, Reuben, Simeon, and Levi. It is tempting to associate this complex blessing with the emergence of David and the preeminent status of Judah at the time of the united monarchy.[19] There can be no doubt that the royal scribes were happy to preserve this piece of Judahite propaganda and to exploit its sentiments to the full in the support of the Davidic dynasty. But I think that Albright is correct in denying that there is any explicit connection with the monarchy in the material or that it is a subtle retrojection from the days of David and Solomon.[20] Typical monarchical terminology is lacking, and there is nothing in the blessing beyond what is said of Joseph in the same testament. The transition from Genesis 49 to Deuteronomy 33 is drastic and surely implies a very serious crisis in the fortunes of Judah. It appears that the tribe has been cut off from its fellows, and there is danger that the separation will be permanent.[21] By the time we reach Judges 5, Judah is no longer on the list; it is unavailable for service in the cause of Yahweh and Deborah and is not even summoned. Presumably the worst has happened, and Judah is no longer sufficiently independent or autonomous to be reckoned among the tribes of the confederation. May we interpret the situation in the light of the Samson story and presume that Judah is now under the control of the Philistines, in short part of a different political power structure?[22] The restoration of Judah and its reunion with the Israelite confederation would have been a major objective of the strategy of leaders like Samuel and Saul, but it would not be fully achieved until the Judahite David shattered the Philistine hegemony over Judah and much of Israel.

---

[17] Josh 17:14-18; cf. Josh 14:4.

[18] See the discussion in "Early Israelite History."

[19] For older views, see the discussion in J. Skinner, *A Critical and Exegetical Commentary on Genesis* (The International Critical Commentary, rev. ed., New York: Scribner's, 1925) 518-25.

[20] *Yahweh and the Gods of Canaan*, 19, n. 49.

[21] For an earlier discussion of this point, see Cross and Freedman, "The Blessing of Moses," *JBL* 67 (1948) 193 and 203, esp. n. 27.

[22] Cf. Judg 15:11.

With respect to Simeon and Levi, these brother tribes are roundly condemned by the speaker in Gen 49:5-7. Whether this statement represents an intertribal judgment for misbehavior in violation of basic protocols, comparable to the internecine battle between the tribal confederation and Benjamin (reported in Judges 19-21) or a veiled reflection of some externally administered defeat, it is clear that the oracle forebodes disaster for these unholy brother tribes. That catastrophe is reflected in the lists of Deuteronomy 33 and Judges 5. Simeon has disappeared entirely from both lists, and we may suppose that some calamity engulfed it. There may be a faint echo of Simeon in the oracle addressed to Judah in Deut 33:7 (note the opening verb *šĕma*ᶜ which seems to play on the name Simeon: *šim*ᶜ*ōn*); since Simeon's territory (after the calamity?) was located entirely inside of Judah, a single oracle may have encompassed both tribes.[23] Since there is no record of Simeon's subsequent revival as a geographic entity, we conclude that the sequence from life to death, from Genesis 49 to Deuteronomy 33 and Judges 5, is logically and chronologically correct and that the reverse is highly unlikely.

The history of Levi is more complicated, but at the beginning we may suppose it shared a common destiny with Simeon. At least Judges 5 gives them equal treatment — silence. Deuteronomy 33, however, offers a novelty. Levi has undergone a transformation, and the secular tribe, denounced and demolished for intransigent violence, has become the stalwart defender of the Mosaic faith in Yahweh.[24] This is the only tribal oracle with an explicit and necessary association with the wilderness wanderings. If the oracle may be trusted as both authentic and ancient, then we have here the transference of tribal status to a group which participated in the Exodus and Wanderings, without, however, a comparable territorial allocation. In Judges 5, there is no mention of Levi, so presumably it did not constitute a tribe for the purpose of the song and battle which is its main subject. Whether Levites were involved at all is not clear, but if they were, it was not on the same basis as the other groups. The status of Levi remained a problem for the biblical historians, and it is treated differently in different lists — generally in two ways reflecting the distinction between Genesis 49 (i.e., as a regular tribe among the twelve) and Deuteronomy 33 (i.e., as a special group, with unique responsibilities for the shrine and ark, but without territorial rights comparable to the other tribes). In any event, it would be much more difficult to explain the history of the tribe of Levi if we were to begin with Judges 5 (i.e., from non-existence to a schizoid split between piety and impious violence) or Deuteronomy 33 (i.e., from a sacral status as guardian of the ark and other holy things to a secular tribe condemned for its atrocities and a period of non-existence along the way). Since in this case we know that Levi officially constituted a sacral group associated with the tabernacle and temple, the status

---

[23]Josh 19:1-9.

[24]Deut 33:8-10.

reflected in Deuteronomy 33 must be toward the end of the development rather than the beginning.[25]

With respect to the other tribes, comparison of the oracles and comments on a cursory basis does not point to any clear chronological lines of development. Closer inspection may reveal otherwise, but we can profitably leave that for another presentation. It remains now to summarize the findings, draw some tentative conclusions, and pose a few questions to those in associated disciplines. Answers to the latter should dispose of the theories presented here in one way or another, but more importantly they may provide a solid basis on which to build a more attractive and convincing reconstruction of early Israelite history.

Our proposals concerning the history of Israel from the late patriarchal period to the end of the pre-monarchic era are as follows:

(1) The organization of a twelve-tribe league denominated Israel and occupying territory in the land of Canaan may be dated some time in the period between the end of the Amarna Age (ca. 1350) and the middle of the 13th century. Since the earliest non-biblical reference to this group is supplied by the Marniptah stele, with the indication that it was of recent origin, I would be inclined to date the emergence of the federation at the end of the 14th or beginning of the 13th century. The founding of the confederation was credited to an immediate ancestor, Jacob, who may well have been a figure of the Late Bronze Age. The origins of some of these groups in Mesopotamia are explicitly attested (e.g., the major group called Joseph) and may be presumed for all or most. The common God of this group is El (Shadday), the deity specifically associated with Abraham, Isaac, and Jacob. The central sanctuary may well have been at Shechem, and the formal relationship between league and deity may have been defined in terms of a covenant.[26]

(2) If we take seriously the statement of the Marniptah stele, an Egyptian punitive expedition around 1230 overran much of Palestine, devastated a number of cities, and put the Israelite league out of commission. While the language of the inscription is typically hyperbolic and we know that reports of the demise of Israel were exaggerated and premature to say the least, it would be reasonable to infer that the confederation suffered a damaging blow, which is

---

[25]In the case of Levi, the most natural order would seem to be: Genesis 49 (a secular tribe); Judges 5 (no longer functional or in existence); Deuteronomy 33 (reconstituted as a sacral entity, with special status). If, however, the connection between Levi and the wilderness experience is authentic, then the order we have posited is correct and the omission in the Song of Deborah is to be explained in another way (as in all likelihood the omission of Judah).

[26]In the light of convincing evidence for the destruction of Shechem in the late Bronze Age (ca. 1300 B.C.) presented by L. Toombs at the Symposium in Jerusalem, it is plausible and attractive to associate the event with the statement in Gen 48:22, to be rendered, following E. A. Speiser in *Genesis* ("The Anchor Bible"; New York: Doubleday & Co., 1964) 356: "As for me, I give you, as the one above your brothers, Shechem, which I captured from the Amorites with my sword and bow." Also deserving attention is the passage in Gen 33:20, "And he [Jacob] erected there [i.e., before Shechem] an altar, and he named it [i.e., dedicated it to] 'El, the God of Israel.'"

reflected in the curtailed lists of Deuteronomy 33 and Judges 5. The apparent disappearance of the tribe of Simeon and somewhat similar fate of Levi suggest that the damage was real and that Israel was a long time in recovering from it. By the middle of the 12th century, Judah should be added to the list of casualties, being cut off from the main group of tribes. Perhaps we find an echo of the tradition preserved in the Samson narratives in which we learn that Judah was subject to the power of the Philistines. The Song of Deborah describes a league of ten northern tribes, which coincides in all important respects with the secessionists at the time of the death of Solomon and accession of Rehoboam. There is a continuous tradition concerning this group from the time of Deborah until the formation of the northern kingdom of Israel — e.g., after the death of Saul, the northern group anoints Ish-baal to be king of Israel, while the southerners select David to be king of Judah (2 Sam 2:1-11). Later on the same distinction is made between northerners and southerners, when David returns to power following the death of Absalom (2 Sam 19:41-44).

(3) Around 1200, or shortly thereafter, the Exodus from Egypt occurred. According to the tradition, Moses led a congeries of people out of bondage to freedom, more specifically from Egypt, across the Reed Sea, to the mountain of God, there to constitute a new community, the people of Yahweh. It is altogether possible, in my opinion, that population elements of the Israelite confederation escaped to Egypt or were brought there as slaves and subsequently joined the Exodus group under Moses. It seems clear that the divine name Yahweh was learned by Moses during his sojourn in the southeastern wilderness, in the general region of Sinai, Paran, Seir, Midian, Edom, in accordance with a persistent tradition in the Bible (preserved in the early poems, including Exodus 15, Judges 5, Deuteronomy 33, and Psalm 68). This name was not known in Canaan or among the Israelite tribes in that area. It is the Mosaic group that brought the religion of Yahweh to Canaan and Israel, and it is only from the time of the Song of Deborah onward that Yahweh is identified as the God of Israel, then located in Canaan; the Song specifically asserts that Yahweh came from the southland, and this view is confirmed by the prologue to the Blessing of Moses (Deuteronomy 33). The date of the Exodus can be fixed from the reference in the Song of the Sea to the four nations which are described as observers of the crossing of the sea and the annihilation of the Egyptian chariot force (Exod 15:14-15). They are described as being struck dumb with terror by this spectacular display of Yahweh's might. These four — Philistia, Edom, Moab, and Canaan — can only have coexisted in their established territories during the 12th century B.C. The Philistines are not mentioned by name any earlier, while the Canaanites presumably did not survive as a national entity beyond the 12th century.[27] Edom and Moab are referred to in Egyptian sources of the 13th century, so their national presence at the time of the Exodus can

---

[27]See the discussion in "Early Israelite History."

hardly be questioned.[28] It seems to me as well that the Oracles of Balaam and the Blessing of Moses reflect a situation only slightly later than that of the Song of the Sea. The Exodus from Egypt is the point of departure (Num 23:22; 24:8), and the present idyllic existence of the people, isolated from other nations, suggests an oasis encampment in the wilderness (Num 24:5-6; Deut 33:28).

(4) From Sinai and its environs, the faith (and at least some of the faithful) spread northward through Transjordan and finally into Canaan, where it was adopted by the Israelite league, either to replace the older (and moribund) El faith, or conjointly with it. Since Yahweh's original name was probably *Yahweh-el* and a descriptive clause like *yahweh ṣĕbāʾōt* was attributed to El, there was an essential compatibility between the gods, which permitted an effective consolidation of aspects and attributes.[29] By the 11th century, Yahweh and El were accepted and worshipped as one god, the god of Mosaic faith, the God of the Fathers and of the Israelite confederation.

(5) Toward the end of the pre-monarchic period, if not before, deliberate efforts are made to restore the twelve-tribe league. Under the leadership of Samuel, Saul, and finally David, Judah (and Simeon) are reunited with Israel. Joseph is permanently divided into two tribes, Ephraim and Manasseh; and this leaves Levi in a somewhat anomalous position as a sacral unit without a territorial allotment. With the establishment of the united monarchy under David and Solomon, the tribal structure itself is replaced by a series of administrative districts in both kingdoms (Israel and Judah), only a few of which coincide with the old tribal names and areas.[30] The tribal lists pass from history into literature and become the stock in trade of nostalgic reminiscences of glories past and projections of future restorations. Essentially, they are of two types, reflecting both ends of the evolution of the tribal pattern from the Late Bronze Age (reflected in Genesis 49) until the end of the 11th century (reflected in various lists): the early list has twelve tribes corresponding to the twelve sons, including both Joseph and Levi. The more common cultic and administrative lists exclude Levi as a special group and divide Joseph between Ephraim and Manasseh.

Poem	*Content*	*Composition*
Genesis 49	14th-13th	11th
Exodus 15	13th-12th	12th
Numbers 23-24	12th	11th
Deuteronomy 33	12th	11th
Judges 5	12th	12th

---

[28]See, e.g., a report from the reign of Marniptah mentioning Edom (*ANET*, 259) and a list of Rameses II which includes Moab (*ANET*, 243).

[29]See my discussion of the name "Yahweh" in an appendix to "Divine Names and Titles" and in the forthcoming article on "Yahweh" in G. J. Botterweçk and H. Ringgren, *Theologisches Wörterbuch zum Alten Testament* (Stuttgart: W. Kohlhammer, 1970-).

[30]See Cross and Wright, "The Boundary and Province Lists of the Kingdom of Judah," *JBL* 75 (1956) 202-26, esp. 224-26.

Early Alphabetic Scripts

FRANK MOORE CROSS
Harvard University, Cambridge, MA

A decade has passed since I last discussed "The Origin and Early Evolution of the Alphabet" in the *Sukenik Memorial Volume*.[1] In this short period of time there have been a number of new discoveries and developments in the study of the Proto-Canaanite alphabet, the Canaanite cuneiform alphabet, and the early Linear Phoenician script.

I. PROTO-CANAANITE (16TH-12TH CENTURIES B.C.)

1. From Raddana comes an inscribed jar handle from the late 13th century B.C. Happily its date is controlled by the stratified context in which it was found as well as by paleography. Three letters are written vertically (see fig. 1): *ʾḥl*[ ], to be completed perhaps *ʾăḥīl*[*ūd*], or perhaps *ʾḥl*[*y*] or *ʾḥl*[ʾ]. Aharoni's attempts to raise the date of the little epigraph to the 14th century are, in my opinion, unsuccessful both on paleographical and archeological grounds. Nor do I believe that the reading of the third letter can be in question. The *lamed* is virtually complete on the handle, and its stance and form are ideal for the period in question.[2]

2. A second Proto-Canaanite inscription has been found at Zarephath (Sarepta) in the University of Pennsylvania excavations.[3] It is a dipinto reminiscent of the Lachish Ewer and the Hazor Sherd. Its script stands close to that of the Beth-Shemesh Ostracon,[4] and its date should not be far from 1200

---

[1]*Eretz-Israel* 8 (1967) 8*-24*.

[2]F. M. Cross and D. N. Freedman, "An Inscribed Jar Handle from Raddana," *BASOR* 201 (1971) 19-22; cf. J. A. Callaway and R. E. Cooley, "A Salvage Excavation at Raddana, in Bireh," *BASOR* 201 (1971) 9-19; Y. Aharoni, "Khirbet Raddana and its Inscription," *IEJ* 21 (1971) 130-35; and S. Yeivin, *Miscellanea Epigraphica I-IV, Bulletin of the Museum Haaretz* 14 (1972) 79-83. Yeivin's attempt to decipher the text in an older writing system is not persuasive. His failure to note that the writer has argued that the Beth-Shemesh Ostracon and the El-Khaḍr arrowheads are written vertically is surprising. We published the Raddana Handle as a vertical text as should be evident from the figures. Vertical (as well as left-to-right and boustrophedon) writing persists through the 12th century. See J. T. Milik and F. M. Cross, "Inscribed Javelin-Heads from the Period of the Judges," *BASOR* 134 (1954) 15f; on the date of the stabilization of writing in horizontal lines, see F. M. Cross, *Eretz-Israel* 8 (1967) 14*-16*.

[3]James B. Pritchard, *Sarepta: A Preliminary Report on the Iron Age* (Museum Monographs; Philadelphia: University Museum, 1975) 101, fig. 55:1.

[4]For a drawing and analysis of the Beth-Shemesh ostracon, see Cross, "The Origin and Early Evolution of the Alphabet," *Eretz-Israel* 8 (1967) 17*-19* and fig. 3.

B.C., the date assigned to the Beth-Shemesh Ostracon.[5] Three letters are complete and a fourth is broken:]*dʾḥ*⌜*k*?⌝[. The writing is probably from right to left. The form and stance of the *ʾalep* are particularly interesting, recalling the archaic "Greek" stance. The rotation of the stance is characteristic of the Proto-Canaanite period when vertical and horizontal writing were both in use.[6]

3. The most important discovery in the field of Proto-Canaanite comes from ʿIzbet Ṣarṭah near Aphek, a sherd upon which five lines of script, some eighty signs, are scratched. The excavator, Moshe Kochavi, who is preparing the text for publication, has kindly sent to me a photograph and drawing of the sherd. Evidently it is a practice text for someone learning the alphabet. Its script suggests a date in the 12th century B.C.; this conforms roughly with the date of the stratum in which it was found. Its publication will immediately bring advances in our knowledge of the rarer letters of the Proto-Canaanite script.[7]

II. PROBLEMATIC TEXTS FROM SYRIA-PALESTINE

1. In 1969 and 1970, Günter Mansfeld published a group of sherds from Kāmid el-Lōz on which are signs which he believes to be Proto-Canaanite.[8] The excavators assign the group to the 15th and 14th centuries; one graffito is upon a Late Mycenean sherd (fig. 3). Two signs are frequent: (1) a circle-and-vertical similar to the Early Linear Phoenician *qop*, Proto-Canaanite *waw* (?),[9] Old South Arabic *y* (<*w*), and (2) a triangle with an extension of two arms in several stances. On five sherds these two signs are repeated and in three instances combined in what is best described as a monogram (see fig. 3).[10] The elements in

[5]Javier Teixidor, who published the text, ignores the stance of *ʾalep*, the most important feature for dating the dipinto and compares forms of the archaic Cyprus Inscription. The form of the Sarepta *ʾalep* also differs from the later Cyprus form in its short crossbar, a feature overlooked by Teixidor. The Sarepta *ʾalep* has its best parallels in form with the Lachish Ewer *ʾalep*, the Raddana Handle, the *Abbaʾ* Seal, and above all with the *ʾalep* of the unpublished ʿIzbet Ṣarṭah inscription, which exhibits little or no breaking through of the cross-bar (see below).

[6]For comparative material, see the preceding note and the article cited in n. 4.

[7]Anson Rainey has made an important contribution in reexamining some of the Serābīṭ el-Khādem inscriptions that remain in place in Sinai: "Notes on Some Proto-Sinaitic Inscriptions," *IEJ* 25 (1975) 106-16. We hope to discuss these texts elsewhere in the near future.

[8]"Deux ostraka incisés à écriture paléo-canaanéene du Tell de Kāmid el-Lōz," *BMB* 22 (1969) 67-75; "Scherben mit altkanaanäischer Schrift vom Tell Kāmid el-Lōz," *Kamid el-Loz — Kumidi*, by D. O. Edzard, R. Hachmann, P. Maiberger, and G. Mansfeld (Bonn: Habelt, 1970) 29-41; W. Röllig and G. Mansfeld, "Zwei Ostraka vom Tell Kamid el Loz und ein neuer Aspekt für die Enstehung des kanaanäischen Alphabets," *WO* 5 (1970) 265-70; cf. G. Garbini, "Gli ostraka di Kamid el Loz," *Annali: Instituto Orientale de Napoli* 22 (1972) 95-98.

[9]Cf. "Origin and Early Evolution of the Alphabet," 16*f.

[10]The fact that the monogram is scratched on a Late Mycenean sherd ("Ostracon 6") argues against taking it as a potter's mark. Sherds with arbitrary marks or symbols are so frequent that one dare not attribute them to the Proto-Canaanite alphabetic system unless they conform in date and typological development to a well-established alphabet. One may illustrate by reference to the marks on Egyptian sherds collected by G. R. Driver, *Semitic Writing* (London: Oxford University Press, 1948, 1954^2) pl. 33.

the monogram may derive from one of the many systems of syllabic writing which flourished in the Late Bronze Age. They do not conform to the Proto-Canaanite pictographic alphabet in contemporary use in Palestine and Sinai.[11]

"Ostracon 2" from Kāmid el-Lōz (fig. 3) is dated by its stratigraphic context to the period before ca. 1400 B.C. It is the only one of the Kāmid el-Lōz sherds that merits special comment. Aside from a *waw*-like sign on the lower right, the sherd contains three clear signs. None of the three appear in the contemporary Proto-Canaanite corpus (16th-13th centuries B.C.). The first sign (reading from right to left) could be taken as *ʾalep*, were the sherd dated to about 1200 B.C.[12] The second and third signs have been identified with similar forms in Old South Arabic, namely *ṯ* and *m*. (The third sign is also found in some epichoric Greek scripts of early date representing *he* [epsilon]!) To be sure, very archaic signs borrowed from the Proto-Canaanite pictographs survive in linear forms in South Arabic. We can date the branching off of the Proto-Arabic script from the Proto-Canaanite to about 1300 B.C. or slightly later.[13] At this time Canaanite *ṯ* and *ś* had merged in South Canaanite dialects.[14] The sign originally *ṯ*, but *ś* in 13th-century and later dialects, was the pictograph of the composite *bow*: Old Canaanite *ṯann*, Phoenician *šan* (Greek *san*).[15] In Proto-Arabic, it was used to represent Semitic *ś*.[16] The Old South Arabic sign for *ṯ* thus is secondary in all likelihood, like Greek *omega* or *psi*. *Mem*, signified by the zig-zag horizontal or

[11]Mansfeld (following Hachmann) attempts to raise dates of the Early Linear Phoenician series (dating ʾAḥirām to the 13th century B.C.). This is to reverse the progress of a generation of epigraphic research. The most recent discoveries of Proto-Canaanite texts in stratified contexts fully confirm the dating of the Proto-Canaanite and Early Linear Phoenician script series laid out in the writer's "The Origin and Early Evolution of the Alphabet" and first sketched following the discovery of the El-Khaḍr arrowheads (*BASOR* 134 [1954] 5-24). Frequently overlooked in this connection is the date of the javelin and arrowheads derived from the typology of the artifacts themselves: see F. M. Cross and J. T. Milik, "A Typological Study of the El Khaḍr Javelin-and Arrow-heads," *Annual of the Department of Antiquities of Jordan* 3 (1956) 15-23.

Edith Porada has dealt with the archeological and art-historical elements of the ʾAḥirām Sarcophagus and puts to rest objections raised by non-epigraphists to a date for the sarcophagus about 1000 B.C.: "Notes on the sarcophagus of Aḥiram," *JANES* 5 [The Gaster festschrift] (1973) 355-72.

[12]Given its date, the sign is best compared with the "A-form" sign on the Shechem Plaque (from the 15th century in all likelihood). See W. F. Albright, *The Proto-Sinaitic Inscriptions and their Decipherment* (HTS 22; Cambridge: Harvard University, 1966) 10f. I am not convinced, however, by Albright's decipherment of the plaque's inscription; the primitive pictographic *reš* goes badly with the linear *ʾalep*, if *ʾalep* it be, and the sign Albright reads as *mem* appears to be far too developed for a 15th-century sign. To be sure, it is possible to have pictographic forms and linear forms contemporary, a formal and a cursive, but scarcely when the alphabetic script is so young.

[13]See "The Origins and Early Evolution of the Alphabet," 19*, and nn. 67-70.

[14]See below on the merging of phonemes in 13th-12th-century Canaanite. In Phoenician, of course, *ṯ*, *ś*, and *š* merged.

[15]F. M. Cross and T. O. Lambdin, "A Ugaritic Abecedary and the Origins of the Proto-Canaanite Alphabet," *BASOR* 160 (1960) 21-26, esp. 26.

[16]After the South Semitic sibilant shift (ś > š and š > s), the sign is etymologically identical with Late Arabic *š*.

vertical line, usually made of seven strokes in early Proto-Canaanite, simplified to a five-stroke wavy line in Linear Phoenician, is one of the best-represented pictographs in decipherable texts. The Kāmid el-Lōz sign (a four-stroke, zig-zag line closed on one side by a vertical) is far too developed for a 15th-century Proto-Canaanite form. Indeed the South Arabic form it resembles is not the earliest South Arabic form, much less the Proto-Arabic ancestor of both the Old South Arabic and Old Thamudic forms.[17]

It must be readily admitted that we do not yet know all the signs of the Proto-Canaanite script, and there is evidence of by-forms (i.e., alternate pictographs) as we should expect in the early evolution of the script. That the three signs of "Ostracon 2" all be hitherto unknown signs, or unknown by-forms of known signs, demands too much of a coincidence; in any case, the values assigned by Mansfeld are wrong.

In short, in view of the fact that only one or two of the Kāmid el-Lōz sherds overlap with contemporary Proto-Canaanite signs and that these like all of the Kāmid el-Lōz marks are highly geometric in form, there is insufficient reason to assign the Kāmid el-Lōz sherds to the Proto-Canaanite corpus.

2. Recently George E. Mendenhall has published a sherd from Tell Jiṣr.[18] He dates the sherd to the Middle Bronze Age and finds on it marks which he attributes to a "signary." Inasmuch as no "sign" repeats itself (unless it be the simple, slightly curved diagonal scratch, his seventh and twentieth sign), he necessarily takes this signary to be a syllabary of some sort. The signs he identifies are vague and nondescript, scratched minutely in the midst of the rope-molding of the sherd's ornamentation. The sharp differentiation necessary between signs to enable easy recognition and identification is lacking.[19] And none is a transparent pictograph. The signs which Mendenhall sees constitute at best a most dubious witness to a writing system. Certainly they have nothing to do with the Proto-Canaanite alphabet. The linear forms Mendenhall posits for the Middle Bronze Age did not evolve into the pictographic forms of the Late Bronze Age. Some will wonder why Mendenhall describes this sherd as documenting "A New Chapter in the History of the Alphabet" and why for comparison he draws upon some thirteen syllabaries and alphabets, some as far separated in time and place as Minoan Linear A and Old North Arabic.[20]

---

[17]See A. Jamme, "An Archaic South-Arabic Inscription in Vertical Columns," *BASOR* 137 (1955) 32-38; and W. F. Albright, *The Proto-Sinaitic Inscriptions*, fig. 1 (opposite p. 12).

[18]"A New Chapter in the History of the Alphabet," *BMB* 24 (1971) 13-18.

[19]One may compare the "inscribed" potsherd most recently republished by G. R. Driver, *Semitic Writing* pl. 50:2; or the imitation of script on a group of seals published by Briggs Buchanan, *Catalogue of Ancient Near Eastern Seals in the Ashmolean Museum I* (Oxford: Clarendon Press, 1966) Nos. 1072-6 (pp. 213f. and pl. 65). The so-called Goetze Seal probably belongs to the same group, and my attempts to decipher it as authentic Proto-Canaanite are best abandoned. Cf. "The Origin and Early Evolution of the Alphabet," p. 10*, n. 14.

[20]The point of most of Mendenhall's comparisons is difficult to fathom, particularly in light of his own statement that "no conclusions can be drawn concerning either derivation or phonetic value from such formal similarities."

Standing behind his endeavor is a theory concerning alphabetic origins. If I understand him correctly, he supposes that alphabets (as opposed to *the* alphabet) evolved naturally out of a welter of syllabaries and were unified out of diversity secondarily by external factors (political, religious, or whatever). The difficulty is that the hard facts in our possession do not accord with Mendenhall's theory.[21] While there can be little doubt that the Proto-Canaanite alphabet was inspired directly or indirectly by hieroglyphic writing, it was not just one of a series. Syllabic writing would have endured had there not been a revolutionary invention. The Proto-Canaanite alphabet came into existence not by an unconscious evolutionary process but by a radical simplification: notation of each consonantal phoneme with a simple pictograph representing an object whose name began with the phoneme in question. Vowels, never initial in West Semitic, were given no notation. By this means the tyranny of complex syllabic systems was broken.

The evolution of the Phoenician alphabet can now be traced from Proto-Canaanite pictographs to the Linear Phoenician script continuously in the case of at least 17 of 22 signs. The ^{c}Isbet Ṣarṭah ostracon will add more. Signs lost after the merger of phonemes (*ḏ>z, ǵ>*^{c}*, ḫ>ḥ, ṯ>š, ẓ>ṣ*) in Canaanite are less well known, though the original value of the surviving sign can often be determined: the sign for *ḏ* prevails over *z,* ^{c} over *ǵ, ḥ* over *ḫ*, and *ṯ* over *š*. In the Proto-Canaanite period, to be sure, variant pictographs or variant forms of a given pictograph existed. The three El-Khaḍr arrowheads illustrate this fact; *ḥ* has a by-form, and *ṣ* has three slightly variant forms. One must remember, however, that the names of the letters, acrophonically based, and in all probability even the order of the letter names in the Proto-Canaanite script go back to its very origin. This is demonstrated beyond doubt, in my opinion, by the Ugaritic abecedaries, particularly the abecedary with Babylonian transcriptions.[22] Thus, there are principles controlling the uniformity of the new alphabetic system from the beginning.

The invention of the Proto-Canaanite alphabet was an act of stunning innovation, a simplification of writing which must be called one of the great intellectual achievements of the ancient world. While older writing systems no doubt were the starting point of the inventor, it must be emphasized that the alphabetic system did not simply emerge of itself in a slow evolutionary fashion from an earlier syllabary. The new system had to be grasped whole, as a *Gestalt*, for the radical simplification to take place. This single system spread to Arabia by the 13th century, and not long after to the Greek and Mediterranean world. All ancient alphabets now known can be traced to it. It should be remembered too that the invention was never repeated in isolated cultures using a syllabic or logographic script.

---

[21]One fears that this theory will flaw Mendenhall's announced decipherment of the Byblian pseudo-hieroglyphs.

[22]See the papers listed in n. 15.

3. A similar lack of discipline is found in Wolfgang Helck's attempt to derive the Phoenician alphabet from Egyptian Hieratic, especially the syllabic writing invented in the Hyksos Age and known from about 1600 B.C.[23] He proposes to compare the syllabic script in use in the 16th and 15th centuries with the earliest forms of the "Phoenician" alphabet. As stated, the procedure is a methodologically sound means to test his hypothesis. However, Helck does not proceed to make comparisons with the earliest stage of the Proto-Canaanite alphabet. He passes over the pictographic phase of the script and rather makes his comparisons with Linear Phoenician and even then not with the 12th-11th-century forms in most cases, but with standard Phoenician of the late 11th and 10th centuries. Indeed in the case of *mem* and *kap* he uses Phoenician forms which evolved only in the course of the 9th century B.C. Such a procedure is unacceptable.

When writing systems consist more or less of linear or simple geometric signs, similarities of form appear frequently whether or not the systems are related in origin. Relationships must be determined by historical-typological sequences. Lack of rigor in historical typology, whether in paleography or in historical linguistics, makes all things possible.[24]

III. CANAANITE CUNEIFORM TEXTS (1400-1200 B.C.)

The corpus of Canaanite texts written in alphabetic cuneiform but coming from Syro-Palestinian sites well to the south of Ugarit continues to grow. In addition to the well-known Beth-Shemesh Tablet, the Tabor Knife, and especially important, the Taanach Tablet fixed in date to ca. 1200 B.C.,[25] two new texts have been found, one in James Pritchard's excavations at Zarephath (Sarepta) on the Lebanese coast, another from Kāmid el-Lōz.[26] The Zarephath inscription comes from a context dated by Carbon 14 to the 13th century B.C. (1290 ± 50 years).

The published non-Ugaritic Canaanite cuneiform texts all belong to a style of cuneiform writing shared by three Ugaritic texts inscribed from right to left, which form a separate corpus at Ugarit.[27] Linguistically, these texts are distinct from Ugaritic in sharing a reduced set of graphemes, reflecting the merging of phonemes in the southern Canaanite dialects. There is direct evidence for the mergers of *ṯ* (>*ś*)>*š*, *ḫ*>*ḥ*, *ẓ*>*ṣ*, and indirect evidence for *ḏ*>*z* and *ǵ*>ᶜ. Proto-Canaanite alphabetic signs give evidence for the same reduction in roughly the same period. Probably all of these texts in the reduced (22-sign) cuneiform

---

[23] W. Helck, "Zur Herkunft der sog. 'phönizischen' Schrift," *UF* 4 (1972) 41-45.

[24] The epigraphist is made much more aware of these issues in a day in which the Americas are made to swarm with pre-Columbian inscriptions left by Old World visitors — including Phoenicians and Jews of the Roman period. For one such inscription, see F. M. Cross, "The Phoenician Inscription from Brazil: A Nineteenth-Century Forgery," *Orientalia* 36 (1968) 437-60.

[25] See F. M. Cross, *BASOR* 190 (1968) 41, n. 1 for bibliography on these several texts.

[26] *Sarepta*, pp. 102-4; pl. 55:2. The Kāmid el-Lōz tablet, to my knowledge, is not yet published.

[27] For bibliography, see n. 25.

alphabet date to the 13th century B.C. At least those with established dates fall into this century. We can then assert that the phonemic mergers and the reduction of the alphabet took place not later than this time.

IV. NEW TEXTS IN EARLY PHOENICIAN LINEAR SCRIPT (11TH CENTURY B.C.)

We are now able to assign twelve texts to the 11th century B.C. This number includes the three El-Khaḍr arrowheads from the beginning of the century, the Ruweiseh and Biqāᶜ darts from the second half of the century,[28] and the Byblus Spatula,[29] all of which I discussed in my 1967 paper. More recently, four additional 11th-century inscriptions have been published or republished and discussed.

1. Two "clay objects" from Byblus (labeled Byblus A and Byblus B for convenience) which bear inscriptions were published by Maurice Dunand in 1954, but went unrecognized until 1973 as 11th century in date (see fig. 6).[30] Byblus A reads *lᶜbdḥmn* and dates from the 11th century; Byblus B reads *lʾḥʾš bbd* and is from the mid-11th century B.C. The names in question are *ᶜAbd-Ḥamōn* (A) and *ʾAḥīʾaš* son of *Bōdī*.

2. From near Jerusalem comes the so-called Manaḥat sherd (see fig. 7).[31] Its reading is clear: *lšdḥ*, presumably *l* "(belonging) to" plus an otherwise unknown personal name, *šdḥ*.

3. Finally we may refer to the Nora Fragment from Sardinia (not to be confused with the famous Nora Stone of the 9th century B.C.[32]). It was published upside down in the *Corpus inscriptionum semiticarum.*[33] After study of a new photograph in color, the writer recognized that the text was written boustrophedon and that the anomalous letters (the first letter in line 1 and the last letter in line 2) fit perfectly in an 11th-century context with the remaining

---

[28]This group of arrowheads, to which the ᶜAzarbaᶜl arrowhead from the beginning of the 10th century B.C. should be added, apparently represents a fad of little more than a century in time during which arrow- and javelin-heads were labeled with personal names. Whatever the function of these arrowheads — *ex votos*, belomancy, or whatever — one suspects that they come from members of archers' guilds.

[29]The most recent treatment of the spatula is the paper of P. Kyle McCarter and Robert B. Coote, *BASOR* 212 (1973) 16-22.

[30]F. M. Cross and P. K. McCarter, Jr., "Two Archaic Inscriptions on Clay Objects from Byblus," *Rivista di Studi Fenici* 1 (1973) 3-8.

[31]The sherd was published by L. E. Stager, "An Inscribed Potsherd from the Eleventh Century," *BASOR* 194 (1969) 45-52; see also J. Landgraf, "The Manahat Inscription: *LŠDḤ*," *Levant* 3 (1971) 92-95; pl. 30.

[32]See most recently, F. M. Cross, "An Interpretation of the Nora Stone," *BASOR* 208 (1972) 13-19.

[33]*CIS* I, 145. Recent treatments and new photographs may be found in M. Amadasi, *Le Iscrizioni fenicie e puniche delle colonie in Occidente* (Rome: Istituto di Studi del Vicino Oriente, 1967) 87f. Tav. 28:2; and Jean Ferron, "La Seconde inscription archaïque de Nora: CIS 145," *Wiener Zeitschrift für die Kunde des Morgenlandes* 62 (1969) 62-75, pl. I (bibliography is brought up to 1969 in Père Ferron's paper).

letter forms, provided the text is reversed.[34] The *ḥet*, a characteristically symmetrical form, and the ᶜ*ayin*, a circle with a point in the center, are regular 12th-11th-century forms (see fig. 8). With the inscription put right-side up, the first letter of line 1 became a familiar ᵓ*alep* which flourished in the 12th century B.C. (rather than a *kap* of the 9th century); the first letter of line 2 (reading from left to right), which has never been satisfactorily explained, became a familiar *lamed*, identical with the *lamed* of line 1, but in a left-to-right stance.

The broken text then can be read:

]*l*ᶜ*p.n*ᵓ[sinistrograde
dextrograde]*lt. ḥṭ*[*r* (?)

Or, converting to our dextrograde convention:

]ᵓ*n.p*ᶜ*l*[
]*lt.ḥṭ*[*r* (?)

The paleographical evidence is clear and consistent. The Nora Fragment was written in a boustrophedon style, a practice not used after the 11th century in Phoenician.[35]

The 11th century is transitional in the styles of writing: (1) the script evolved from pictographic forms to linear forms in the course of the century, and (2) the direction of writing was standardized as the century passed. At the beginning of the century vertical, dextrograde, sinistrograde, and boustrophedon modes of writing were still in use. By century's end one direction of writing had become standard. All 10th-century inscriptions extant are inscribed from right to left. Both the developing linear letter-forms and the persistence of multi-directional writing caused uncertainty in the stance of the letters. During the pictographic stage there was little difficulty in giving letters their proper stance (the signs faced away from the direction of the writing). Stances could be changed according to the direction of writing without confusion. With the development of linear forms, the "proper" stance could easily be forgotten. In fact, characteristic of the 11th-century script is confusion of right-to-left and left-to-right stances. Of the twelve epigraphs listed above, no fewer than ten exhibit deviations from the standard right-to-left stance in some one or more of their letters.

The last examples of vertical and (horizontal) boustrophedon writing occur in the first half of the 11th century. In the subsequent history of the Phoenician script examples of confused stance are almost nonexistent.[36] The rotation of letter stances produced by confusion in shifting between horizontal and vertical

---

[34]F. M. Cross, "Leaves from an Epigraphist's Notebook. 2. The Oldest Phoenician Inscription from the Western Mediterranean," *CBQ* 36:4 [Patrick W. Skehan festschrift] 490-93.

[35]The practice survived in Old South Arabic and in archaic Greek (see the discussion below).

[36]Some few occur on seals where the engraver is trying to make letters in the negative and becomes confused.

directions in writing ceased by ca. 1050 B.C. The last extant examples of rotation are found on the El-Khaḍr darts and the Byblus "clay objects." This is, of course, in utter contrast to Proto-Canaanite of the 15th through the 12th centuries, where most letters rotate by ninety degrees once and often twice in the course of three centuries (see fig. 11). The form proper of signs (as opposed to stance) also is standardized by the end of the 11th century. The last striking variants occur in the El-Khaḍr arrowheads about 1100 B.C., namely in the forms of *ʾalep, ḥet, ʿayin,* and *ṣade* (see figs. 10 and 11).

These data are important in determining the time when the national scripts, notably Proto-Arabic and Greek, branched away from the line of development which runs through the Proto-Canaanite and Linear Phoenician scripts.

V. THE SPREAD OF THE PHOENICIAN ALPHABET TO THE GREEKS

The inventory of early Phoenician inscriptions found in the Mediterranean world apart from the Phoenician mainland is becoming increasingly impressive. The earliest is the Nora Fragment from 11th-century Sardinia, followed by the Nora Stone of the 9th century B.C. If the writer's interpretation of the Nora Stone is correct for the last lines of the stele,[37] there is evidence that Phoenician forces under a certain "Milkatōn, general of (King) Pummay" were in the field in Sardinia and set up a victory stele. The Pummay of the Nora Inscription is in our view a personal name of a type well-known in Phoenicia. It is the hypocoristicon of Pummayyatōn, Greek Pygmalion, the Tyrian king who ruled 47 years, from 831-785 B.C.[38] From Cyprus comes the Kition Bowl of ca. 800 B.C., as well as the well-known archaic Cyprus Inscription of the early 9th century B.C.[39] Spain has yielded up a Phoenician inscription dedicated to Hurrian Astarte dating to the mid-8th century B.C.[40] From Carthage comes the Gold Pendant Inscription now to be dated in the second half of the 8th century B.C.[41]

In view of these data, the traditional date for the founding of Carthage, in the seventh year of Pygmalion's reign (825 B.C.), need no longer be doubted, and the classical dates for the founding of Utica and Cadiz (ancient *Gader*), at the

---

[37]The beginning of the stele is still uncertain; in my opinion, the top of the stele was cut off when the stone was reused. I am convinced, however, that my interpretation of the last three lines is sound. See the paper cited in n. 32.

[38]On the chronology of the Tyrian kings, see "An Interpretation of the Nora Stone," p. 17, n. 11, where our reconstruction of Tyrian chronology is given and references listed.

[39]See provisionally, P. K. McCarter, "The Early Diffusion of the Alphabet," *BA* 37 (1974) 62-66; and especially his monograph *The Antiquity of the Greek Alphabet and the Early Phoenician Scripts* (Harvard Semitic Monographs 9; Missoula, MT: Scholars Press, 1975). For the Kition Bowl, see Robert B. Coote, "The Kition Bowl," *BASOR* 221 (1975) and the bibliography cited there.

[40]F. M. Cross, "The Old Phoenician Inscription from Spain Dedicated to Hurrian Astarte," *HTR* 64 (1971) 189-95 (where bibliography is listed).

[41]On the problems of dating the Carthage Pendant, see J. Brian Peckham, *The Development of the Late Phoenician Scripts* (Harvard Semitic Series 20; Cambridge: Harvard University, 1968) 119-24.

end of the 12th century B.C., need no longer be dismissed as complete fantasy. I think that there can be no doubt that the Phoenicians were establishing colonies in the Western Mediterranean in the heyday of Pygmalion the Great before the end of the 9th century B.C. Furthermore, there seems some reason to believe that Phoenician merchantmen were plying the Western Mediterranean in the copper trade as early as the 12th century B.C. and that trading posts and refineries were established in far-away Spain and Sardinia long before systematic colonization of the West commenced. Traders in metal go to where the commodity is to be found, and distance, I believe, was not a primary consideration.

At the same time, increasing evidence of the 8th-century date of the earliest Greek inscriptions has accumulated.[42] The most surprising of the new discoveries are the Phrygian inscriptions from Gordion published by Rodney Young.[43] Six of the Phrygian inscriptions can be fixed stratigraphically to the middle and second half of the 8th century. Such early dates for Phrygian, a derivative of the Greek alphabet, were unexpected. In the opinion of Rhys Carpenter, whose views long dominated classicists' discussion of the date of the borrowing of the Greek alphabet, the Phrygian script developed from the Greek script after 600 B.C.

Given the distance the earliest of the Greek and Greek-derived scripts have evolved independently, the date of the borrowing can be no later than the late 9th century, which in turn falls in the era of Pygmalion. This is also the latest possible date according to the typology of the Phoenician scripts, so that it cannot be doubted, in my opinion, that the Greek scripts lost contact with their Phoenician ancestor no later than 800 B.C.

A new direction has been given to the discussion by a brilliant and audacious proposal of Joseph Naveh.[44] Beginning with the writer's reconstruction of the early development of the Proto-Canaanite and Early Linear Phoenician scripts, he noted that the earliest Greek inscriptions were written in multiple directions: sinistrograde, dextrograde, and boustrophedon, precisely as was the Phoenician practice before the end of the 11th century B.C. Thus, early Greek writing exhibits the same shift of stance and rotation of forms which characterize Proto-Canaanite (and the earliest Linear) writing and its other early descendant, the Old South Arabic system of writing. Naveh also pointed to some archaic letter-forms in early Greek inscriptions which were

---

[42]See McCarter's monograph cited in n. 39, where full bibliography is given. A convenient review of the discussion of classicists concerning the date of the Greek borrowing of the Phoenician alphabet can be found in *Das Alphabet: Enstehung und Entwicklung der griechischen Schrift*, ed. G. Pfohl (Darmstadt: Wissenschaftliche Buchgesellschaft, 1968), including reviews of the monumental study of L. J. Jeffery, *The Local Scripts of Archaic Greece* (Oxford, 1961). Another study which is often of use is B. Einarson, "Notes on the Development of the Greek Alphabet," *Classical Philology* 62 (1967) 1-24.

[43]"Old Inscriptions from Gordion: Toward a History of the Phrygian Alphabet," *Hesperia* 38 (1969) 252-96.

[44]"Some Semitic Epigraphical Considerations on the Antiquity of the Greek Alphabet," *AJA* 77 (1973) 1-8.

traced most easily to Proto-Canaanite and/or Early Linear forms. Most striking were the "dotted" ᶜ*ayin* (i.e., the ᶜ*ayin/omicron* with the vestigial pupil of the pictographic eye preserved), the symmetrical, box-shaped *ēta/ḥet*, the legless, five-stroke *mu/mem*, the legless or short-legged *he/epsilon*, short-legged, large-headed *rhō/reš*, and short-legged *xi/samek* (see fig. 12). Naveh concludes that the Greeks borrowed the alphabet about 1100 B.C.

Kyle McCarter in his monograph on the antiquity of the Greek scripts has examined Naveh's hypothesis with great care.[45] He lists a number of criticisms and queries. Is the legless, five-stroke *mem* derived from Proto-Canaanite, or is it an inner-Greek development from the five-stroke form with the fifth stroke elongated? The short-legged forms of *he, samek,* and *reš* are not far distant from the 10th-9th-century forms and may exhibit a new Greek tendency to conform to a baseline. Naveh's attempt to relate stemless, trident-formed *chi* to early Phoenician *kap* is not persuasive, argues McCarter; *chi* belongs with the Greek signs invented to represent Greek aspirates, phonemes not found in Canaanite. Greek *kappa* in fact must derive from a 9th-century form of *kap* — unless it evolved in Greek script by chance in a fashion parallel to the evolution of the Phoenician *kap*, from a trident-shaped form in the 10th century B.C. to a form with the right, final stroke breaking through to form a leg.

Naveh's arguments from stance of letters and direction of writing remain persuasive, and the survival of ᶜ*ayin* with pupil in "dotted omicron" and the box-like *ḥet* in Greek *ēta* is difficult to deny. Indeed, Greek preserved two forms of *ḥet*, the early box or frame-shaped form, and the form which appears quite late in Greek: the "H" form (see fig. 12). Both types of *ḥet/ēta* have their precise equivalents in the El Khaḍr forms of ca. 1100 B.C. There is some likelihood, I think, that the "H" form in both scripts may be a natural simplification and need not be borrowed. The coincidence of the two types occurring as by-forms in Early Linear Phoenician and in the Greek scripts is nevertheless striking. Even more extraordinary is the occurrence in an 11th-century inscription from Nora, boustrophedon writing, the "dotted" ᶜ*ayin*, and the box-shaped *ḥet*, all three absent from Phoenicia after the 11th century B.C., all three found in earliest Greek.[46]

McCarter proposes an alternate hypothesis to account for the complex data:

> It is reasonable to suppose at least — and perhaps at most — that the Greeks, though their script did not diverge as an independent tradition before ca. 800, had experimented with the Semitic alphabet as early as ca. 1100 . . . . The memory of the earlier experimentation survived long enough — perhaps in an isolated moribund tradition somewhere — to exert a limited influence upon the final

---

[45]See above, n. 39.

[46]I have been tempted to read the Nora Fragment in Greek in order to reduce its date to the 9th century! The Phoenician elements, especially the word *p*ᶜ*l*, the exclusively Phoenician form of ᵓ*alep*, and like arguments, prevent.

formulation of the Greek alphabet years later. The similar influence of older indigenous writing systems upon the borrowing of the Asianic alphabets (such as Carian) from a Greek model is well documented.[47]

I am not sure that there is sufficient evidence to establish firmly either the case of Naveh or that of McCarter. At all events, the initiatives of Naveh and McCarter have brought the discussion into a new phase and complicate old problems which seemed at the point of solution.

From the standpoint of the orientalist, certain standard arguments of classicists for a late date of the borrowing of the alphabet no longer carry weight.

(1) The argument that the Phoenicians were not in the West until the 8th century or later is simply wrong, a classic instance of the fallacy of *argumentum e silentio*. The Phoenicians were in commercial contact with the islands and shores of the western Mediterranean from the 11th century on, and as early as the 9th century were in the West in force establishing colonies.

(2) The theory of a prolonged dark age of Greek illiteracy, based on the absence of Greek inscriptions appears to be crumbling. Certainly the terminal date of the Dark Age must continue to be raised as classicists have recognized. To the orientalist this theory, based principally on an argument from silence, appears most precarious. As Naveh has pointed out, the gap between the latest Nabatean inscriptions and the earliest texts in the North Arabic script, a derivative of Nabatean, is some two centuries. An even better example is the extraordinary period of silence between the branching apart of the ancestral Proto-Arabic script from the Proto-Canaanite in the 13th century B.C., and the earliest inscriptions in Old South Arabic dating to the 8th century B.C., a span of five hundred years. In Israel there is a remarkable paucity of inscriptions in the 10th and 9th centuries B.C. Only one Hebrew inscription of the 10th century is extant, the Gezer calendar.[48] One newly found inscription dates to the end of the

---

[47]P. K. McCarter, "The Early Diffusion of the Alphabet," *BA* 37 (1974) 68.

[48]Klaus Beyer, "Die Problematik der semitischen Konsonantenschrift," *Zeitschrift der Vereinigung der Freunde der Studentenschaft der Universität Heidelberg* XIX Jahrgang, Band 42 (December, 1967) 12-17 argues that the Hebrew alphabet was borrowed from the Arameans, not from the Phoenicians. Such a view I believe is wholly wrong. Phoenician (or North Israelite) letter names, dialectically distinct, survive in Judahite usage: *bet, mem,* and *yod* to name the more obvious examples. It seems unlikely that these were borrowed through Aramaic. Almost certainly during the United Kingdom Phoenician Linear styles were adopted for chancellery usage, including the 22-letter alphabet representing the Phoenician (and perhaps North Israelite) phonemes, but omitting the Judahite contrast between the sibilants *śin* and *šin*. Earlier Proto-Canaanite was in use in Palestine, and the shift to Linear Phoenician was a matter of following fashion rather than taking up alphabetic writing for the first time. A direct argument can be made: the Gezer Calendar of the 10th century B.C., written in "Phoenician" orthography must be called a Hebrew inscription, signed as it is by a certain *ᵓby⌜w⌝*, *ᵓAbīyaw*. An indirect argument can be made also. The national script of Moab in the 9th-century inscription of Mešaᶜ can be distinguished from 9th-century Aramaic. It is allied to the Gezer Calendar and later Hebrew despite its adoption of the Aramean system of final *matres lectionis*. On the contrary, Ammonite is a branch of Aramaic becoming independent about 750 B.C.

9th century: an inscribed stone bowl from Kuntillet ʿAjrūd in Sinai. The text reads: *lʿbd[y]w bn ʿdnh brk hʾ lyhw,*[49] "Belonging to ʿAbdyaw son of ʿAdnah. Blessed be he to Yahweh." The inscription is written with one instance of a final *mater lectionis* (a Hebraic trait); its script also is moving in the direction of Hebrew. *ʾAlep* with large, rounded point cannot be later than the 9th century and could be pushed earlier. *He* shows no sign of the upper horizontal breaking through the vertical to the right; the leg of *he* is short, reminiscent of *he* of the ʾAḥiram Sarcophagus; *dalet* is written without a tail, an archaic trait which did not survive later than the mid-8th century B.C. *Waw* is inscribed in the style of the 10th- and 9th-century Phoenician forms. On the other hand, the long letters and fluid style anticipate the style of the early 8th century. *Kap* appears with the right down-stroke lengthened, a trait developing in the late 10th century. In short, our evidence points to a date about 800 B.C., leaving a long gap of two centuries filled only by one substantial inscription.[50]

The paucity of Hebrew inscriptions in the 10th and 9th centuries is even more striking when we remember that Palestine is the most intensively excavated area of the pre-Roman world. To sum up: the use of an argument from silence to reduce the date of the borrowing of the alphabet is perilous at best and, to judge from analogies, particularly dangerous in dealing with the borrowing of the alphabet and the development of national scripts.

(3) The widely-held view that the Greek script was borrowed immediately before the earliest extant Greek inscriptions (now dated to the second half of the 8th century B.C.) is wrong. We must posit a considerable time span between the time the script was borrowed and its appearance in the earliest known Greek inscriptions in order to explain the distance between the earliest Greek scripts and any point in the sequence of the Proto-Canaanite and Linear Phoenician script types. The very existence of the derived Phrygian alphabet of the mid-8th century requires such a period of evolutionary changes. As McCarter has shown,

---

[49]See provisionally Z. Meshel and C. Meyers, "The Name of God in the Wilderness of Zin," *BA* 39 (1976) 6-10, fig. 2. I am most grateful to Dr. Meshel for sending me a glossy print of this inscription. [Note *Yahweh* is written in "Phoenician" orthography; we are not to read *yahū*.]

[50]There are in addition to the two inscriptions discussed above some extremely fragmentary graffiti from the mid-9th century B.C., found in Stratum VIII at Hazor. Three have strongly Phoenician traits: Nos. 1, 3, 4 (Y. Yadin et al., *Hazor II* [Jerusalem, Magnes Press, 1960] 70-72; pls. 169 and 170. No. 1 which reads]*ʾwʾ*[exhibits a Phoenician *waw*, a form developed in both Phoenician and Aramaic in the course of the 9th century B.C., but not found in Hebrew. No. 3 reads *bt z. symbol*, "This *bat* (-jar). symbol." If our interpretation is correct, *z* is written in Phoenician style without a final *mater lectionis*. The *bet* with the lower leg twisted back to the right is known hitherto only in the 10th-century Byblian inscriptions. No. 4 appears to read [*l*]⌜*m*⌝*ttʾ*[*l*], "Belonging to Mattitʾel". The two *taws* are incised with the vertical lengthened downward below the cross-bar. This form developed in the 9th century B.C. in Phoenician and Aramaic. It did not develop in Hebrew. No. 2 reads *lʾy*[*DN*]. A number of names begin with the element *ʾy*, "where is?" plus the divine name or epithet. It is tantalizing, of course, to fill out the name *ʾy*[*zbl*], "Jezebel," one such name in which the epithet *zbl*, "prince," refers to Baʿl. The angular *lamed* is another northern trait in the 9th century B.C.

there can be no question of the Greek borrowers being ill-informed about the Phoenician system or drawing their letters sloppily. Contact between Phoenicians and Greeks existed for a considerable period. Moreover, the special stances of such letters as *alpha, beta, gamma,* and *lamda* took time to evolve. It was not ignorance which brought them into being but typical evolution in a period when multidirectional writing flourished. The special form of *iota, san* (*ṣade*), and *tau* in the earliest Greek scripts requires a considerable period of time for evolving from the distant Phoenician letter forms — whatever the date of borrowing.

The letter *kap* has long seemed to require a late date for its borrowing. The trident-shaped *kap* of the 10th century B.C. and the "reversed K-shaped" *kap* of the 9th century B.C. overlap in use at least for a period toward the end of the 10th century. We do not know, however, how long this overlap lasted. It may be that the two types of *kap* were by-forms for a long period, evolving from a common ancestor, the "K" form finally becoming standard in the 9th century B.C. Such a development can be documented in detail for ᵓ*alep*. At the end of the 12th century B.C., two ᵓ*aleps* were in use, the older form with a large "head" closer to the pictograph of the ox, and a younger form resembling somewhat the letter *K*. Both ᵓ*aleps* appear on the El-Khaḍr Arrowheads (see figs. 10 and 11) and continue in use in the 11th and 10th centuries. A special form of the "K" type flourished at Byblus in the 10th century B.C. In the course of the 9th century the older type rose again in popularity and in a short time ousted its rival.

There is some reason to believe that behind the trident form of *kap* of the 10th century, and the "reversed-K" form of the 9th, there may stand a common ancestor, a trident with its middle line elongated downward (or rather a stylized hand and wrist). In such a case, *kappa*/*kap* would raise no problems for a borrowing either in the 11th century or in the 9th.[51]

At least three forms of *ḥet* existed through the 11th to the 9th century (see fig. 11), the symmetrical, "double-frame" *ḥet*, the ladder-like *ḥet* which is also close to the pictograph and continued to evolve in the 9th century B.C., and "H" or *ēta*-shaped *ḥet*. It would not be surprising if more than one was borrowed in the Greek world.

Alternately, we may explain the "late" forms of *kappa* with its right down-stroke lengthened and *mem* similarly with its right down-stroke lengthened as instances of parallel or convergent evolution. The lengthening of a final down-stroke is quite frequent in the evolution of the Linear Phoenician script: *dalet* (9th century), *he* (9th century), *mem* (9th century), *nun* (10th and 9th centuries), *samek* (10th and 9th centuries), and *reš* (10th and 9th centuries). The same tendency may have operated in the archaic Greek scripts.

(4) No theory of the Greek script will long stand which does not offer an adequate explanation for the marked concentration of archaic features (i.e.,

[51]The Gezer Calendar has the form of *kap* with the right leg lengthened as does the Aramaic script which branched apart from Phoenician in the course of the 11th century B.C.

typologically old) in the alphabet of Crete, Thera, and Melos. I am strongly inclined to believe that Phoenicians in the West rather than Greeks in the East were the primary agents in the initial spread of the alphabet.[52]

POSTSCRIPT

We have not commented on the significance of the invention and perfection of the alphabet. We wish to make only one or two observations. With the creation of the alphabet came the first opportunity for the democratization of culture. The older cultures of the ancient Near East were carried primarily by a scribal elite, secondarily in folk oral traditions. With the invention of alphabetic writing, literacy spread like wildfire and a new epoch of cultural history may be said to begin with the emergence of the Linear alphabet. The congruence of the history of the alphabet with the history of Israel is intriguing. The pictographic Proto-Canaanite alphabet flourished in the late Patriarchal Age. The creative events of Israel's history fall into the era of transition from Proto-Canaanite pictographs (together with the Canaanite cuneiform alphabet) to the Early Linear character. Israel's emergence as an imperial state is coeval with the Israelite national script and its use in the chancelleries of David and Solomon; it is the time when Israel's fundamental epic tradition was recast in prose and put into classical form. I suspect that there may be a correlation between Israel's peculiar religious concern with history and preoccupation with egalitarian legislation and the parallel democratization of culture effected by alphabetic writing. If so, it is a thesis to be defended on another occasion.

[52] Cf. Margherita Guarducci, "Der Geburtsort des griechischen Alphabets," *Das Alphabet*, 197-213.

Fig. 1. The Raddana Handle from the late 13th century B.C. *The signs read vertically:* ʾḥl[ ].

Fig. 2. A painted potsherd from Zarephath from ca. 1200 B.C. *The signs from right to left read:*]dʾḥ⌜k?⌝ [.

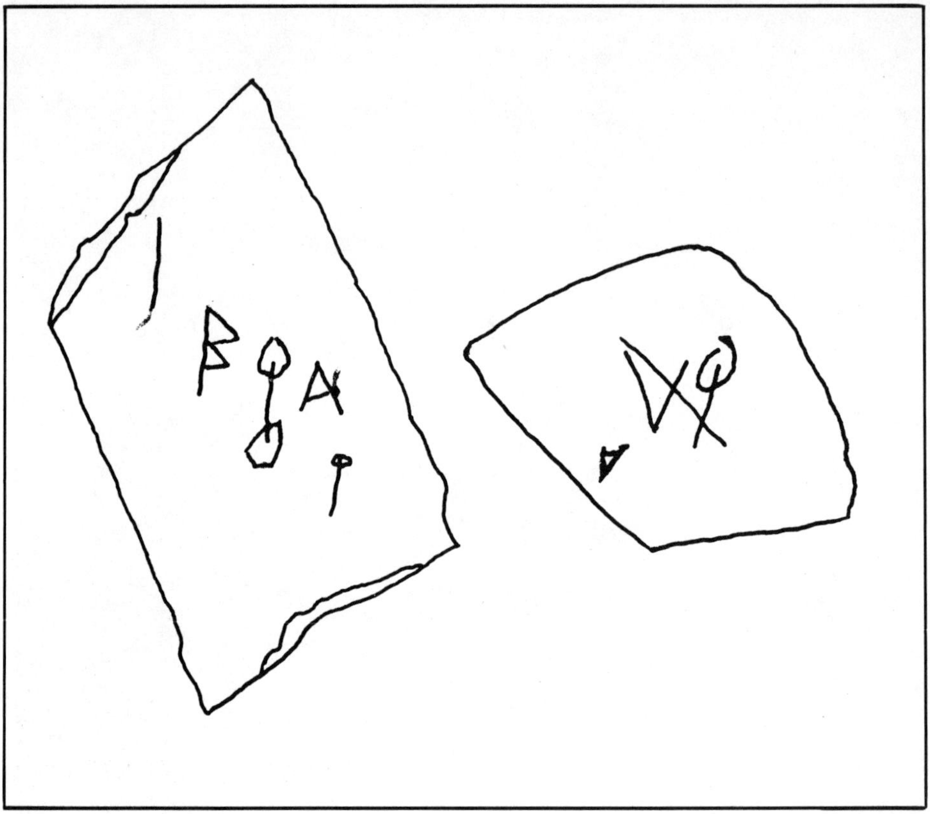

Fig. 3. Graffiti on sherds from Kāmid el-Lōz. On the left is a drawing of a Mycenean sherd inscribed with a monogram (?); on the right is "Ostracon 2."

Fig. 4. An inscribed ewer from Lachish dating to the 13th century B.C. *The inscription, which is painted on together with the decoration, reads as follows:* mtn. šy l[rb]ty ᵓlt *"Mattan. An offering to my Lady Elat."*

Fig. 5. Another side of the Lachish Ewer.

Fig. 6. *Inscribed clay objects from Byblus. No. 7765 (Byblus A) from the early 11th century* B.C. *reads* lʿbdḥmn, *"Belonging to ʿAbd-Ḥamōn." No. 11687 (Byblus B) from the mid-11th century* B.C. *reads* lʾḥʾš bbd, *"Belonging to ʾAḥīʾaš son of Bōdī."*

Fig. 7. The Manaḥat sherd from the mid-11th century B.C. *It reads:* lšdḥ.

Fig. 8. The Nora Fragment from the 11th century B.C. *The first line reads (from right to left)*]ʾn.pʿl[*and the second line (from left to right) reads:*]lt. ḥṭ[. *This inscription is the earliest Phoenician text from the Western Mediterranean.*

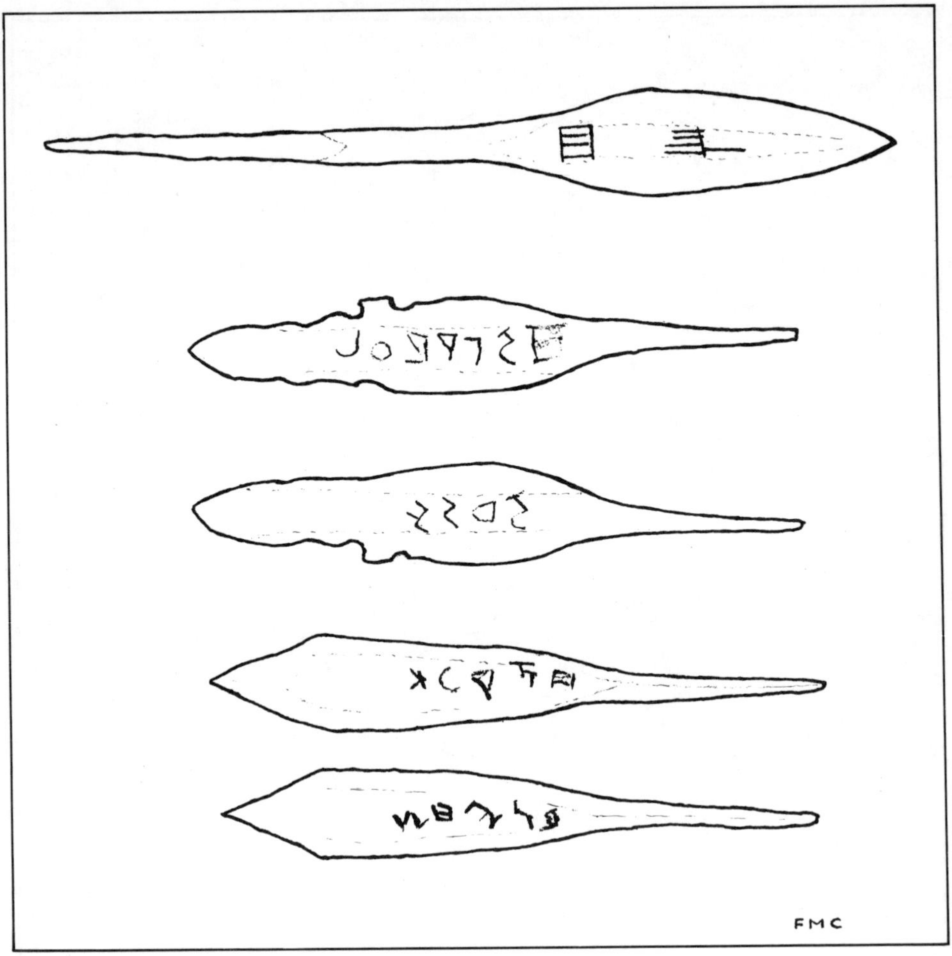

Fig. 9. Inscribed Arrowheads. The first is an archaic arrowhead from the Middle Bronze Age inscribed in cuneiform; the second, from the mid-11th century B.C., ḥṣ grbʿl ṣdny; *"Dart of Gerbʿl the Sidonian"; the third from the mid-11th century* B.C. *reads* ḥṣ rpʾ bn yḥš, *"Dart of Rapaʾ, son of Yaḥoš."*

Fig. 10. An arrowhead from El-Khaḍr. The text, which also appears on two other arrowheads found in the hoard, reads ḥṣ ᶜbdlbᵓt, *"Dart of ᶜAbd-Labīᵓt." It dates from about 1100 B.C.*

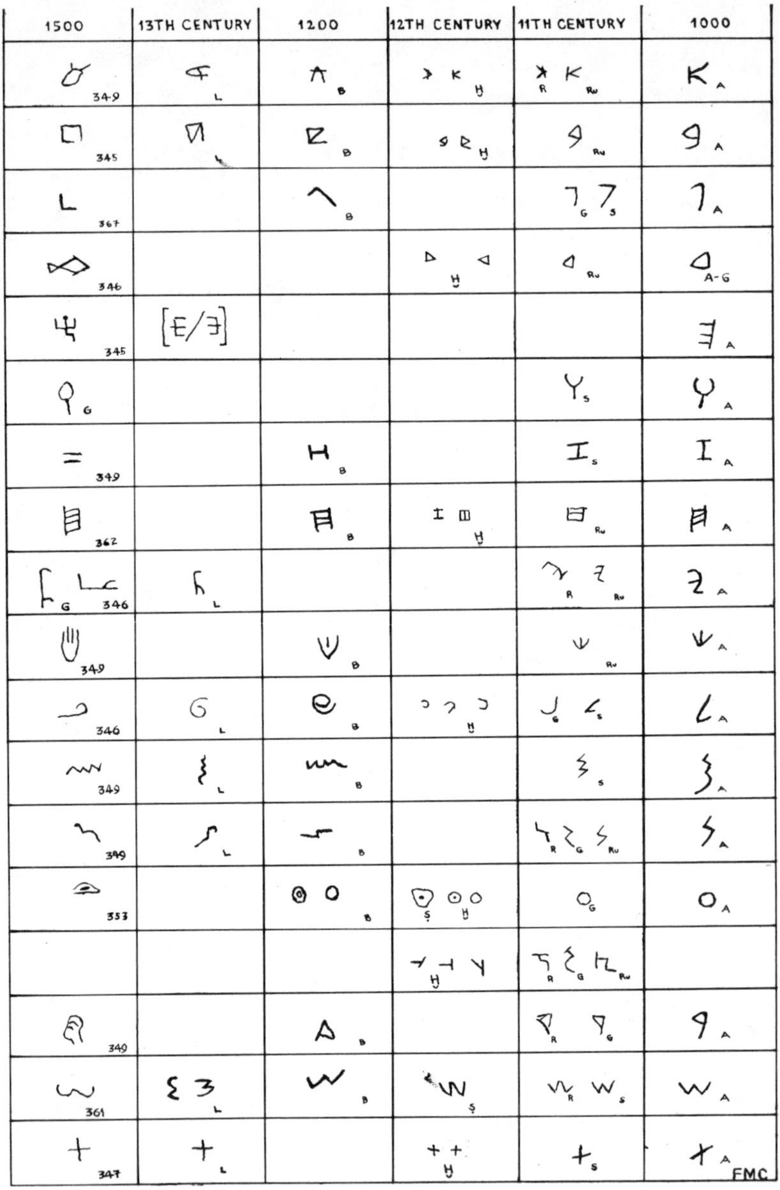

Fig. 11. *The Development of the Proto-Canaanite Script. In column 1, text numbers refer to the Proto-Sinaitic inscriptions; in column 2, "L" refers to the Lachish Ewer and Bowl; in column 3, "B" stands for the Beth-Shemesh Ostracon; in column 4, "Ḫ" stands for the El-Ḫaḍr arrowheads, "Ṣ" for the Tell eṣ-Ṣarem Sherd; in column 5, "Ru" stands for the Ruweiseh Arrowhead, "R" for the Rapaʾ Arrowhead, "G" for Gerbʿl Dart, "S" for the Byblian Spatula; in column 6, "A" stands for the ʾAḥirām Sarcophagus, "A-G" for the ʾAḥirām Shaft Inscription.*

Fig. 12. Archaic Greek Letters in Ideal Form. From the left epsilon/he, ēta/ḥet, *a by-form of* ēta/ḥet, mu/mem, *a by-form of* mu/mem, xi/samek, omicron/^{c}ayin, rhō/reš.

Ashdod at the End of the Late Bronze Age and the Beginning of the Iron Age

MOSHE DOTHAN
University of Haifa, Haifa

Ashdod is the only city of the Philistine Pentapolis where the transition from the Late Bronze Age city to the Philistine city has been observed stratigraphically. Two of the remaining four cities, Gath and Ekron, have not so far been conclusively identified.[1] The excavations of the identified cities, Ashkelon and Gaza, were little more than sections, having been carried out more than fifty years ago when Palestinian archeology was in its infancy.[2] The results of these excavations were far from being satisfactory examples of stratigraphy. It is to be remembered that even at Ashkelon, where the scope of the excavations was much larger than at Gaza, the excavators often dealt with mixed and very thick layers of deposits as single units, making it impossible to conclude more than that the city was destroyed at the end of the Late Bronze Age.

The excavations at Ashdod can tell us far more precisely what happened in one of the main coastal cities at the end of the Late Bronze and beginning of the Early Iron Age. The relevant areas and strata were excavated mainly in the fourth and fifth seasons during 1968-69, but the final reports from these seasons have not yet been published.[3] There are three areas at Ashdod, all of them on the acropolis, where Late Bronze and Early Iron strata were found: Areas A and B, Area G, and Area H. In each of these areas the last Late Bronze stratum is XIV, the first Iron strata are XIII and XII (fig. 1).

Areas A and B, which for the purposes of this discussion can be considered a single area, are continuous, but the surface level of Area B is considerably

---

[1]W. F. Albright, *AASOR* 2-3 (1921-22) 11; *BASOR* 17 (1925) 8; S. Yeivin, *First Preliminary Report on the Excavations at Tel Gat* (Seasons 1956-58), Jerusalem, 1961; S. Buelow and R. A. Mitchell, *IEJ* 11 (1961) 101-10; R. Amiran and A. Eitan, *IEJ* 14 (1964) 219-31; R. Amiran and A. Eitan, *Archaeology* 18 (1966) 113-23; W. F. Albright, *BASOR* 15 (1924) 8; *BASOR* 17 (1925) 5-6; J. Naveh, "Khirbet al-Muqanna — Ekron: An Archaeological Survey," *IEJ* 8 (1958) 166-70.

[2]J. Garstang, *PEFQ* (1921) 12-16, 73-75; 162ff.; *PEFQ* (1922) 112-19; *PEFQ* (1924) 24-25; W. J. Phythian-Adams, *PEFQ* (1921) 163-69; *PEFQ* (1923) 11-36.

[3]For the final reports of the first three seasons at Ashdod, see: M. Dothan and D. N. Freedman, *Ashdod I* (1962), ʿAtiqot 7 (1967); M. Dothan, *Ashdod II-III* (1963-65), ʿAtiqot 9-10 (1971). For the preliminary reports of the fourth and fifth seasons, see M. Dothan, "Notes and News: Ashdod," *IEJ* 18 (1968) 253-54; *IEJ* 19 (1969) 243-54. Also, M. Dothan, "Ashdod," in *Encyclopedia of Archaeological Excavations in the Holy Land*, Vol. I (Jerusalem, 1975) 103-19.

lower than that of A, some 4 m of stratified deposits having been removed in the modern period by local inhabitants (fig. 2; cf. *Ashdod* I, pl. 1:2). The upper strata of Area B are therefore continuous with the lower levels of Area A.

In Area B, Stratum XIV was uppermost, but had been exposed to the elements for so long a period that it was eroded extensively. The floor was traceable only in a few scattered places, and the only structural remains were two large storage pits. In the vertical section however, between Areas A and B, the full depth of this stratum can be seen. It consists mostly of a thick destruction layer (ca. 85 cm), containing ashes, which indicate that this stratum, in Area A-B, ended in a heavy conflagration. Since the later strata had been removed in this area, as mentioned above, we had to excavate nearby in Area A and descend toward Stratum XIV from the surface, through 4 m of deposits (cf. *Ashdod* I, p. 16). The area which could be excavated in the earliest strata was consequently rather limited and was found to contain no discernible building remains.

The finds from Stratum XIV in this area are characteristic of the end of the Late Bronze Age (*Ashdod* I, pp. 81-83; II-III, p. 25-26). The bowls, cooking pots, storage jars, jugs, and juglets all belong to this period, and the same is true of the decorated ware. The closest parallels come from Tell Beit Mirsim, Lachish (Fosse Temple), and Megiddo (VII) (*Ashdod* I, pp. 81-82). Cypriot pottery is quite abundant and includes knife-pared juglets, Base Ring (bilbil), and White Slip II ware, mainly of the milk bowl variety. A sizable amount of Mycenean sherds includes some from a stirrup jar, a kylix, a krater bearing a chariot scene, fiddle figurines, and others. All these have parallels in the Mycenean IIIb ware found in this country or in Mycenean IIIb ware from such sites as Ugarit or Enkomi (*Ashdod* I, II-III). These finds point to the second half of the 13th century as a chronological setting for Stratum XIV.

Let us see now what succeeded the thick destruction level of Stratum XIV. The debris found above this stratum was about 80 cm thick (local Stratum 13). It was later tentatively correlated with that above Stratum XIV and with Stratum XIIIb in other areas. It contained several local pottery types of the late Late Bronze and Early Iron Ages, as well as some Cypriot sherds of the latest White Slip II types, a single Mycenean fragment, and a few Philistine sherds (*Ashdod* II-III, p. 26-27). If the Philistine sherds are not intrusive, they may indicate Philistine occupation of this area of the city (identifiable perhaps with Stratum XIIIa, local Stratum 12), possibly after the local abandonment which followed the destruction of the Canaanite city. It is difficult, however, to draw chronological conclusions on the basis of the situation of Stratum XIII in Area A-B.

Stratum XII (local 11) is the earliest Iron I level which has well-defined building remains in Area A-B. It inaugurates a series of local Philistine phases continuing until Stratum X. The finds include such characteristic vessels as kraters with bichrome checkerboard pattern over white slip. Here we found for the first time the greenish Mycenean IIIc1b ware which elsewhere had already appeared in Stratum XIIIb. On the whole, however, the information obtained from the small section in Area A was rather meager (*Ashdod* II-III, pp. 27-29).

If we had terminated the excavations at Ashdod after the second season, which was before we penetrated the Late Canaanite and Early Iron periods in any area, we would have been unable in any way to decide on the detailed chronology of the critical strata and unable to draw any soundly based conclusions. I do not wish to imply that, having excavated more complete and detailed sequences in Areas G and H, we are now in possession of all the facts; but we can now at least begin to explain some of the archeological finds, and by relating them to known historical events, propose a soundly based historical hypothesis. For this purpose I will now briefly outline the situation in Areas G and H.

Area G is situated on the northern perimeter of the acropolis (fig. 3). Part of the fortifications of the city, or perhaps of a fortified palace, which was found there existed with only minor changes throughout the Late Bronze Strata XVI-XIV. In Stratum XIV a formidable structure built of thick brick walls on stone foundations was uncovered. This structure may have stood near a gate of which all trace has been removed, perhaps by erosion.[4] (The first city gate of the Middle Bronze IIc period was found slightly to the north of the preserved northern wall of this structure.) Three parallel lines of rooms and courts were uncovered, together with a plastered water pool and a cistern. The finds from the floors of Stratum XIV include local pottery typical of the 13th century: bowls, storage jars, and some decorated vessels. The imported ware included White Slip II, Base Ring II, and Mycenean IIIb. To this stratum also must have belonged objects found in secondary use in Stratum XIII and in the fill of Stratum XII. One of these is a segment of a stone lintel — which may have been part of a gate lintel of Stratum XIV — bearing a hieroglyphic inscription of the late 19th Dynasty, possibly dating to the reign of Rameses II. Fragments of a glass vessel with a cartouche of Rameses II and of a palette belong to the same period. The structures and the finds indicate a flourishing Canaanite city which probably remained loyal to Egyptian rule, since it is never mentioned in the texts as having rebelled against Egypt or as having been conquered by it.

The destruction of the city in this area seems to have been thorough, although the actual debris was less evident than in Areas A-B. The main point to be stressed, however, is that the character of the area changed completely between Strata XIV and XIII. The walls built at right angles to the above-mentioned parallel rooms on their northern side were destroyed, and only the inner, parallel walls, surviving to a height of ca. 1.20 m, and their partition walls remained. Thus the site of the fortified building in the northern part of the area in Stratum XIV was occupied by an open space with some small rooms in

---

[4]The buildings and finds from this stratum were mentioned briefly in "Notes and News: Ashdod," *IEJ* 18 (1968) 253; *IEJ* 19 (1969) 243-44; cf. *Encyclopedia*, Vol. I, 107.

Stratum XIII.[5] In this open space, what appears to have been a High Place was discovered. It consists of a square structure of plastered bricks and the stone base for a round pillar. On the surface of the brick structure, sherds and bones were found. The surface of the stone base (certainly reused from Stratum XIV) bore traces of burning. To the south of these structures, which may have served as an altar and a base for an image, a wall built of three interconnected sections made of large, reused stones is preserved. The brick walls uncovered in this stratum are much thinner than those found in Stratum XIV, and the builders reused some of the stones from Stratum XIV in order to strengthen these walls.

On the floor of one of the rooms a large amount of charred wood, probably from a kiln, was found. Nearby, a group of 27 pottery vessels, consisting mostly of bowls, was left, each turned upside down, on the floor. This room seems to have been a store or a shop, perhaps belonging to a potter's workshop. From this floor came most of the pottery attributed to the lower phase of Stratum XIII. It resembles the Mycenean IIIc1 vessels to be found mainly in Cyprus, but also in the Aegean and the Eastern Mediterranean. Together with this type of ware, some bearing monochrome decoration, usually of simple motifs known as bands, also appear, of a type mainly known from Cypriot sites such as Sinda (Stratum III), Kouklia, and more important, from Enkomi (Stratum IIIa).[6]

The upper phase of Stratum XIII (A) is different only in minor details from the lower phase (B). There are some changes in the layout, and floors were laid in some of the rooms. The change, however, is recognized more clearly from the finds. Here for the first time we have a number of typical Philistine sherds. Although one or two such sherds had been found in Phase B, it appears that these were intrusive. But only in Stratum XII were we able to see the extent to which Philistine pottery becomes the main distinctive element of the Early Iron Age at Ashdod.

The next stratum (XII) showed a complete change in Area G.[7] Stratum XIII appears to have been of short duration. The best evidence for this is the fact that the people of Stratum XII were still able to use some of the remains of the fortified complex of Stratum XIV. The outer wall of this building was widened and now became the outer wall of the city. The space between the outer and the parallel walls was divided, partly by using old partition walls, and partly by adding new ones, and thus became virtually a casemate wall. The space between the walls was packed with fill. Debris from Strata XIV and XIII was also used for raising the levels of the floors. Some of the rooms inside the city were used for industrial purposes. In one of these a clay larnax-like bathtub was

---

[5] M. Dothan, "Notes and News: Ashdod," *IEJ* 19 (1969) 244; cf. *Encyclopedia*, Vol. I, 109.

[6] M. Dothan, *Relations Between Cyprus and the Philistine Coast in the Late Bronze Age (Tel Mor, Ashdod)*, in *Praktikon tou protou diethnous Kyprologikon synedriou*, Nicosia, 1972, 54-56, pls. 8-9.

[7] M. Dothan, "Notes and News: Ashdod," *IEJ* 18 (1968) 253; M. Dothan, *Qadmoniot* 17 (1972) 6 (Hebrew); cf. *Encyclopedia*, Vol. I, 108-9.

found, together with the remains of a kiln, a stone stool, mortars, and a large lump of glass. Many typical Philistine vessels were found in this and other rooms; beer jugs, stirrup jars, bell-shaped bowls, and kraters. The designs were also typical and consisted of stemmed decorative spirals between metopes and birds facing in opposite directions.

Let us now view the situation in the last relevant area — Area H.[8] This is situated on the western slope of the acropolis, and the Late Bronze town was found to extend westward beyond the systematically excavated area (fig. 4). Its outer walls were found to have been eroded, as had occurred elsewhere on the tell. Stratum XIV (local 7), the last city of the Late Bronze Age at Ashdod, was reached here only in a few places, and the few foundations of brick walls and sections of floors which were uncovered were too fragmentary to allow coherent building units to be identified.

The finds from this stratum illustrate a situation similar to that which emerges from Stratum XIV in other areas. The pottery, both local and imported, includes a repertoire characteristic of the latter part of the 13th century B.C.E.: cooking pots, storage jars, pilgrim flasks, Cypriot White Slip II, Mycenean IIIb sherds, and some Egyptian "flower pots."[9]

The destruction of Stratum XIV was not completely uniform; in some places the remains were buried under about 1 m of ash, while in others the Stratum XIII foundations were laid directly on top of the remaining walls of Stratum XIV.[10] The layout of the new structures differs completely from that of the preceding occupation. The main feature of this area was a street about 3.5 m wide dividing two complexes of buildings, a feature which it shares with Stratum XII in this area. To the north of the street a large building, at least 17 by 13 m, was uncovered, consisting of a courtyard and a few rooms, bounded on one side by a double wall. Several of the walls here were preserved to a height of ca. 1.5 m, and in some places two phases, XIIIa and b, were recognized.

The relatively few finds in this stratum show some continuity of the Canaanite pottery tradition, mainly in Phase XIIIb, examples being the four-handled storage jar and a bowl with a characteristically painted palm motif. The most distinct group of pottery however, is of the Mycenean IIIc1 type, which had already appeared in Area G, where it was mostly undecorated.[11] The decorative motifs, in addition to horizontal stripes, consisted of wavy lines, antithetical stemmed spirals (some of these with a net design center), and vertical zig-zag patterns forming parts of triglyphs. The greenish pottery and the buff pottery with monochrome decoration is most similar to the Mycenean IIIc1b

---

[8] M. Dothan, *Ashdod II-III*, 155-58; M. Dothan, "Notes and News: Ashdod," *IEJ* 18 (1968) 253-54; cf. *Encyclopedia*, Vol. I, 108.

[9] M. Dothan, *Ashdod II-III Plates*, figs. 81, 82:1; pl. 75; *Encyclopedia*, Vol. I, 108.

[10] M. Dothan, "Notes and News: Ashdod," *IEJ* 18 (1968) 253; *Encyclopedia*, Vol. I, 108.

[11] M. Dothan, *Ashdod II-III Plates*, pl. 76; *Relations Between Cyprus and the Philistine Coast*, pls. 8-9; M. Dothan, *Qadmoniot* 17 (1972) 6 (Hebrew); *Encyclopedia*, Vol. I, 108.

pottery from Cyprus. It did not appear earlier than Stratum XIII and continued in Stratum XII alongside Philistine pottery. The layout of the buildings in Area H in Stratum XII partly follows that of Stratum XIII, and the transition between the strata seems to have been peaceful. The best-preserved complex of buildings lies to the north of the street. The southern part of this northern complex is rectangular and consists of a courtyard with rows of rooms to the west and to the north of it. Its main feature is an apsidal structure, built above a rectangular substructure.[12] The northern part of the complex consists of a central hall, with several rooms to the north and to the south of it. Here two stone column bases which supported the roof were found. A rectangular structure (1.8 x 1.3 m) made of white plastered bricks was attached to one of the columns.

Among the finds from this stratum the large amount of typical Philistine pottery should be stressed. It is mostly of the bichrome variety, sometimes on a white background, with a stylized bird as its main decorative motif. In addition to the pottery a large quantity of other finds includes jewelry, scarabs, ivory objects, a stamp, etc., showing some Egyptian, but chiefly Aegean influence. Of special significance is a clay figurine of a seated female deity. It is likely that at the time of Stratum XIIIa and certainly in Stratum XII the local cult already centered around this goddess, whose prototype was the Great Mother of the Mycenean cult.[13]

CONCLUSIONS

Before drawing any conclusions, let me summarize what we know of the end of the Late Bronze Age and the beginning of the Iron Age at Ashdod from our excavations in the relevant areas and strata. Stratum XIV was a flourishing Canaanite city. Its connections with the outside world are evident from the Mycenean and Cypriot pottery found there and from the rich Egyptian finds, which attest to continued Egyptian supremacy until as late as the second half of the 13th century B.C.E. Additional evidence of the city's importance in this period is to be found in the Ugaritic texts. Not only do we find that Ashdod is one of the three Palestinian cities which are mentioned as having commercial relations with Ugarit, but also that many Ashdodites were actually living in Ugarit, probably as merchants or as agents of their city.[14]

The Canaanite city of Ashdod was conquered and much of it was destroyed, possibly as a result of one of the large and powerful movements which included the Sea Peoples. This may have been the wave which destroyed a number of cities along the Syro-Palestinian coast and in Cyprus, including

[12]The preliminary plans and photographs appear in M. Dothan, *Ashdod II-III*, plan 26; *Plates*, pl. 74:2; M. Dothan, "Ashdod" in *Encyclopedia*, Vol. I, 109.

[13]*Ashdod II-III*, 20-21, 128; *Encyclopedia*, Vol. I, 109; *Qadmoniot* 17 (1972) 8 (Hebrew).

[14]*Ashdod II-III*, 18 and n. 7; 17 and nn. 9-15.

Ugarit, Tell Abu Hawam, and Enkomi 11b. The archeological evidence for dating the event includes the abrupt end of the Mycenean and Cypriot imports, finds such as Marneptah's dagger in the destroyed last stratum at Ugarit, and Tausret's cartouche on the faience vessel from Tell Deir ᶜAlla.[15] This provides us with a latest approximate date for the destruction of Ashdod XIV of ca. 1200 B.C.E. This must be placed somewhat earlier if we are to accept the higher chronology, but it cannot be far from the very end of the 19th Dynasty and the beginning of the 20th Dynasty, or shortly before the reign of Rameses III. The next city, Stratum XIII, seems to have been much smaller, unfortified, and to have had a different ground plan. Not only were the physical structures of the city changed, but the new inhabitants brought with them a different cultural background. The finds indicate that they were influenced greatly by late Mycenean culture. The forms and decorations of their pottery are particularly close to those of Mycenean IIIc1 pottery in Cyprus.

The people of Stratum XIII changed the character of the city but were not able to settle the entire area of the Canaanite city or to fortify it. The people who destroyed the last Canaanite city of Ashdod were the vanguard of more Sea Peoples who came to settle there. They were led to participate in a process which would, in due course, bring to an end the Egyptian hegemony over Canaan and direct rule over certain Canaanite cities.

It seems that Ashdod XII was taken over peacefully by people akin to the inhabitants of Stratum XIII. These new inhabitants, who according to their material culture were Philistines, came apparently not as conquerors but as settlers. This agrees with the biblical tradition that the Philistines settled mainly along the southwestern coast of Canaan. This must have happened after the defeat of the Sea Peoples in the 8th year of the reign of Rameses III. The beginning of Stratum XII should therefore be dated according to the accepted chronology, to ca. 1190 or 1180 B.C.E. This city, which covered the whole mound, was both fortified and well planned and survived for several generations, probably until the end of the 12th century. The city plan and the finds in Stratum XII reflect the rapidly developing material culture of a city-state, on a political and military level by the fortifications, and socio-religiously by the cult of the Great Mother. Ashdod, at the beginning of the 12th century, was ready to enter the Early Iron Age of Palestine as one of the principal elements of the Philistine Pentapolis.

---

[15]See "Historical Notes on the Excavation Results," *Ashdod II-III*, 18-23, for the historical setting. For Marneptah's dagger, cf. M. C. Astour, "New Evidence on the Last Days of Ugarit," *AJA* 69 (1965) 253-58; for Tausret's cartouche, H. J. Franken, "Deir Alla," *VT* 14 (1964) 377ff.

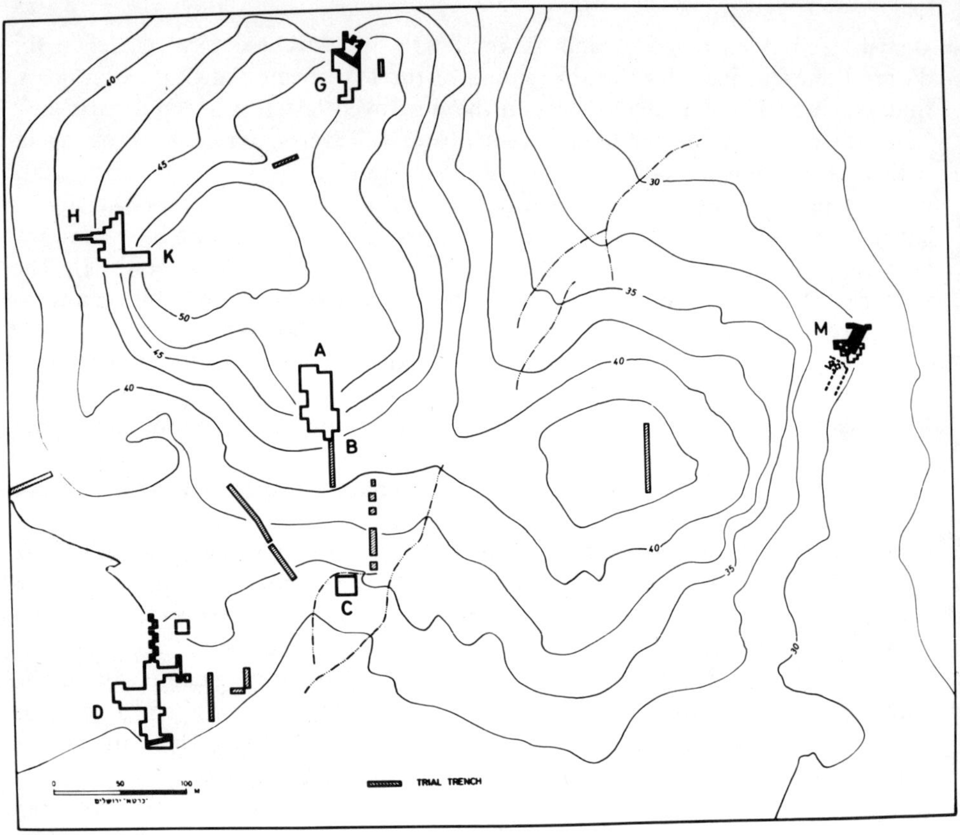

Fig. 1. The topography of Tel Ashdod, 1969.

Fig. 2. Aerial photo of Areas A-B.

Fig. 3. Aerial photo of Area G.

Fig. 4. Aerial photo of Areas H-K.

Volume 2

Archaeology and the Sanctuaries of Israel

The Temple in The Ugaritic Myth of Baal

RICHARD J. CLIFFORD
Weston School of Theology, Cambridge, MA

The temple in the ancient Near East is not merely a building which archeology can excavate. Inseparably woven into the fabric of public and private life of antiquity, it performed functions in society which modern students would analyze as economic, cultural, religious, and political. It was at once a municipal or national vault, a seat of learning and repository of sacred traditions, a place of worship and theophany, a platform where the king and his role in the divine governance of the world might be displayed and given legitimacy.

It is the last-named function of the temple, an instrument in divine-human governance, that is the special concern of this paper. Fortunately there exists a body of texts from the 14th-13th centuries B.C.E., written in alphabetic cuneiform, that illustrate the temple's importance in creation and kingship. The texts are in the Ugaritic language, and in language, prosody, and to some extent in subject matter show remarkable affinities to the earliest Hebrew poetry. That Ugaritic literature provides evidence for the beliefs of peoples well beyond the environs of the city of Ugarit is clear from the range of place-names and from the agreements with biblical poetry of southern provenance.

Within the Ugaritic corpus, there are six major tablets all concerned with the rise to kingship of the storm god Baal through his victory over *Yammu* "Sea" and *Môtu* "Death." These supply a somewhat unified corpus for analysis of the meaning of the temple in Late (and perhaps Middle) Bronze Age in Canaan. Andrée Herdner, the editor of the critical edition of the texts, has numbered them in tentative sequence 1-6[1] and has characterized them as "Cycle de Ba^cal et ^cAnat." Though Herdner's sequence of tablets reflects the opinion of many scholars, no genuine consensus has so far emerged on how the six tablets are to be related to each other. Only two of the six are in undoubted sequence. Tablet 6 continues immediately the goddess Anat's mourning for Baal described in the last column of tablet 5. It has often been assumed that tablet 5 follows tablet 4 immediately. Difficulties stand in the way of the assumed continuity

[1]Abbreviations used in the paper: *CTCA*, Andrée Herdner, *Corpus des tablettes en cunéiformes alphabétiques* (Mission de Ras Shamra 10; Paris: Imprimerie Nationale, 1963); *PRU II, Le palais royal d'Ugarit* (Mission de Ras Shamra 7; Paris: Imprimerie Nationale, 1957). Another widely used system of designating the tablets is that of Cyrus H. Gordon, *Ugaritic Textbook* (Analecta Orientalia 38; Rome: Pontifical Biblical Institute, 1965). *CTCA* 1 = *UT* ^c*nt*: pl. 9, pl. 10; 2 = 137, 129, 68; 3 = ^c*nt*; 4 = 51; 5 = 67; 6 = 49 + 62.

both from the context and from the number of lines that would have to be posited in the last column of tablet 4.

It is assumed in this paper that *CTCA* 1-6 contain two variants of the same basic myth of the victory of the storm god rather than, as is often assumed, of a single connected story of a conflict with Sea followed by a conflict with Death. One finds instead a combat with Sea, intercession of a goddess (either Anat or Asherah) with El, construction and consecration of a temple alongside a variant of a conflict with Death, intercession of a goddess, construction of a temple. The language and logic of the two variants are of course similar. Nonetheless, there are differences. Tablets 1 and especially 2, which describe the conflict of Baal and Yam, show clear parallels to the Akkadian creation epic *Enūma eliš* which are not found in the Baal-Mot story: Yam "Sea" and Tiamat "Sea," the prominence of the assembly of the gods (Akkadian *puḫrum* = Ugaritic *pḫr*) and the bold threat to that body by Sea (in the Baal-Mot story El acts rather than the assembly).[2] Tablets 4-6 describe the Baal-Mot struggle. Tablets 3 and 4 appear to be variants at least in the long accounts of the goddess' intercessory journeys to El.

However one resolves the problem of the sequence of the tablets, it is only necessary for the present paper to establish a sequence of states or actions in Baal's accession to kingship. The admittedly artificial isolating of stages clarifies the function of the temple in divine-human governance at Ugarit. Four separate stages in Baal's rise to royal power can be discerned in the texts.

Stage One. Baal lacks political power before his victory over Yam and Mot which is symbolized by his not having a temple/palace.

Stage Two. Even after his victory Baal is without the kind of royal power a temple would provide. He must ask a goddess to obtain from El and the assembly a decree authorizing construction of a temple.

Stage Three. El and the assembly decree a temple. A temple is built.

Stage Four. The festive consecration of the temple and the manifestation of Baal's kingly power.

In stage one Baal's powerlessness is shown most dramatically in the assembly scene from the Baal-Yam story, in *CTCA* 2.1. Even before the arrogant messengers of Yam coerce the assembly into giving up Baal into the hands of their master, Baal has a subordinate role in the assembly, *baᶜlu qama ᶜalê ᵓili* "Baal stands before El." How precarious Baal's position actually is appears from the readiness of El and the assembly to surrender him.

---

[2]Thorkild Jacobsen has suggested that the Akkadian story of the combat between the storm god and Tiamat originated among the West Semites where the sea would play a dominant role in the religious imagination, "The Battle between Marduk and Tiamat," *JAOS* 88 (1968) 419-26. He has recently returned to the theme in "Religious Drama in Ancient Mesopotamia," in *Unity and Diversity: Essays in the History, Literature and Religion of the Ancient Near East* (eds. H. Goedicke and J. J. M. Roberts; Baltimore: Johns Hopkins University, 1975) 65-97.

The appearance in the distance of the two messengers of Sea sets the following scene in motion.

Then they (two messengers) set face
Toward the Mount of El (text: *ll*)
Toward the meeting of the council.
The gods were sitting to eat,
The holy ones, to dine.
Baal was standing before El.
As soon as the gods saw them,
Saw the messengers of Yam,
The envoys of Judge River,
The gods dropped their heads
Onto their knees,
Down on their princely thrones.
Baal rebuked them,
"Why have you lowered, O gods,
Your heads upon your knees
And on your princely thrones?
I see, O gods, you are terrified
From fear of the messengers of Yam,
The envoys of Judge River.
Lift up, O gods, your heads
From upon your knees
From your princely thrones.
And I will answer the messengers of Sea
The envoys of Judge River.
The gods lifted up their heads
From upon their knees
From their princely thrones. (*CTCA* 2.1.19-29)

The messengers arrive and present their demand.

"Give up the god whom you harbor,
Him whom the assembly harbors.
Give up Baal and his followers,
The son of Dagan that I might take his gold(?)"
And answered Bull, his father El,
"Your servant is Baal, O Yam,
Your prisoner is Baal, O River,
The son of Dagan is your captive.
He will be borne as your tribute.
Yes, El will bring tribute,
And the holy ones, your gift. (*CTCA* 2.1.34-38)

Baal's attack on the messengers comes to nothing and is even restrained by Ashtart, a member of the assembly. Three columns later — the intervening two are unfortunately not preserved and a fragment (*CTCA* 2.3[?]) cannot be placed within the action — Baal defeats Yam, "Yam is dead. Baal reigns." (*CTCA* 2.4.32).

What happens between the assembly's capitulation in column one and Baal's victory over Yam in column four is not known because of the destroyed intervening two columns. One can, however, conjecture concerning events consequent upon the defeat of Yam in column four by exploiting the general similarity of the Akkadian epic *Enūma eliš*, noted above, and two possible biblical parallels, Psalms 24 and 29.

In the Akkadian epic, after the story of the creation and the successful handling of the first threat to cosmic order by Apsu through the wisdom of Ea, a new threat arises. Tiamat, "Sea" threatens the assembly. No one is strong enough to lead an army against her and her entourage. After the assembly recovers from their terror, the gods choose a young god, Marduk, he of the storm, evidently not yet a powerful member of the assembly. Marduk insists that the assembly grant royal authority to him before he fights in their name. He successfully defeats Tiamat, forming the cosmos out of her carcass and then creating man. The gods construct a temple, Esagila, for the victorious god and then as a gathering place for themselves. A banquet is then celebrated. With the Akkadian parallel in mind, one can assume that El and the assembly hail Baal after his victory over Sea, grant him the power appropriate to his victory, and build him a temple.

Two biblical parallels may cautiously be adduced. Baal's call to the gods to lift up their heads, quoted above, appears to be reflected in Ps 24:7-9.

> Lift up, O gates, your heads.
> Lift yourselves up, O ancient doors.
> The king of glory shall enter.
> Who is this king of glory?
> Yahweh, mighty and valiant,
> Yahweh the warrior.

The words of the psalm, now of course in a different context, may well have had their origin in cries of processionists in the victorious god's train as they approached the temple where the divine assembly was thought to reside. In the Israelite perspective the members of the assembly have been changed to architectural features of the temple. But it appears that the victorious god takes up and reverses a statement made earlier in the assembly in a kind of inclusio.[3]

Psalm 29, acknowledged by many scholars as an adapted Canaanite hymn to Baal, seems also to portray the welcoming of the warrior god to the assembly

---

[3]For further discussion, see F. M. Cross, *Canaanite Myth and Hebrew Epic* (Cambridge: Harvard University, 1973) 91-93.

and the grant to him of the authority rightfully his by the victory over chaos. With no change in the consonantal Hebrew text and by reading enclitic *mem* instead of the plural, one can read

> Ascribe to Yahweh, sons of El,
> Ascribe to Yahweh glory and strength,
> Ascribe to Yahweh his glorious name.

After his entry into the temple, Yahweh seats himself on Flood (another name for Sea), presumably the remnant of the slain monster from which he has created the cosmos.[4]

These conjectures have taken us into later stages. Analysis of *CTCA* 2 has shown, however, that before his victory over Yam, Baal was out of power in the assembly.

What distinguishes the second stage is that Baal is still without independent royal power despite his victory and needs to go to El and the assembly for a temple-granting decree. Important evidence is found in *CTCA* 4.1.4-19. The identity of the speaker is not certain but is probably Anat or Baal.

> He cries out to Bull El his father
> The king who created him.
> He cries out to Asherah and her sons,
> The goddess and her brood of lions(?).
> Look, Baal has no house (*bt*) like the gods,
> No court like the sons of Asherah.
> The dwelling of El is the shelter of his son,
> The dwelling of Lady Asherah of the Sea,
> The dwelling of the perfect brides,
> The dwelling of Pidrayya, daughter of Light,
> The shelter of Talliyya, daughter of Showers,
> The dwelling of Earthie, daughter of y^{c}*bdr*.
> (*CTCA* 4.1.4-19, 4.4.47-57, 3.5.43-52)

The logic is simple. Having his own temple would enable Baal to move out of El's household and to establish his harem independently.[5] It would also make him equal to "the gods/the sons of Asherah" providing a hall for divine banquets and a place to commemorate his victory and to proclaim his sovereignty.

The goddesses Asherah (*CTCA* 4.4.47-57) and Anat (*CTCA* 3.5.43-52) use the same words in their pleas before El on behalf of Baal, *after* the victory but

---

[4]For a recent treatment with bibliography, see A. Fitzgerald, "A Note on Psalm 29," *BASOR* 215 (1974) 61-63.

[5]Total dominion over a harem seems to be important in displaying independent royal power. Cf. the symbolism of Absalom's going into David's harem in 2 Sam 16:20-23.

before the temple is granted. They also add

> Our king is Aliyan Baal
> Our judge and there is none above him.
> All of us carry his *q-š*.
> All of us carry his *k-s*. (*CTCA* 4.4.43-46; 3.5.40-42)

Even though these two important members of the assembly call Baal their king, a decree is needed from El.

In discussing stage two it is appropriate to mention several features of the battle and victory of Baal. There is no single standard description of the storm god's battle in the Ugaritic texts but rather several, with a variety of motifs and a fluidity of actors. In *CTCA* 2.4, Baal alone defeats Yam with Koshar's magic weapons. In *CTCA* 3.3.34-4.48, Anat reveals that she was a participant in the battle and that there were many monsters in Yam's army.

> Did I not smite the beloved of El, Yam?
> Did I not destroy El's River, Rabbim?
> Did I not muzzle the dragon? I muzzled him.
> I crushed the crooked serpent,
> Shilyat with the seven heads.
> I smote the beloved of El, Ar(-).
> I destroyed El's bullock, Atak.
> I smote the divine bitch, Fire.
> I destroyed the house of El Dbb.
> I battled for the silver, I possessed the gold,
> Of him who would thrust Baal from the heights of Zaphon
> - - - - - - - - - - - - - - - - - -
> Of him who would chase him from his royal throne,
> From the dais, the throne of his power.

A fragment, not from the Baal cycle, describes Anat's battle with the dragon as taking place not on Zaphon but on Lebanon.

> In the land of *Mḫnm* he (the dragon) swirled the sea,
> His double-tongue licked the heavens;
> His twin tails churned up (?) the sea.
> She fixed the unmuzzled dragon.
> She bound him to the heights of Leban(on). (*PRU* II 3.8-10)

On one occasion, Baal and Mot fight in single combat on Mt. Zaphon.

> They shake one another like wild camels.
> Mot is strong. Baal is strong.
> They gore one another like buffaloes.
> Mot is strong. Baal is strong.
> - - - - - - - - - - - - - - - -
> They butt like chargers.
> Mot is exhausted. Baal is exhausted. (*CTCA* 6.6.16-22)

At this point the sun goddess Šapšu warns off Mot and Baal is seated as king.

A second feature of the battle is that it always takes place on a mountain. The texts just cited show that the battle is either at Zaphon, the mountain near the city of Ugarit, or at Lebanon. In the Hebrew Bible, motifs attached to Mt. Zaphon are attached to Mt. Zion. In Ps 48:3, Mt. Zion is even called Zaphon.

The third point has likewise been made in the texts already cited, that the battle on the mountain is for kingship. Those who attack want to drive Baal from the heights of Zaphon, from his royal seat. It is by the same token a battle for creation since Baal by his victory overcomes death and chaos.

In the third stage of the process of Baal becoming king, El issues a decree establishing the temple and Koshar wa-Hasis the divine craftsman sees to its construction. When Anat and Asherah ask El for permission for the temple, they celebrate El's decree.

> Your decree, O El, is wise.
> Your wisdom lasts forever.
> A life of good fortune is your decree. (*CTCA* 4.4.41-43; 3.5.38-39)

The life-bestowing nature of El's decree is clearly seen in the Krt and Aqht epics where by its power a child is granted to a childless ruler. It is appropriate here as well since the storm god will direct his life-giving rains from his temple. El gives his decree in response to the goddesses' plea.

> Let a temple be built for Baal like the gods,
> A court like the sons of Asherah. (*CTCA* 4.4.62-5.63)

Asherah's hymn of response tells what Baal will do in his temple — continue the imposing of that order upon the cosmos initiated by the defeat of Yam or Mot.

> And now let Baal appoint his rains,
> Let him appoint the seasons of wetness(?) with snow(?).
> And let him thunder in the clouds,
> Let him flash his thunders in the earth. (*CTCA* 4.5.68-71)

When Koshar arrives to build the temple, the raw materials of gold, silver, and precious stones have already been gathered. At the completion of the structure, Baal rejoices,

> My temple I have built of silver,
> My palace indeed of gold. (*CTCA* 4.6.35-38)

The climactic couplet, repeated as an inclusio later in *CTCA* 4.8.32-36, frames the manifold proclamation of Baal's kingship in the heavens, on the earth, and in the underworld.

The fourth stage, the festive consecration of the temple by a banquet and the proclamation of sovereignty in the storm, is really an explication of Baal's statement, "My house I have built of silver, my palace indeed of gold." He summons the members of the heavenly court, the seventy sons of Asherah — now he is their equal — for a banquet. The preserved text of over 41 lines does not tell us what went on at the banquet except for prodigious feats of eating.

One can conclude little from the broken first lines of column seven which follows the description of the banquet, certainly nothing about a conflict with Yam as some commentators have tried. The seizing of 66/77 and 80/90 cities and towns by Baal is not clear. Perhaps it is the manifestation of sovereignty in the localities around Mt. Zaphon where Baal's devotees live. Baal then manifests his kingship on earth while his enemies scatter.

> He opened a window in the temple,
> A casement in the midst of the palace.
> Baal opened clefts in the clouds.
> Baal uttered his holy voice.
> Baal discharged the utterance of his lips.
> His holy voice shook the earth.
> - - - - - - - - the mountains.
> The distant - - - were quaking - - (?)
> - - - - - the sea.
> The high places of the earth tottered.
> The enemies of Baal took to the wooded heights.
> The haters of Haddu to the - - of the mountain.
> And Aliyan Baal said,
> "Enemies of Haddu, why are you quaking?
> Why are you quaking, attackers of the Valiant One?"
> The eye of Baal anticipated his hand,
> When - - the cedar (club) in his right hand.
> Indeed Baal is enthroned in his temple.
> "No king or commoner,
> A land of sovereignty shall establish.
> Tribute I will not send to the son of El, Mot,
> Gifts of homage(?) to the beloved of El, Ghazir." (*CTCA* 4.7.25-47)

There remains now the proclamation of his kingship to Mot in the underworld, who thinks that "he alone shall rule over the gods, yea, shall fatten gods and men, who shall satiate the multitudes of the earth" (*CTCA* 4.7.47-52). This Baal does by dispatching the messengers to the underworld to announce his rule in terms of the completion of his temple, "My temple I have built of silver, my palace indeed of gold."

These four stages illumine the significance of the temple in the Baal cycle. Without a decree of El (and the assembly) and a temple/palace, Baal is unable to be on a par with the other members of the assembly and has no place in which to continue the work of ordering and ruling the cosmos initiated in the defeat of his enemies. There are of course other texts in the six tablets which show that Baal falls into the power of Yam and Mot and suggest strongly that Baal's kingship is seasonal and must be ever won anew.

In deliberate contrast to the palace of Baal is the tent of El the high god. Within these six tablets El always dwells in a *ᵓahl/mškn* "tent"/"tabernacle." El's power does not seem to be seasonal but certainly is not always adequate for the governing of the universe. In one text, quoted above, El is coerced by the messengers of Yam. He is virtually seduced by his wife Asherah in her pursuit of his decree while Anat threatens the old god with physical violence for the same purpose. A frequently repeated description of El's dwelling reveals that it is the source of the cosmic waters which give life to the world.

> Then they set face
> Toward El at the sources of the Two Rivers,
> In the midst of the pools of the Double Deep.
> They entered (i.e., rolled back the tent flaps) the tent of El and went into
> The tent shrine of the king, the father of years. (*CTCA*).

Beside being at the source of cosmic waters that fertilize the earth, El's tent is a place of decrees and the meeting place of the assembly of the gods.[6] It is not necessary to postulate, as many scholars have, that Baal and El are hostile to one another. There is no record of hostility in the texts, and evidence used from other ancient Near East theogonies must be used with extreme caution. Rather, two types of royal rule are portrayed, the one patriarchal with the archaic tent as the royal dwelling and which relies on wisdom and consensus, the other, national kingship with the temple/palace, relying on youth and military power. The two can coexist and the balance between them that is found in the Ugaritic texts expresses quite well the complexity of human (and divine) rule that is to be found in many nation-states of the time.

Whether the temple of Baal excavated at Ugarit re-presented liturgically on earth the heavenly temple described in the texts just considered cannot be decided. For an extended treatment of the earthly mountain and its temple, one must turn to the Hebrew Bible, particularly the psalms, but that is beyond the limits of this paper.

---

[6]See further R. J. Clifford, *The Cosmic Mountain in Canaan and the Old Testament* (Harvard Semitic Monographs 4; Cambridge: Harvard University, 1972) 35-57.

Iron Age Sanctuaries and Cult Elements in Palestine

Yigal Shiloh
The Hebrew University, Jerusalem

The subject of cult sites, cult elements, and sanctuaries is one of the most interesting to discuss, but at the same time one of the most problematic and controversial in all of the research conducted on the material culture of Palestine during the Iron Age. It is precisely because of the continuously proliferating multiplicity of archeological finds that those who are investigating this specific field encounter considerable difficulty with regard to comparing, interpreting, and identifying them correctly and integrating them with the fund of new information that has accumulated in the areas of religious and historical research. This research has undergone a great many fluctuations from the close of the preceding century up to the present time. Today it appears that all of us negate the method that prevailed in the past, according to which a cultic interpretation was bestowed on every unusual structure or other object to which such a designation could conceivably be attached. Thus, for example, we now know that the two large four-room houses at Tell en-Naṣbeh, which Badé and Thiersch defined as temples, are in fact important public buildings concordant with the town-planning program of this Israelite city.[1]

We deny the cultic interpretation which a number of the Megiddo excavators ascribe to structure IA of Megiddo VA-IVB, whose stone pillars they define as sacred standing stones — *maṣṣēbôt*.[2] The correct interpretation is the architectural one, that the prevailing construction technique was the use of rows of stone pillars, built of monoliths or of links of stone that were so widespread in Israelite houses during the Iron Age. This eliminates their definition as cultic *maṣṣēbôt*.[3] Fisher and May pursued a similar rationale when they defined the

---

[1]W. F. Badé, *PEFQS* (1930) 12ff.; H. Thiersch, *ZAW* 50 (1932) 73-86. See also the full discussion on the subject of the four-room houses, their plan, and their place in the Israelite town-plan: Y. Shiloh, *IEJ* 20 (1970) 180-90; *Eretz-Israel* 11 (Jerusalem, 1973) 277-85; S. Yeivin, *Eretz-Israel* 11 (Jerusalem, 1973) 163.

[2]H. G. May, *Material Remains of Megiddo Cult* (Chicago, 1935) 10, pls. 8-9; R. S. Lamon and G. M. Shipton, *Megiddo I* (Chicago, 1939) 3-4.

[3]See their repeated appearance as pillars in the storehouses and four-room houses: Y. Shiloh, *IEJ* 20, figs. 1, 4, 5; W. F. Albright, *The Excavation of Tell Beit Mirsim III* (*AASOR* 21-22 [1943]) 53-55. We join in the opinion of C. F. Graesser (*BA* 35 [1972] 54-55), who rejects Kenyon's interpretation of the two stone pillars she found in the structure dug up on the eastern slope of the Ophel, as cultic *maṣṣēbôt* (K. M. Kenyon, *Digging up Jerusalem* [London, 1974] 137-38).

magnificent Building 338 of Megiddo IVA as a temple.[4] The rejection of this definition by Guy and Loud, on the basis of their examination of the structure's plan and the absence of any cultic find inside it, is accepted now by most scholars.[5]

Currently, the severest repudiation of this method appeared in Yeivin's latest study dealing with a number of structures of the Bronze and Iron Age which had been described as temples.[6] The title of the article, "Temples They Were Not," is self-explanatory. However, no doubt attaches to the fact that there existed for cultic purposes temples, altars, high places (= *bāmôt*), and sacred standing stones (= *maṣṣēbôt*). Many scriptural descriptions depict a variegated picture of the cultic particulars as they were practiced in Palestine, from the central temple in Jerusalem, through local community temples and tribal cultic sanctuaries, to *bāmôt, maṣṣēbôt*, and altars of families and clans, and a broad variety of cult objects.[7]

A parallel symposium conducted in Jerusalem in July, 1975, discussed in detail those aspects that pertain to Iron Age I. In that discussion, the view was expressed clearly that parallel to the sharp, clear-cut extinction of a number of significant Canaanite centers dating to the end of the Bronze Age — as, for example, Hazor — the remnants of the Canaanite culture stretch on into Iron Age I in those cities which the Israelites did not conquer, such as Megiddo and Beth-shean (Judg 1:27).

The existence of the remnants of the Canaanite civilization, especially in the valleys, the settled Israelite communities in the mountains, and the Philistine cities in the maritime plain in the Iron Age I, assuredly set mutual influences in motion in the realm of material culture. On the cult theme, the mutual influences find highly tangible expression in the various archeological finds.

The short time at our disposal prevents our dealing with new cultic sites belonging to the neighboring cultures, such as the Philistine temple at Tell Qasile, dating to the 12th-11th centuries B.C.E., which was excavated recently by A. Mazar,[8] or the temple in Ashdod Area D, of the 8th century B.C.E., which was excavated by Dothan and Freedman,[9] or the Egyptian temple in Timna near Elat, which its excavator, B. Rothenberg, dates to the 14th-12th centuries B.C.E.[10]

This paper will attempt to present some of the new archeological finds which were amassed chiefly during the past decade and which characterize the

---

[4]Cf. H. G. May, *Material Remains*, 4-9.

[5]R. S. Lamon and G. M. Shipton, *Megiddo I*, 58-59.

[6]S. Yeivin, *Eretz-Israel* 11, 163-75.

[7]For a detailed survey of these subjects, see R. de Vaux, *Ancient Israel* (New York, 1961) 271-339, 406-14; S. Yeivin, *Encyclopedia Biblica* 5 (Jerusalem, 1968) 322-28.

[8]A. Mazar, *IEJ* 23 (1973) 65-71; *BA* 36 (1973) 42-48.

[9]M. Dothan and D. N. Freedman, *Ashdod I* (*Atiqot* 7 [1967]) 132-34.

[10]B. Rothenberg, *Timna*, (London, 1972) 125-76.

Israelite settlements in particular. By limiting our discourse to an analysis of the material finds alone, we are of course restricting the scope of our deliberations. Nevertheless, we hope that this attempt to present the details — first and foremost on the basis of the finds — the resultant critiques, and the up-to-date discoveries relating to the Holy Land in this period will constitute a modest contribution toward the correct direction and productive results of the discussions conducted in the course of this symposium.

I

First, let us consider some examples from the field of urban architecture. The "sacred area" of Canaanite Megiddo is famous for the continuity of the monumental temples existing within it from the beginning of the third millennium B.C.E. until the beginning of the Iron Age I.[11] In Israelite Megiddo, the renewed Israelite royal center which was built by Solomon in the 10th century B.C.E., many of the elements that comprised the previous town-plan were preserved: the system of fortifications, the gate, and the palaces. But the sacred area was completely eradicated. The fact that in Stratum IVA from the 9th century B.C.E. on it was replaced by the northern complex of stables[12] serves to emphasize the change that transpired in Israelite Megiddo in contrast to Canaanite Megiddo.

To the best of our knowledge at the present time, evidence was found in Megiddo of small cultic corners (chapels) dating to the Israelite period. The most familiar example of this is the one that was discovered by Loud in Building 2081 of Stratum VA, near the city gate.[13] A group of cult objects was uncovered in a corner of the forepart of the structure, apparently the courtyard, and included a set of obviously cultic utensils, two horned limestone altars, chalices, cultic stands of stone and clay, as well as plain pottery. There is no doubt that this corner, with all the utensils it contained, served for cultic practices which revolved principally around the small stone altars. Similar altars were found at this level in other structures as well in the eastern part of the city, most of which was occupied in the 10th century by residential quarters.[14] The analogous picture is plain: if cultic remnants were extant in Israelite Megiddo, they were not the monumental temples typical of the Bronze Age, but rather cult corners located in residential sections and buildings.

Conversely to Megiddo, where the Canaanite culture continued into Iron Age I, Canaanite Hazor, in which four monumental temples dating from the Bronze Age were uncovered, was totally destroyed at the close of the Bronze Age.[15] On its ruins the Hazor expedition directed by Yadin discovered two strata

---

[11]G. Loud, *Megiddo II* (Chicago, 1948) 57-105.
[12]R. S. Lamon and G. M. Shipton, *Megiddo I*, 41-47; Y. Yadin, *Hazor* (London, 1972) 150-64.
[13]G. Loud, *Megiddo II*, 45-46, figs 100-2.
[14]H. G. May, *Material Remains*, 12-13, pl. 12.
[15]Y. Yadin, *Hazor*, 67-105.

(XII-XI) from the settlement period. To one side of the residential buildings in Stratum XI, Area B, an installation described as a high place — *bāmâ* — was found.[16] Beside the *bāmâ* a votive jar was exposed. It contained various votive objects that included weapons and bronze figurines of a god wearing a cone-shaped helmet, thus adding a pagan tinge to this collection of items. The *bāmâ* is not connected to any specific structure; it appears that it was found among the common buildings of this Israelite settlement which only several decades later, in the days of Solomon (Stratum X), was again to become an important royal center in the northern section of the country.

Another group of cultic utensils was discovered by Aharoni in 1968 at Lachish in the area excavated beneath the Hellenistic solar shrine. Among the other structures on Level V dating from the 10th century B.C.E. there was unearthed a rectangular room fitted with shelves and having normal dimensions (3 x 4 m); on the floor was discovered a horned stone altar, cultic stands, chalices, and ordinary clay utensils. This too is evidently a group of cultic utensils ascribable to a local cult-place at Israelite Lachish during the 10th century B.C.E., comparable to the ones brought to light at Megiddo and Hazor.[17]

The horned limestone altars which were characteristic of most of the cult collections noted above are known to us from various Iron Age sites that Israelites inhabited. Similar ones have been found at Gezer, Shechem, Tell Beit-Mirsim, Megiddo, Arad, Tell Qadesh in the Jezreel Valley, and recently also at Lachish and Tell Dan.[18] There is no doubt that these altars, which may have burned incense and animal fat, were the essential elements of the different cultic corners in the Israelite habitations. Two similar altars in Arad form a nexus between the rather limited cultic installations noted heretofore and the temple in Arad which will be discussed further. A number of the cult utensils discovered in these groups, such as the incense stands, resemble those familiar to us from alien cult sites, either the Canaanite or the Philistine.[19] In several cases, as for example at Megiddo, Taanach, and Hazor, statuettes representing a god were found among the other cult objects. This connotes unequivocal evidence of the manifestly pagan influences that emanated from the neighboring cultures. One such instance is the description of the existence of an altar to Baal and a grove

---

[16] Y. Yadin, *Hazor*, 132-34; Y. Yadin and others, *Hazor III-IV* (Jerusalem, 1961) pls. 38, 204-5.

[17] Y. Aharoni, *IEJ* 18 (1968) 157-69, 254-55; *Qadmoniot* 2 (1969) 131-34, pl. 3; *Investigations at Lachish* (*Lachish V*; Tel Aviv, 1975) 3-11, 26-32. See there Aharoni's view on the cultic and contextual relationship between the Arad temple discussed in this article and the Hellenistic solar shrine of Lachish. For another view, see S. Yeivin, *Eretz-Israel* 11, 173-75.

[18] A. Biran, *BA* 37 (1974) 106-7.

[19] R. Amiran, *Ancient Pottery of the Holy Land* (Jerusalem/Ramat Gan, 1969) 302-6; R. Amiran and J. Perrot, *Israel Museum News* 9 (1972) 56-61; R. Rowe, *The Four Canaanite Temples of Beth Shan* (Philadelphia, 1940) pls. 56A-62A; A. Mazar, *IEJ* 23, pls. 16-18.

in the village of Gideon (Judg 6:25-33). But on the whole, the cult practiced in these Israelite sites seems to have been the Israelitish-Yahwistic cult.[20]

II

Already in 1902 Sellin found in Taanach an ornamented object which he defined as a *Raucheraltar*, an incense altar.[21] In 1968, Lapp unearthed another utensil of this type, likewise ornamented, but he preferred — and correctly so — to describe it in more general terms as a "cultic stand," dating it to the 10th century B.C.E.[22] Five years previously, in 1963, Lapp discovered in the same excavation area in which these two stands had been disclosed a two-room building from the 10th century B.C.E.[23] On its floor were found two small stelae, a mold for casting statuettes of Ashtoreth, and other items. Lapp defined this as a "cultic structure," bolstering his view by reference to the basin constructed of slabs of stone sunk in the courtyard of this building, in which he reconstructed a stone stela-*maṣṣēbâ* that was found lying beside it. This basin had already been excavated in 1902 by Sellin, who declared it to be an "olive press."[24]

Thus goes the play of history among us archeologists, too. In the case of Taanach, Lapp did not agree with Sellin regarding the secular nature of this installation since he considered it a cultic installation. As a matter of fact, thirty-five years before, in 1928, a similar dispute occurred between the two German excavators of Shechem, Sellin and Welter.[25] At the time, it was in fact Sellin who placed the *maṣṣēbôt* on their bases in the forefront of the structure, which he correctly termed a temple of the Bronze Age in contradiction to Welter, who deemed this structure to be a fortress and therefore defined the bases of the *maṣṣēbôt* as the horses' drinking troughs. We have cited these differences merely to stress our weaknesses as archeologists, for to this day we still lack criteria on which we can all agree.

If we accept Lapp's reconstruction and grant that the stone found beside the basin is a stela-*maṣṣēbâ*, then we will be justified in agreeing with Lapp in the parallel he brings from a similar installation, also from Iron Age II, which was unearthed in 1950 in northern Tell Farᶜah-Tirzah, by the late Father de Vaux.[26] This installation is situated in the inner space of the city gate. Here too there is a basin sunk in the floor of the square and lined with slabs of stone. A monolith 6 feet high was found lying beside it (Level I, Locus 112); de Vaux reconstructed

---

[20]Cf. W. F. Albright, *Archaeology and the Religion of Israel* (Baltimore, 1956) 95-129; *Yahweh and the Gods of Canaan* (London, 1968); F. M. Cross, *Canaanite Myth and Hebrew Epic* (Cambridge, 1973).

[21]E. Sellin, *Tell Taᶜannek*, (Wien, 1904) pls. 12-13.

[22]P. W. Lapp, *BASOR* 195 (1969) 42-44.

[23]P. W. Lapp, *BASOR* 173 (1964) 26-32.

[24]E. Sellin, *Tell Taᶜannek*, 76; S. Yeivin, *Eretz-Israel* 11, 172-73.

[25]See the detailed description of the excavations of the German expedition in G. E. Wright, *Shechem* (New York, 1965) 33-34; G. R. H. Wright, *ZAW* 80 (1968) 1-25.

[26]R. de Vaux, *RB* 58 (1951) 428.

it as a *maṣṣēbâ* that stood beside the basin. De Vaux deduced the significance of this installation from the fact that it had been in place from Stratum III up to Stratum I (where the gate was in fact blocked up, but the installation preserved within an enclosure built around it).[27]

In this context, it would perhaps be worthwhile to examine another installation that was discovered in the northern part of Israel in the Tell Dan excavations directed by Biran since 1966. In the inner square within the city gate, dating to the end of the 10th century B.C.E., an installation of uncommon form came to light. Built on the floor of the square in the shape of a hollow box (basin), its walls are made of three large ashlar stones.[28] In three of its four corners were found rounded stone bases, ornamented with a bas-relief of leaves. These served as bases for wooden columns which apparently supported a canopy.

From among the various possibilities for interpreting the role of this installation, Biran chose the view which perceives in it the basis of a throne for an important personage seated within the city gate, as would accord with many cases described in the Bible (2 Sam 19:8; Ruth 4:1). However, it may be that in the light of our present deliberations it is appropriate to reexamine the function of the installation in the Dan gate, similar as it is to the one seen at Tell Farᶜah.[29]

Lapp proposed linking these cultic installations, whose leading components were the water basin and the standing stone, to the rituals connected with the water cult,[30] religio-political rituals recently discussed by Father de Vaux (Gen 14:7; 21:31; 1 Kgs 1:33-40).[31] The cult functions of these installations, two of which, at Tell Farᶜah and Dan, were located within the city gates, are further emphasized by the biblical description, which notes the existence of cult installations within the city gate (2 Kgs 23:8).[32]

III

Let us now resume our consideration of a number of large structures. First, we will turn our attention again to one of the most impressive recent discoveries of the Iron Age, the large structure which is the *bāmâ* at Tell Dan.[33] In the

---

[27]R. de Vaux, *RB* 58, 6-8.

[28]A. Biran, *BA* 37 (1974) 43-47.

[29]Biran stated in a private discussion that, if the cultic interpretation here being investigated be accepted, it would explain the presence of a large, flat, stone monolith (*maṣṣēbâ*?) which was found lying at random in the same square before the gate and the above-described installation.

[30]P. W. Lapp, *BASOR* 173, 32.

[31]R. de Vaux, *Ancient Israel*, 277-78.

[32]In the light of these details, it will be necessary to examine once again the large water basin situated in the first compartment of the gate at Gezer, keeping in mind the question: did it have a similar connotation, or was collecting water its only everyday purpose? See W. G. Dever, *BA* 34 (1971) 116, figs. 1, 8.

[33]A. Biran, *BA* 37, 40-43.

northern part of the tell a big podium was uncovered which measured approximately 18 x 18 m. The podium is enclosed by framing walls and its interior is filled with basalt and fieldstones. The framing walls are made of ashlar stones and built according to the technique that characterized the Israelite ashlar masonry prevalent in Palestine during the 10th and 9th centuries B.C.E. Excavators point out two principal stages in the life of the structure during the Israelite period. In their view, this is the large *bāmâ* which was erected by Jeroboam the son of Nebat, who set up the golden calves in Dan and in Bethel (1 Kgs 12:28-31) and which later, in the 9th century B.C.E., was enlarged by Ahab. As the digging continues, when the vestiges of the Greek and Roman periods which still cover a considerable portion of the Israelite high place are removed, it will be possible to determine unequivocally whether this podium was indeed a high place that stood uncovered beneath the heavens, an area which has no parallel for spaciousness, or whether the framing walls of this podium served as foundations for a system of walls in a splendid building to which the people ascended by means of a broad stairway.[34] It should be remembered that many of the main buildings in the royal centers throughout the country, especially those that were built in Ahab's time, in the 9th century B.C.E., were erected on a podium which elevated them by artificial means above the level of the city of their time; thus it was with the commander's building in Megiddo 338,[35] the Iron Age II fortress at Hazor, Area B,[36] the Israelite palace at Lachish,[37] and a number of the *Bêt ḥilāni* structures in the cities of Northern Syria during this period.[38] On the other hand, the cultic character of this structure is further emphasized by the discovery of a seven-spouted clay oil lamp on a tall base, by fragments of figurines, and by a horned stone altar, all of which were found beside it.[39]

IV

Apart from Dan, we learn from the Bible of the existence of some ten communities scattered throughout Israel and Judah, such as Shiloh, Bethel, Mizpah, Shechem, and others where local temples very likely may be found, or which may have been places intended for mass assemblies related to the political and religious activities of the Israelites, dating as far back as the settlement period.[40] But for the time being, we can refer from an archeological standpoint to both the sanctuary at Shiloh and the temple in Jerusalem solely on the basis of indirect testimonies.[41]

---

[34]A. Biran, *BA* 37, fig. 13.

[35]H. G. May, *Material Remains*, pl. 6.

[36]Y. Yadin and others, *Hazor II* (Jerusalem, 1960) 53, fig. 2.

[37]O. Tufnell, *Lachish III*, (London, 1953) 78-86.

[38]Cf. H. Frankfort, *Iraq* 14 (1952) 120-25.

[39]A. Biran, *BA* 37, 41, fig. 14; Biran, *BA* 37, 107, fig. 15.

[40]For references, see above.

[41]Cf. T. A. Busink, *Der Temple von Jerusalem I* (Leiden, 1970).

One of the key discoveries in this sphere occurred, as it happened, at an unexpected site. Within the fortress of Arad, in the valley of Beer-sheba, Aharoni uncovered in 1963 the first Israelite temple ever discovered in the course of archeological excavations conducted in the Holy Land.[42] We shall limit ourselves to noting a number of particulars which have an important bearing on our present discussions.

The plan of the temple, which was erected in Stratum XI in the 10th century B.C.E., comprised a large open courtyard surrounded by small chambers. At its western end, there was a broad space which was described as an ʾ*ûlām* or *hêkal* and which contained in its center a kind of cella-*dĕbîr*, square in shape and with small dimensions (1.5 x 1.5 m). This compartment protruded from the western wall of the temple and clung on to the inner side of the wall of the fortress dating to the 10th century B.C.E. The various installations that we have mentioned in the course of this paper as being characteristic of cult corners as a whole here appear in different parts of the temple, although not all of them were built at the same time or served throughout the temple's entire existence. To the right of the entrance into the large courtyard was a large altar, constructed — as biblical law directs (Exod 20:25) — of uncut field stones, measuring 2.5 x 2.5 m (in other words, a square "five cubits long and five cubits broad" as it is described in Exod 27:1). At its head was a slab of flint encircled by plastered channels — intended perhaps to receive the blood of the sacrifices? On the other side of the entrance there was added at Level VIII a large basin built of stone.[43] On the two sides of the entrance into the Holy of Holies (*dĕbîr*) there were two stone altars in secondary use. In their original function they stood one on each side of the entrance into the *dĕbîr*. These two altars are similar in form to the horned altars found in the north, although those in Arad have no horns. At their head are preserved the remnants of burned organic material. Found lying on the stone-paved floor of the compartment was a stone stela-*maṣṣēbâ* very skillfully wrought. Its head is rounded and on its face a little red paint still remains. An additional *maṣṣēbâ* was found sunken into the wall of the *dĕbîr*. A number of ostraca which were exposed in the adjoining chambers or on the slope have various Hebrew names inscribed on them. Most important for our purpose are those which note the names of priestly families known to us from the Bible, as, for example, Pashur and Meremoth (Jer 20:1; Ezra 8:33)[44] who may have been connected with the priestly administration of this temple.

In his latest analyses Aharoni tended to compare the plan of the temple at Arad with the plan of the tabernacle at Shiloh.[45] He accepted the thesis advanced by Cross and Busink[46] in analyzing the problems of the temple of

---

[42] Y. Aharoni, *BA* 31 (1968) 18-32.

[43] *Ancient Arad*, Catalogue No. 26 (Israel Museum, Jerusalem, 1967) figs. 13, 17.

[44] Y. Aharoni, *BA* 31, fig. 17.

[45] Y. Aharoni, *BA* 31, 25-26.

[46] F. M. Cross, *BA* 10 (1947) 45-68; T. A. Busink, *Der Tempel*.

Jerusalem and the descriptions of the tabernacle, and hypothesized that the plan of the temple at Arad preserves the tradition associated with the plan of the tabernacle and is influenced only slightly by the plan of the Jerusalem temple. This tradition relating to the plan antedates Solomon's time and is a heritage deriving from the days of the tabernacle in the period of the Judges and of David.

The fact that some of the ostraca mention the Kittim (*ktym*)[47] — apparently the Greek mercenaries who received their supplies from the storehouses in the fortress of Arad — impelled Yeivin to suggest that the temple served the foreign soldiers stationed there.[48] One has to agree with Aharoni that in the light of the cumulative data on the temple itself and of the assortment of finds from the fortress, particularly the ostraca from Arad, it is feasible to assume that the temple — which was organically integrated into the plan of the fortress, occupying a substantial part of its area — served above all the Israelite inhabitants.

The time that Aharoni assigns the temple is from the 10th century B.C.E. until the days of Josiah in the 7th century B.C.E., when a new network of fortifications was completed in Arad and the temple ceased to exist. Aharoni holds that the Arad temple was destroyed deliberately, in keeping with the reforms introduced by Josiah (2 Kgs 23:4-25). Some scholars reject this premise, basing their objections on details of the architecture and stratigraphy of the late casemate wall.[49] In their opinion, all of the above-mentioned changes should be post-dated to the Iron Age, with the temple serving therefore, according to this view, undisturbed, until the close of the Iron Age.

As to the fact of a temple's existence in Arad, the excavator infers that in border fortresses such as Arad, Bethel, and Dan, royal temples were erected to sanctify the boundaries of the kingdom in a manner similar to the *maṣṣēbôt* of the border.

When in 1969 Aharoni began his excavations at Tell Beer-sheba, he hoped on the basis of this rationale to find an additional temple there, the one mentioned in Amos 5:5. Thus far the Israelite temple itself has not been discovered, but there have come to light in the walls of the city's royal storehouses at Level II, from the 8th century B.C.E., ashlar stones in secondary use which, when reconstructed, produced a splendid horned altar of particularly large dimensions.[50] A curving line engraved on one of the stones may be interpreted as representing the brass serpent[51] (2 Kgs 18:4). Contrary to the case in Arad where the altar was made of uncut field stones, fitting the biblical description of the altar in the tabernacle (Josh 8:31), the stones of the temple in

---

[47] Y. Aharoni, *BA* 31, 14.
[48] S. Yeivin, *PAAJR* 34 (1968) 152-54.
[49] Y. Yadin, *IEJ* 15 (1965) 180; C. Nylander, *IEJ* 17 (1967) 56-59.
[50] Y. Aharoni, *BA* 37 (1974) 2-6; *Tel Aviv* 2 (1975) 154-56.
[51] Y. Aharoni, *BA* 37, fig. 2.

Beer-sheba were skillfully cut. In its outline contours it is identical with the small stone horned altars that we have reviewed. It would appear that those altars, as also this one in Beer-sheba, imitated in their shape and especially in their four horns, the famous horned altar which stood in the courtyard of the temple in Jerusalem (1 Kgs 1:50; 2:28), or in other central cult-places such as Bethel (Amos 3:14).

Until such time as the temple in Beer-sheba is discovered and the existence of such a structure proved also in this site, we shall not know where this altar should be placed.[52] Since the altar's stones were found in secondary use in Stratum II from the 8th century B.C.E., Aharoni surmises that this is an example of destroying the high places which took place in the days of King Hezekiah who, according to 2 Kgs 18:22, "hath taken away . . . the high places and . . . altars . . . and hath said to Judah and Jerusalem, Ye shall worship before this altar in Jerusalem."

V

In this brief survey we have noted examples of all the types of cultic finds from the Iron Age in Israel and Judah, beginning with stelae-*maṣṣēbôt*, small horned altars, and the accompanying cultic utensils such as cultic stands and votive vessels. A minor number of the finds belongs to the actual period of settlement; one such instance is the *bāmâ* and the votive finds in Stratum XI at Hazor. Most of the finds which attest to the existence of the small cult-corners — chapels in cities such as Megiddo, Lachish, and Taanach — date from the 10th century B.C.E., the period when the United Kingdom was flourishing.[53] The erection of the temple in Arad also is dated to the 10th century B.C.E. This particularization shows that parallel to historical information with regard to the work of erecting and operating the temple in Jerusalem — the House of God, the main and central cult-place in which the religious and national rituals were performed on holidays and festivals — archeological finds of the past decade have added distinct evidence concerning the existence and character of cult-places, large and small, in all parts of the country. We knew of these sites from the biblical accounts which allude to altars, high places, houses of high places, and even local temples in places of assembly.

[52] Aharoni contends that there existed in Beer-sheba a temple built like the Arad temple. This has not been discovered in the excavation on this site to date. One of the latest assumptions of the excavators is that this structure was dismantled and removed on purpose from its location which was in the center of the tell before Stratum II was constructed in the 8th century B.C.E. Y. Aharoni, *Tel Aviv* 2 (1975) 156-65. For a different view, see Y. Yadin, *BASOR* 222 (1976) 5-17.

[53] Recently, Ruth Amiran advanced the hypothesis that the two stone objects, a statuette of a lion and a libation tray, which came to light in the Tell Beit Mirsim excavations and were attributed by Albright to a cult place in Stratum C of the Late Bronze Age should be dated to the Iron Age. Thus, in her view, these objects attest the evidence of a cult place in Israelite Tell Beit Mirsim. W. F. Albright, *The Excavation of Tell Beit Mirsim II, AASOR* 17 (1936-37) 65-68, pls. 23-24; R. Amiran, *Proceedings of the Third Archaeological Conference in Israel* (Jerusalem, 1975) 17.

An examination of the individual items of the entire corpus of cult objects makes it clear that some of them, such as the stelae-*maṣṣēbôt* and the cultic stands, are well known from the Canaanite culture, which extends from the Bronze Age somewhat into Iron Age I, and may be borrowed from it. Other items, as for example, the stone type of horned altar, occupy an independent position which is specific to the Israelite cult, even though the very use of an altar for cultic needs, as detailed in the Bible, is also familiar from other cults. A separate subject in its own right is the question of the origin and the influence in the plan of the Jerusalem temple, at which we have only hinted. The conclusions of the overall picture are the same as those reached by analyzing other components of the material culture in this period: evidence of influences and contacts with the previous local Canaanite culture and with the cultures of the Iron Age such as those of the North Syrian, Neo-Hittite, and Phoenician cities on the one hand and on the other hand independent expression specific to the formal cult of the kingdom of Judah and Israel, both in the main temple in Jerusalem and in other centers such as Megiddo and Lachish, as well as distant border fortresses such as Arad, Beer-sheba, and Dan.

Jewish Shrines of the Hellenistic and Persian Periods

EDWARD F. CAMPBELL, JR.
McCormick Theological Seminary, Chicago, IL

My predicament herein is to attempt a portrayal of Jewish sanctuaries which are not where they are expected, are where they are not expected, and are to be reconstructed as to their appearance and religious practice from literary data which are difficult to assess. For the Hellenistic period, we have what I shall claim to be two sanctuary platforms without clear remains of a temple on them, at Tell er-Râs and Tell el-Yehūdîyeh; a temple at ᶜArâq el-Emîr, which Josephus does not mention; and a temple at Lachish which is claimed to follow a Jewish architectural plan but does not appear to be Jewish. For the Persian period, the current state of our knowledge is meager and therefore less perplexing. We are led by the Elephantine papyri, especially numbers 30 and 31, to expect an impressive temple structure at that site, but a random, and rather devastating, search has produced no candidate. As for Jerusalem, from which all our comparisons would most naturally start, we know so little that Dame Kathleen Kenyon, the doyenne of soil deposition archeologists, resorts to comparative masonry technique in order to yield a suggestion as to the approximate location of the Second Temple. The same seam in the masonry of the east wall of the Ḥarâm esh-Sharîf which she invokes is nominated as the indicator of the Seleucid Akra by Y. Tsafrir.[1]

But we are gaining ground. A year ago in Washington, Frank M. Cross gave a brilliant paper on the historians and the history of the Persian period.[2] We thereby gained a stronger skeleton, together with further evidence of the high quality of Josephus' sources and in general of his interpretation. And more and more clearly we are coming to recognize the fascinating panorama of Judaism in the Hellenistic period.

We begin, then, with the Hellenistic period and with the discoveries on Tell er-Râs, the peak at the end of the north spur of Mt. Gerizim directly above

---

[1]K. M. Kenyon, *Digging up Jerusalem* (London & Tonbridge, 1974) 111ff. and pls. 35-36, supported by observations of M. Dunand; Y. Tsafrir, "The Location of the Seleucid Akra in Jerusalem," in *Jerusalem Revealed* (Jerusalem, The Israel Exploration Society, 1975) 85-86. Cf. now B. Mazar et al., *The Mountain of the Lord* (Garden City, 1975) 203-4, 216, which maintains a Hasmonean date for the structure north of the seam.

[2]F. M. Cross, "A Reconstruction of the Judean Restoration," *JBL* 94 (1975) 4-18 = *Interpretation* 29 (1975) 187-203.

ancient Shechem. Here Robert J. Bull and his colleagues have brought to light a complex which well-nigh inescapably belongs to the Samaritan sanctuary on the Samaritan holy mountain. The Hellenistic structures had been overbuilt and encased by the massive solidification work of Hadrian's engineers as they prepared to build a temple to Zeus Olympius on this sacred spot. Excavation has been able to break through the Roman overlay only at relatively few places, but the data resulting from this effort give a pretty clear picture of what is — and is not — there.[3]

There stands at the center of the complex a solid mass of coursed masonry rising from bedrock through some eighteen courses, to a preserved height of nearly 8 m. Indications suggest that in fact it originally stood even taller. The horizontal dimensions of this masonry block are just under 21 m north-south by just over 18 m east-west. Flush against the west face of the main block is a 2-m-wide stretch of masonry, similar in construction to the main block but not bonded to it and preserved only to a height some 2 m short of the height of the main block. If this stretch be taken as an integral part of the block, the east-west dimension becomes just over 20 m and the horizontal dimensions become very nearly those of a square. But in sanctuary architecture, a miss of this size is as good as a mile. The difference in the two dimensions is 80 cm, even when the west-face stretch is included. Without that addition, which seems very likely to be a buttress, the original block measures 20.93 by 18.19 m on its top, roughly 40 by 35 cubits on the Egyptian long cubit of 525 mm. It stands within a rectangular enclosure of sturdy walls; the original Hellenistic enclosure walls had the thicker Roman walls built against their outer faces. The northwest and northeast interior corners have been found and they make it certain that the Hellenistic court was longer on its north-south axis than it was on its east-west one. At the mid-point of the north enclosure wall is a gate more than 8 m wide, marking what is surely the major entrance to the court; search along the east enclosure wall has produced no sign of an entrance from that direction. In short, in Hellenistic as in Roman times the orientation of both court and central block is north-south.

In the deliberations of the Shechem staff, we were unable to reach a conclusion concerning the identity of the central block. Dr. Bull has now come down on the side of calling it the altar of sacrifice of the Samaritans.[4] A corollary of this claim would almost have to be that there was no Samaritan *temple* as such at this location, only an immense altar. Let me defend an alternate hypothesis here, which bears on the overall topic under discussion.

Among the many references in Josephus to the Samaritan temple, two say something about the similarity it bore to the Jerusalem temple. In *Ant* 13.256, which reports on John Hyrcanus' campaign against Shechem and Gerizim, the

---

[3]R. J. Bull and E. F. Campbell, Jr., "The Sixth Campaign at Balâṭah (Shechem)," *BASOR* 190 (April, 1968) 4-19 and figs. 1-12.

[4]Bull, "An Archaeological Context for Understanding John 4:20," *BA* 38 (1975) 54-59.

Gerizim temple is said to have been "built after the model of the sanctuary at Jerusalem." In *Ant* 11.310, Josephus reports the plan of Sanballat to install Manasseh as high priest on Mt. Gerizim, promising to build there "a temple similar to that in Jerusalem." We cannot be certain what model Josephus himself had in mind here, whether the Solomonic temple, or that of Zerubbabel. Of the latter we know very little, although Ezra 3:12-13 and Hag 2:3 suggest that it disappointed those who recalled the destroyed one. Let it be said at once that a temple of the dimensions of the Solomonic one, 20 cubits wide by 70 long (including the porch) would not fit on the masonry block on Tell er-Râs, whether it were oriented north-south or east-west. A structure half that size would fit, but if oriented east-west, only barely.

In *Ant* 13.73ff., a report is given of a quarrel between Alexandrian Jews and Samaritans who are presumably also in Egypt. As Josephus tells it, they are arguing over which of their temples, the Jerusalem or the Gerizim one, conforms to the laws of Moses. The sanctuary at stake in the law of Moses would of course be the Tabernacle, not the Solomonic temple. The historicity of this debate in Egypt is highly dubious, but the particular feature of it, about conformity to Mosaic law, has an air of plausibility to it; it may even suggest that the Jerusalem Second Temple and the Samaritan sanctuary both conformed to the Tabernacle. Two things about such a prospect are interesting. First, the ideal size would then be 30 cubits long and 10 wide, with the 5 cubit by 5 cubit altar for burnt offering out in front of the Tabernacle — a combination which could well fit on the Tell er-Râs block, especially if the orientation were north-south. Second, it could mean that the structure was impermanent, thus accounting for the absence of any large stone structural members on the top of the block — at least so far as we know at this stage of the archeological investigation.

There are obvious problems. A north-south orientation contradicts the Exodus 27 instructions, and it borders on excessive ingenuity to suggest that that is what the Jews and Samaritans in Egypt were quarreling about according to Josephus. And yet, a north-south orientation would line the sanctuary up looking toward the summit of Mt. Ebal across the pass, and there may be factors involved with that which should be taken into account.[5] Another problem: the enclosure walls on Tell er-Râs *are* permanent, and they do not mark out a precinct 100 cubits by 50 cubits as the Tabernacle model calls for, but rather a much larger area.

Finally we do not yet know how access to the top of the masonry block was achieved. The rise would be very steep from the entrance in the north enclosure wall to the top of the block. But this problem confronts us no matter how the block was used — as altar or as podium for a Tabernacle-model sanctuary.

---

[5]T. A. Busink, *Der Tempel von Jerusalem von Salomo bis Herodes* (Leiden, 1970) 252-56, defends anew the hypothesis that the eastward orientation of the Solomonic temple is due to the intention to face the ancient holy site on the Mount of Olives (2 Sam 15:30ff., and cf. 1 Kgs 11:7-8).

So there are reasons for hesitancy, but I submit that a sanctuary, probably impermanent, on the masonry block makes better sense than an immense altar and no temple. We will have to make some peace with its north-south orientation. But a Tabernacle-like sanctuary fits well the overall picture we can piece together about the Samaritans from the Bible (2 Kgs 17:24-34a; 2 Chr 30:1-12; 34:9; Jer 41:4-5) and from Josephus. It suggests that the Samaritans were less heterodox than is often claimed, and that the more distinctive thing about them was that they strove to anchor their tradition in ancient Yahwistic worship and believed that they were true to Israelite faith. They became increasingly an alternative to non-Hellenized Jerusalem Judaism, but if Cross and Purvis (among others) are correct,[6] they were not in irrevocable conflict with Jerusalem until Hyrcanus destroyed their sanctuary in 128 B.C.E.; instead they were one among a number of the faces of Judaism of their time.

There is one other curious problem about the Gerizim sanctuary to be noted. The pottery which dates the enclosure and the block belongs to the 3rd century rather than the 4th — where Josephus would clearly place its building. This judgment is anchored in the close stratigraphy of the Shechem mound, where the distinction between late 4th- and early 3rd-century pottery is pretty well established.[7] In this regard, it reminds one of the circumstances characterizing the ᶜArâq el-Emîr in Transjordan, to which we now turn.

The careful stratigraphic excavation at three points within the large site of ᶜArâq el-Emîr in Transjordan, about ten miles WSW of Amman, was carried out by Paul W. Lapp and ASOR in 1961 and 1962.[8] The excavation was designed to test the relationship of this site to a series of literary indications pertaining to the Transjordanian activities of the Tobiad family. Tobiah, the Ammonite governor, appears with Sanballat the Horonite and Geshem the Arab as the constant thorns in Nehemiah's side as he seeks to rebuild the Jerusalem wall. A century and a half later, another Tobiah plays a role in the Zenon papyri, and then Josephus presents to us the story of Joseph and his son Hyrcanus, members of the Tobiad family, and of Hyrcanus' construction of a *baris*, "fortress," in Transjordan during the years 182-175. This phase concludes with Hyrcanus' death in 175 by his own hand.

Lapp and his colleagues focused their excavation on the megalithic Qaṣr el-ᶜAbd, long confidently associated with Hyrcanus' "fortress," on a square building north of the Qaṣr, and on a probe in the village half a kilometer to the northeast. In the village probe, a public building with fine plaster walls came to

---

[6]Cross, "Aspects of Samaritan and Jewish History in Late Persian and Hellenistic Times," *HTR* 59 (1966) 201-11; J. D. Purvis, *The Samaritan Pentateuch and the Origin of the Samaritan Sect* (Cambridge, 1968) 88-118.

[7]See provisionally N. R. Lapp, "Pottery from Some Hellenistic Loci at Balâṭah (Shechem)," *BASOR* 175 (Oct., 1964) 14-26; F. Zayadin, "Early Hellenistic Pottery from the Theater Excavations at Samaria," *ADAJ* 11 (1966) 53-64 and pls. 27-31.

[8]P. W. Lapp, "Soundings at ᶜArâq el-Emîr, " *BASOR* 171 (Oct., 1963) 8-39; M. J. B. Brett, "The Qaṣr el-ᶜAbd: A Proposed Reconstruction," *BASOR* 171 (Oct., 1963) 39-45.

light, as well as house-walls and a lengthy stretch of what could be a defense perimeter. All three public buildings, the Qaṣr, the square building, and the plaster building, combined with the village stratigraphy to yield a loud and clear chronological conclusion: all came into being at the very earliest in the 2nd century B.C.E. From a stratigraphic point of view, the next earlier occupation level at ᶜArâq el-Emîr belongs to the 11th century B.C.E.

We cannot go into detail about the remarkable Qaṣr building. Lapp and his architect Michael Brett have made a compelling case that the structure is a temple, standing comfortably within the developing tradition of Syrian architecture as influenced by Greek canons. The staircase tower at its northeast corner especially underscores its cultural affinities and relates it to known temples in Syria, admittedly of a substantially later date. The impressive decorative features of the building are especially eloquent in demanding the conclusion that this is no mere fortress. The most striking is the feline-like composite animal carved in high relief on a lower course block of dolomite breccia, a stone yielding an arresting spotted effect. The animal's mouth is a water spout. Dorothy Hill has analyzed the piece as being within the Greek provincial tradition and datable again to the early 2nd century.[9] One other observation about this temple: it was abandoned before it was finished.

So we have another Hellenistic temple, but this time an unexpected one. It is clearly the building which Josephus calls a fortress; he describes features of it which fit the ruins perfectly, and he describes the nearby caverns and the still-visible water works, but nowhere does he mention a temple. And yet the building must have been used by Jews if a Tobiad built it, and furthermore it probably had more than purely local significance. True, the temple is near two population centers — a village of about two acres and the caverns, designed to be living quarters. But indications from the Zenon papyri are that there was in the middle of the 3rd century a "*Land* of Tobiah" where Zenon traveled, a location which is distinct from the place called "Sōrabitt" in the papyri, a name which doubtless refers to ᶜArâq el-Emîr, called in Greek "Tyros" by Josephus (equivalent to Hebrew *ṣōr*) and riding on the banks of the Wadi eṣ-Ṣîr. In a region called "Tobiad-land" there must have been large numbers of Jews, increasingly disenchanted with the Jerusalem temple and politically opposed to the Jerusalem alignments, for whom the ᶜArâq temple would have become the religious center. Here, apparently, Hellenization was welcome, judging from the temple's architecture. Here also, we may surmise, vestiges of the old Tobiad-Samaritan association persisted. James Purvis has argued that this association included a political ingredient, namely a pro-Ptolemaic stance, down to 198 B.C.E. anyway, when the Battle of Panias brought Palestine under Seleucid authority, and Shechem and the Samaritans with it.[10] As for Hyrcanus, he appears to have sustained an anti-Seleucid posture over against his brothers and

---

[9] D. K. Hill, "The Animal Fountain of ᶜArâq el-Emîr," *BASOR* 171 (Oct., 1963) 45-55.
[10] Purvis, *The Samaritan Pentateuch*, 111, 127-29.

Simon the Just in Jerusalem by going to ᶜArâq el-Emîr in 182, with many dissidents accompanying him; there he held out until the accession of Antiochus Epiphanes probably played its part in leading him to suicide. So short had been his epoch there that the grand temple he had constructed was left unfinished at his death.

There remain open questions about ᶜArâq el-Emîr. Is the early 2nd-century date of the earliest Hellenistic stratum really definitive for the start of the site's Hellenistic existence? A few sherds of the 3rd century and of the Persian era do occur in fills and in pockets in the bedrock. The famous Tobiah inscriptions carved in the facades of the cave mouths up above the temple are to be dated confidently, in agreement with Frank Cross, to the late 4th or early 3rd centuries.[11] Then there is the *Sōrabitt* reference in the Zenon papyri of the mid-3rd century. There is, furthermore, a network of foundation walls beneath the floor of the temple which appears not to have been put to use in the structure whose ruins we now can see; do they attest a pre-Hyrcanus phase? It is clear that someone must take up Paul Lapp's own determination to return to ᶜArâq el-Emîr for further excavation, both at the caves and at other locations on the terraces down to the Temple.[12]

The third outlying temple is the Oniad one at Tell el-Yehūdîyeh/Leontopolis. Let me leave aside the tangled problem of Josephus' identification of the Onias involved; it seems that those favoring Onias IV and a date around 155-145 B.C.E. are carrying the day.[13] In reading Josephus on the subject of this temple, one gains the impression that Josephus turns to it almost too often — at least at six different points — for it to be of no significant importance as an alternative to Jerusalem for Egyptian Jewish loyalty. Indeed, the Oniad temple may have been similar to the Tobiad one in appealing to a wider population of Jews in the Delta region than simply the military contingent which Onias is supposed to have brought with him when he left Jerusalem around 162 B.C.E. Victor

---

[11]Cross, "The Development of the Jewish Scripts," in G. E. Wright, ed., *The Bible and the Ancient Near East* (Garden City, 1961) 191, 195, (nn. 13 and 75 respectively).

[12]Since this essay was written (Autumn, 1975), the Jordanian government has begun major reconstruction work at the Qaṣr el-ᶜAbd, under the supervision of Ernst Will and Francois Larché of the French Archaeological Institute normally based in Beirut. Among other important finds are a matching feline fountain block on the side opposite the first one found, several undamaged blocks from the lion frieze on the top preserved row of the Qaṣr walls, and parts of a massive eagle carving from a corner block of the top courses. The movement of these blocks from their fallen positions opened up some areas of undisturbed soil near the walls. Robin Brown, a member of the Andrews University Expedition staff at Ḥesban (Heshbon), was able to stay in Jordan during the autumn of 1976 and carry out several soundings near Lapp's trenches. Her results confirmed his later Hellenistic dates for the existing strata and revealed no early Hellenistic stratified deposits. The French efforts as well as Brown's may yield some new perspectives on the date of the Qaṣr's founding on further analysis, but so far no new evidence changes the chronological picture described above.

[13]*Encyclopedia Judaica* (Jerusalem, 1971) *s.v.* "Onias"; M. Delcor, "Le temple d'Onias en Égypte," *RB* 75 (1968) 188-203.

Tcherikover, while advocating the position that the Oniad temple was a local phenomenon, its establishment the "act of an adventurer, an act with no religious or national significance," does observe that the Zenon papyri portray many Jews out in the rural areas of the Nile Delta who were not attracted to Alexandrian Judaism and its sophisticated ways.[14]

Just a brief look here at Petrie's exploration of Tell el-Yehūdîyeh.[15] Of late, his ingenious reconstruction of the temple and the "New Jerusalem" at the site has been looked upon with jaundiced eyes. It is true that his fancy mathematical footwork with the poorly preserved ruins of a brick-and-sand, stone-encased platform east of the Hyksos camp is a bit dazzling. But many of his insights may be very much on the mark. The platform does indeed seem to have been artificially made, in one operation. At its south end, where the platform narrows to a thin strip, the traces of foundation walls do suggest a building substantially longer than it is wide; Petrie felt he could establish a 2:7 proportion and, furthermore, that the structure was about 10 by 35 cubits, half the size of the Solomonic temple, and (he wondered in print) perhaps then of the same size as the poor and unimpressive Second Temple in Jerusalem. The pottery in the mud-brick platform was, he claimed, of 2nd-century B.C.E. date; he speaks of amphora fragments distributed throughout the platform fill, and there is reason to think that Petrie could be counted upon to know Rhodian jars when he saw them. His dedicatory sacrifices, buried in the sides of the platform, are not that much different from those at Qumrân, in spite of de Vaux's demurrers.[16] And finally, the nearby cemetery and other artifacts found at the site certainly attest a Jewish population here. For my part, I suspect a good bit of Petrie's reconstruction is valid. It may well be the case, what is more, that Onias did build his temple here with an eye to imitating the architecture *and* the topography of Jerusalem, as Petrie maintained.

Admittedly, this last judgment is influenced by what the archeology of Tell er-Râs and ᶜArâq el-Emîr seems to suggest. Each of these three places is probably the center for flourishing alternatives to Jerusalem Judaism, and each is led by people with priestly connections to the Jerusalem Temple. In each case, it is at least possible that the architecture of the sanctuary reflected the particular orientation and emphasis involved. To my mind it is incorrect to dismiss any of these alternatives as essentially politically motivated and therefore not important religiously; each had a mixture of political, social, and also theological warrant. That having been said, it is easy to include in our survey the Essene community at Qumrân — that is, to include it as an analogue to the others in the panorama of Jewish pluralism in the 2nd century B.C.E. (Let me say

---

[14] V. A. Tcherikover and A. Fuks, *Corpus Papyrorum Judaicarum* (Cambridge, 1957) Vol. I, 43-46; cf. Tcherikover, *Hellenistic Civilization and the Jews* (Philadelphia, 1959) 275-87.

[15] W. M. F. Petrie, *Hyksos and Israelite Cities* (London, 1906) 19-27 and plates.

[16] See his remarks on pp. 204-5 of *RB* 75 (1968) in a postscript to the Delcor article above in n. 12.

at once that S. H. Steckoll's attempt to turn Room 77, the great common room of the Qumrân community, into a temple is ridiculous, as Père de Vaux has rather too kindly pointed out.[17])

Three Jewish sanctuaries of the Hellenistic period; is there a fourth in the so-called Solar Temple at Lachish? Yohanan Aharoni has claimed that this structure bears a close architectural similarity to the final phase of the Judean sanctuary at Arad, destroyed in 586.[18] When he checked the Wellcome-Marston expedition's chronological judgment with a probe of his own, however, he proved it to be as they said — Hellenistic. Does it then carry forward into the Hellenistic era a sanctuary tradition stemming from the last years before the 586 fall? My judgment would be that the indications do not support that conclusion. An inscribed "incense altar" from a cave at the foot of the Lachish mound cannot be read as Aharoni has proposed (he reads a combination *lyh* as meaning "to Yahweh"), and without that reading, it does not bear on the identification of the deity worshiped in the sanctuary; indeed, Albright has probably established that the incense altar is not an altar at all.[19] We can afford to keep the question open in the hope that new data will help us to comprehend this anomalous building.

I have arrived at the conclusion of these remarks and have not touched upon Elephantine. That evidences the frustration of the archeological search for the Temple of Yahweh there.[20] In its bizarre way, however, Elephantine points up the general conclusion to our whole inquiry, that Hellenistic Jewry was multifaceted and that the same was true to a degree in the preceding era. It may seem that no injunction of the Torah was transgressed more roundly than was the one calling for the centralization of worship at one place — except of course that Jews at each of the places we have viewed doubtless felt that somehow they were honoring that injunction.

What archeological work should gain priority from all this? I have already urged that digging be resumed at ᶜArâq el-Emîr. If it is any longer possible, a renewed exploration of Tell el-Yehūdîyeh is called for, especially in view of the reported opinion of Du Mesnil du Buisson that Petrie's mud-brick platform is in fact part of the Hyksos camp. For a better understanding of Samaritan origins, we would do well to undertake excavations at the twin site of Sālim/Khirbet esh-Sheikh Naṣrallah three miles due east of Shechem, to which Samaritan tradition points in exegeting Genesis 14 and where surface exploration has

---

[17]S. H. Steckoll, "The Qumran Sect in Relation to the Temple of Leontopolis," *RQ* 6 (1967) 55-69; De Vaux, *RB* 75 (1968) 204-5.

[18]Y. Aharoni, "Trial Excavation in the 'Solar Shrine' at Lachish," *IEJ* 18 (1968) 157-69; note also pp. 254-55.

[19]On the reading of *lyh*, see Cross, *BASOR* 193 (Feb., 1969) 24. On the "altar," see W. F. Albright, "The Lachish Cosmetic Burner and Esther 2:12," in H. N. Bream et al., eds., *A Light unto My Path: Old Testament Studies in Honor of Jacob M. Myers* (Philadelphia, 1974) 25-32.

[20]See the excellent portrayal by E. G. Kraeling, *The Brooklyn Museum Aramaic Papyri* (New Haven, 1953) 64-82.

yielded good evidence of Hellenistic occupation.[21] A small expedition should, as soon as it is feasible, conduct a meticulous excavation of a lonely ruin on the top of Mt. Ebal, toward which one looks as he stands on the platform of the temple complex on Tell er-Râs. For the Persian period we do not yet know enough to plan. But a corpus of securely dated Persian pottery forms will emerge from the publications of the Tell el-Ḥesi and En-gedi expeditions, ready to control explorations. Our best hopes here, however, may lie again with ᶜArâq el-Emîr. And I close with the report of a recent nightmare, which pictured Robert Bull carefully lifting, with the longest lever ever seen, the masonry block on Tell er-Râs, to see what is underneath!

[21] Campbell, *BASOR* 190 (April, 1968) 26.

INDEX

Boldface page numbers indicate a major entry—that is, a direct and substantial discussion of a topic. Minor entries are indicated by regular type; they are brief references without detailed discussion. All biblical references, no matter how incidental, have been included.

A

B

C

G

H

I

J

K

R

S

T

U

Ugaritic texts
—Anat and Baal cycle **137-45**
Utica
—founded 105-6

W

water cult
—at Tell Dan and Tell Far^{c}ah 152
Wilusa
—Homeric equivalent 4

Y

Yehūdîyeh, Tell el
—temple **164-65**
Yeivin, S.
—Palestine Bronze and Iron Age temples 148

Z

Zarephath see Sarepta

SCRIPTURE REFERENCES